An Assessment of Research-Doctorate Programs in the United States: *Biological Sciences*

Committee on an Assessment of Quality-Related Characteristics of Research-Doctorate Programs in the United States

Lyle V. Jones, Gardner Lindzey, and Porter E. Coggeshall, *Editors*

Sponsored by

The Conference Board of Associated Research Councils

American Council of Learned Societies
American Council on Education
National Research Council
Social Science Research Council

NATIONAL ACADEMY PRESS
Washington, D.C.   1982

QH
319
.A1
A871
1982
REF

Library of Congress Catalog Card Number 82-62670

International Standard Book Number 0-309-03340-3

Available from

NATIONAL ACADEMY PRESS
2101 Constitution Avenue, N.W.
Washington, D.C. 20418

MEASURES COMPILED ON INDIVIDUAL RESEARCH-DOCTORATE PROGRAMS
IN THE BIOLOGICAL SCIENCES

Program Size[1]   (See pages 18-19.)
01 Reported number of faculty members in the program, December 1980.
02 Reported number of program graduates in last five years (July 1975
    through June 1980).
03 Reported total number of full-time and part-time graduate students
    enrolled in the program who intend to earn doctorates, December 1980.

Characteristics of Graduates[2]   (See pages 19-22.)
04 Fraction of FY1975-79 program graduates who had received some national
    fellowship or training grant support during their graduate education.
05 Median number of years from first enrollment in graduate school to
    receipt of the doctorate--FY1975-79 program graduates.[3]
06 Fraction of FY1975-79 program graduates who at the time they completed
    requirements for the doctorate reported that they had made definite
    commitments for postgraduation employment.
07 Fraction of FY1975-79 program graduates who at the time they completed
    requirements for the doctorate reported that they had made definite
    commitments for postgraduation employment in Ph.D.-granting universities.

Reputational Survey Results[4]   (See pages 22-27.)
08 Mean rating of the scholarly quality of program faculty (scale = 0 to 5).
09 Mean rating of the effectiveness of the program in educating research
    scholars/scientists (scale = 0 to 3).
10 Mean rating of the improvement in program quality in the last five years
    (scale = 0 to 2).
11 Mean rating of the evaluators' familiarity with the work of the
    program's faculty (scale = 0 to 2).

University Library Size[5]   (See pages 27-28.)
12 Composite index describing the library size in the university in which
    the program is located, 1979-80 (scale = -3 to +3).

Research Support   (See pages 28-29.)
13 Fraction of program faculty members holding research grants from the
    National Institutes of Health, the National Science Foundation, or the
    Alcohol, Drug Abuse, and Mental Health Administration at any time during
    the FY1978-80 period.[6]
14 Total expenditures reported by the university for research and
    development activities in a specified field, FY1979[7] (in thousands of
    dollars).

Publication Records[8]   (See pages 29-31.)
15 Number of published articles attributed to the program, 1978-79.
16 Estimated "overall influence" of published articles attributed to the
    program, 1978-79 (raw values are not reported).

[1]Based on information provided to the committee by the participating
universities.
[2]Based on data compiled in the NRC's Survey of Earned Doctorates.
[3]In reporting standardized scores and correlations with other variables, a
shorter time-to-Ph.D. is assigned a higher score.
[4]Based on responses to the committee's survey conducted in April 1981.
[5]Based on data compiled by the Association of Research Libraries.
[6]Based on matching faculty names provided by institutional coordinators
with the names of research grant awardees from the three federal agencies.
[7]Based on data provided to the National Science Foundation by universities.
[8]Based on data compiled by the Institute for Scientific Information and
developed by Computer Horizons, Inc.

Acknowledgments

In conducting this assessment the committee has benefited from the support and advice of many individuals and organizations. The assessment was conducted under the aegis of the Conference Board of Associated Research Councils, and special thanks go to Roger Heyns, Robert M. Lumiansky, Jack W. Peltason, Frank Press, Kenneth Prewitt, Eleanor Sheldon, John William Ward, and the late Philip Handler for their efforts in overseeing the planning and execution of this project. Financial support was provided by the Andrew W. Mellon Foundation, the Ford Foundation, the Alfred P. Sloan Foundation, the National Institutes of Health (NIH), the National Science Foundation (NSF), and the National Academy of Sciences. Without the combined support from these organizations the project would not have been undertaken. The committee appreciates the excellent cooperation it received from the staff officers at these organizations--including John Sawyer and James Morris at Mellon; Mariam Chamberlain, Gladys Chang Hardy, and Sheila Biddle at Ford; Albert Rees and James Koerner at Sloan; Helen Gee at NIH; and Bernard Stein at NSF. Some supplemental funds to enhance the study were furnished by the Association of American Geographers, the American Psychological Association, and the American Psychological Foundation.

The committee is most appreciative of the cooperation it received from individuals in the 228 universities participating in the assessment. In particular we thank the university presidents and chancellors who agreed to participate and offered the assistance of staff members at their institutions; the graduate deans, department chairmen, and many other university personnel who helped to compile information about the research-doctorate programs at their own institutions; and the nearly 5,000 faculty members who took the time to complete and return reputational survey forms. This assessment would not have been feasible without the participation of these individuals. Nor would it have been complete without the suggestions from many individuals within and outside the academic community who reviewed the study plans and committee reports.

The committee also acknowledges the contributions of Francis Narin and Paul R. McAllister, whose innovative work in the area of publication productivity in science and engineering fields has been a valuable resource. We thank H. Roberts Coward and his colleagues at the Institute for Scientific Information for their help in compiling publications data as well as William Batchelor and John James at NIH and David Staudt at NSF for their help in acquiring data on individual research grant awards.

Within the National Research Council many individuals have assisted in the planning and completion of this project. Robert A. Alberty, Harrison Shull, and W. K. Estes, former chairmen of the Commission on Human Resources, and William C. Kelly, Executive Director of the commission (now the Office of Scientific and Engineering Personnel), offered assistance and helpful counsel during all phases of the study. Lindsey R. Harmon and C. Alan Boneau contributed greatly to the planning of the assessment.

To Porter E. Coggeshall, Study Director, the committee expresses thanks for a job extremely well done. His ability to translate the committee's directions into compiled data and analyses must be given a large share of the credit for the completion of this project. He has been ably assisted by Prudence W. Brown, who supervised the data collection activities; Dorothy G. Cooper, who provided excellent secretarial support; George A. Boyce, whose programming expertise was invaluable; and Kathleen Drennan and Linda Dix, who helped in preparing final copy of the manuscript.

Committee on an Assessment of Quality-Related
Characteristics of Research-Doctorate Programs
in the United States

Preface

The genius of American higher education is often said to be in the close association of training and research--that is, in the nation's research-doctorate programs. Consequently, we are not surprised at the amount of worried talk about the quality of the research doctorate, for deterioration at that level will inevitably spread to wherever research skills are needed--and that indeed is a far-flung network of laboratories, institutes, firms, agencies, bureaus, and departments. What might surprise us, however, is the imbalance between the putative national importance of research-doctorate programs and the amount of sustained evaluative attention they themselves receive.

The present assessment, sponsored by the Conference Board of Associated Research Councils--comprised of the American Council of Learned Societies, the American Council on Education, the National Research Council (NRC), and the Social Science Research Council--seeks to correct the imbalance between worried talk and systematic study. In this effort the Conference Board continues a tradition pioneered by the American Council on Education, which in 1966 published An Assessment of Quality in Graduate Education, the report of a study conducted by Allan M. Cartter, and in 1970 published A Rating of Graduate Programs, by Kenneth D. Roose and Charles J. Andersen. The Cartter and Roose-Andersen reports have been widely used and frequently cited.

Some years after the release of the Roose-Andersen report, it was decided that the effort to assess the quality of research-doctorate programs should be renewed, and the Conference Board of Associated Research Councils agreed to sponsor an assessment. The Board of Directors of the American Council on Education concurred with the notion that the next study should be issued under these broader auspices. The NRC agreed to serve as secretariat for a new study. The responsible staff of the NRC earned the appreciation of the Conference Board for the skill and dedication shown during the course of securing funding and implementing the study. Special mention should also be made of the financial contribution of the National Academy of Sciences which, by supplementing funds available from external sources, made it possible for the study to get under way.

To sponsor a study comparing the quality of programs in 32 disciplines and from more than 200 doctorate-granting universities is to invite critics, friendly and otherwise. Such was the fate of the previous studies; such has been the fate of the present study. Scholarship, fortunately, can put criticism to creative use and has done so in this project. The study committee appointed by the Conference Board reviewed the criticisms of earlier efforts to assess research-doctorate programs, and it actively solicited criticisms and suggestions for improvements of its own design. Although constrained by limited funds, the committee applied state-of-the-art methodology in a design that incorporated the lessons learned from previous studies as well as attending to many critics of the present effort. Not all criticism has thus been stilled; nor could it ever be. Additional criticisms will be voiced by as many persons as begin to use the results of this effort in ways not anticipated by its authors. These criticisms will be welcome. The Conference Board believes that the present study, building on earlier criticisms and adopting a multidimensional approach to the assessment of research-doctorate programs, represents a substantial improvement over past reports. Nevertheless, each of the diverse measures used here has its own limitations, and none provides a precise index of the quality of a program for educating students for careers in research. No doubt a future study, taking into account the weaknesses as well as strengths of this effort, will represent still further improvement. One mark of success for the present study would be for it to take its place in a continuing series, thereby contributing to the indicator base necessary for informed policies that will maintain and perhaps enhance the quality of the nation's research-doctorate programs.

For the more immediate future the purposes of this assessment are to assist students and student advisers seeking the best match possible between individual career goals and the choice of an advanced degree program; to serve scholars whose study site is higher education and the nation's research enterprise; and to inform the practical judgment of the administrators, funders, and policymakers responsible for protecting the quality of scholarly education in the United States.

A remarkably hard-working and competent group, whose names appear on page vii of this report, oversaw the long process by which this study moved from the planning stage to the completion of these reports. The Conference Board expresses its warmest thanks to the members of its committee and especially to their co-chairmen, Lyle V. Jones and Gardner Lindzey.

Conference Board of Associated
Research Councils

Committee on an Assessment of Quality-Related Characteristics of Research-Doctorate Programs in the United States

LYLE V. JONES (Co-Chairman), Director of the L. L. Thurstone Psychometric Laboratory, University of North Carolina at Chapel Hill

GARDNER LINDZEY (Co-Chairman), Director, Center for Advanced Study in the Behavioral Sciences

PAUL A. ALBRECHT, Vice-President and Dean, Claremont Graduate School

MARCUS ALEXIS, Department of Economics, Northwestern University

ROBERT M. BOCK, Dean of the Graduate School, University of Wisconsin at Madison

PHILIP E. CONVERSE, Institute for Social Research, University of Michigan

JAMES H. M. HENDERSON, Department of Plant Physiology, Tuskegee Institute of Alabama

ERNEST S. KUH, Department of Electrical Engineering and Computer Sciences, University of California, Berkeley

WINFRED P. LEHMANN, Department of Linguistics, University of Texas at Austin

SAUNDERS MAC LANE, Department of Mathematics, University of Chicago

NANCY S. MILBURN, Dean, College of Liberal Arts and Jackson College for Women, Tufts University

LINCOLN E. MOSES, Department of Statistics, Stanford University

JAMES C. OLSON, President, University of Missouri

C. K. N. PATEL, Director, Physical Research Laboratory, Bell Laboratories

MICHAEL J. PELCZAR, JR., President, The Council of Graduate Schools in the United States

JEROME B. SCHNEEWIND, Department of Philosophy, Johns Hopkins University

DUANE C. SPRIESTERSBACH, Vice-President, Educational Development and Research, University of Iowa

HARRIET A. ZUCKERMAN, Sociology Department, Columbia University

Study Director

PORTER E. COGGESHALL, Office of Scientific and Engineering Personnel, National Research Council

Contents

LIST OF FIGURES

LIST OF TABLES

I
Origins of Study and Selection of Programs

Each year more than 22,000 candidates are awarded doctorates in engineering, the humanities, and the sciences from approximately 250 U.S. universities. They have spent, on the average, five-and-a-half years in intensive education in preparation for research careers either in universities or in settings outside the academic sector, and many will make significant contributions to research. Yet we are poorly informed concerning the quality of the programs producing these graduates. This study is intended to provide information pertinent to this complex and controversial subject.

The charge to the study committee directed it to build upon the planning that preceded it. The planning stages included a detailed review of the methodologies and the results of past studies that had focused on the assessment of doctoral-level programs. The committee has taken into consideration the reactions of various groups and individuals to those studies. The present assessment draws upon previous experience with program evaluation, with the aim of improving what was useful and avoiding some of the difficulties encountered in past studies. The present study, nevertheless, is not purely reactive: it has its own distinctive features. First, it focuses only on programs awarding research doctorates and their effectiveness in preparing students for careers in research. Although other purposes of graduate education are acknowledged to be important, they are outside the scope of this assessment. Second, the study examines a variety of different indices that may be relevant to the program quality. This multidimensional approach represents an explicit recognition of the limitations of studies that rely entirely on peer ratings of perceived quality-- the so-called reputational ratings. Finally, in the compilation of reputational ratings in this study, evaluators were provided the names of faculty members involved with each program to be rated and the number of research doctorates awarded in the last five years. In previous reputational studies evaluators were not supplied such information.

During the past two decades increasing attention has been given to describing and measuring the quality of programs in graduate education. It is evident that the assessment of graduate programs is highly important for university administrators and faculty, for employers in

1

industrial and government laboratories, for graduate students and prospective graduate students, for policymakers in state and national organizations, and for private and public funding agencies. Past experience, however, has demonstrated the difficulties with such assessments and their potentially controversial nature. As one critic has asserted:

> . . . the overall _effect_ of these reports seems quite clear. They tend, first, to make the rich richer and the poor poorer; second, the example of the highly ranked clearly imposes constraints on those institutions lower down the scale (the "Hertz-Avis" effect). And the effect of such constraints is to reduce diversity, to reward conformity or respectability, to penalize genuine experiment or risk. There is, also, I believe, an obvious tendency to promote the prevalence of disciplinary dogma and orthodoxy. All of this might be tolerable if the reports were tolerably accurate and judicious, if they were less _prescriptive_ and more _descriptive_; if they did not pretend to "objectivity" and if the very fact of ranking were not pernicious and invidious; if they genuinely promoted a meaningful "meritocracy" (instead of simply perpetuating the _status quo ante_ and an establishment mentality). But this is precisely what they cannot claim to be or do.[1]

The widespread criticisms of ratings in graduate education were carefully considered in the planning of this study. At the outset consideration was given to whether a national assessment of graduate programs should be undertaken at this time and, if so, what methods should be employed. The next two sections in this chapter examine the background and rationale for the decision by the Conference Board of Associated Research Councils[2] to embark on such a study. The remainder of the chapter describes the selection of disciplines and programs to be covered in the assessment.

The overall study encompasses a total of 2,699 graduate programs in 32 disciplines. In this report--the fourth of five reports issuing from the study--we examine 616 programs in six disciplines in the biological sciences: biochemistry, botany, cellular/molecular biology, microbiology, physiology, and zoology. These programs account for more

---

[1] William A. Arrowsmith, "Preface" in _The Ranking Game: The Power of the Academic Elite_, by W. Patrick Dolan, University of Nebraska Printing and Duplicating Service, Lincoln, Nebraska, 1976, p. ix.
[2] The Conference Board includes representatives of the American Council of Learned Societies, American Council on Education, National Research Council, and Social Science Research Council.

than 90 percent of the research doctorates awarded in these six disciplines. It should be emphasized that the selection of disciplines to be covered was determined on the basis of total doctoral awards during the FY1976-78 period (as described later in this chapter), and the exclusion of a particular discipline was in no way based on a judgment of the importance of graduate education or research in that discipline. Also, although the assessment is limited to programs leading to the research-doctorate (Ph.D. or equivalent) degree, the Conference Board and study committee recognize that graduate schools provide many other forms of valuable and needed education.

PRIOR ATTEMPTS TO ASSESS QUALITY IN GRADUATE EDUCATION

Universities and affiliated organizations have taken the lead in the review of programs in graduate education. At most institutions program reviews are carried out on a regular basis and include a comprehensive examination of the curriculum and educational resources as well as the qualifications of faculty and students. One special form of evaluation is that associated with institutional accreditation:

> The process begins with the institutional or programmatic self-study, a comprehensive effort to measure progress according to previously accepted objectives. The self-study considers the interest of a broad cross-section of constituencies--students, faculty, administrators, alumni, trustees, and in some circumstances the local community. The resulting report is reviewed by the appropriate accrediting commission and serves as the basis for evaluation by a site-visit team from the accrediting group. . . . Public as well as educational needs must be served simultaneously in determining and fostering standards of quality and integrity in the institutions and such specialized programs as they offer. Accreditation, conducted through nongovernmental institutional and specialized agencies, provides a major means for meeting those needs.[3]

Although formal accreditation procedures play an important role in higher education, many university administrators do not view such procedures as an adequate means of assessing program quality. Other efforts are being made by universities to evaluate their programs in graduate education. The Educational Testing Service, with the sponsorship of the Council of Graduate Schools in the United States and the Graduate Record Examinations Board, has recently developed a set of

---

[3]Council on Postsecondary Accreditation, The Balance Wheel for Accreditation, Washington, D.C., July 1981, pp. 2-3.

procedures to assist institutions in evaluating their own graduate programs.[4]

While reviews at the institutional (or state) level have proven useful in assessing the relative strengths and weaknesses of individual programs, they have not provided the information required for making national comparisons of graduate programs. Several attempts have been made at such comparisons. The most widely used of these have been the studies by Keniston (1959), Cartter (1966), and Roose and Andersen (1970). All three studies covered a broad range of disciplines in engineering, the humanities, and the sciences and were based on the opinions of knowledgeable individuals in the program areas covered. Keniston[5] surveyed the department chairmen at 25 leading institutions. The Cartter[6] and Roose-Andersen[7] studies compiled ratings from much larger groups of faculty peers. The stated motivation for these studies was to increase knowledge concerning the quality of graduate education:

> A number of reasons can be advanced for undertaking such a study. The diversity of the American system of higher education has properly been regarded by both the professional educator and the layman as a great source of strength, since it permits flexibility and adaptability and encourages experimentation and competing solutions to common problems. Yet diversity also poses problems. . . . Diversity can be a costly luxury if it is accompanied by ignorance. . . . Just as consumer knowledge and honest advertising are requisite if a competitive economy is to work satisfactorily, so an improved knowledge of opportunities and of quality is desirable if a diverse educational system is to work effectively.[8]

Although the program ratings from the Cartter and Roose-Andersen studies are highly correlated, some substantial differences in successive ratings can be detected for a small number of programs--suggesting changes in the programs or in the perception of the programs. For the past decade the Roose-Andersen ratings have generally been regarded as

---

[4] For a description of these procedures, see M. J. Clark, Graduate Program Self-Assessment Service: Handbook for Users, Educational Testing Service, Princeton, New Jersey, 1980.

[5] H. Keniston, Graduate Study in Research in the Arts and Sciences at the University of Pennsylvania, University of Pennsylvania Press, Philadelphia, 1959.

[6] A. M. Cartter, An Assessment of Quality in Graduate Education, American Council on Education, Washington, D.C., 1966.

[7] K. D. Roose and C. J. Andersen, A Rating of Graduate Programs, American Council on Education, Washington, D.C., 1970.

[8] Cartter, p. 3.

the best available source of information on the quality of doctoral programs. Although the ratings are now more than 10 years out of date and have been criticized on a variety of grounds, they are still used extensively by individuals within the academic community and by those in federal and state agencies.

A frequently cited criticism of the Cartter and Roose-Andersen studies is their exclusive reliance upon reputational measurement.

> The ACE rankings are but a small part of all the eval-
> uative processes, but they are also the most public,
> and they are clearly based on the narrow assumptions
> and elitist structures that so dominate the present
> direction of higher education in the United States.
> As long as our most prestigious source of information
> about postsecondary education is a vague popularity
> contest, the resultant ignorance will continue to pro-
> vide a cover for the repetitious aping of a single
> model. . . . All the attempts to change higher educa-
> tion will ultimately be strangled by the "legitimate"
> evaluative processes that have already programmed a
> single set of responses from the start.[9]

A number of other criticisms have been leveled at reputational rankings of graduate programs.[10] First, such studies inherently reflect per-ceptions that may be several years out of date and do not take into account recent changes in a program. Second, the ratings of individual programs are likely to be influenced by the overall reputation of the university--i.e., an institutional "halo effect." Also, a dispropor-tionately large fraction of the evaluators are graduates of and/or faculty members in the largest programs, which may bias the survey re-sults. Finally, on the basis of such studies it may not be possible to differentiate among many of the lesser known programs in which rel-atively few faculty members have established national reputations in research.

Despite such criticisms several studies based on methodologies similar to those employed by Cartter and Roose and Andersen have been carried out during the past 10 years. Some of these studies evaluated post-baccalaureate programs in areas not covered in the two earlier reports--including business, religion, educational administration, and medicine. Others have focused exclusively on programs in particular disciplines within the sciences and humanities. A few attempts have been made to assess graduate programs in a broad range of disciplines, many of which were covered in the Roose-Andersen and Cartter ratings, but in the opinion of many each has serious deficiencies in the methods and procedures employed. In addition to such studies, a myriad of ar-

---

[9] Dolan, p. 81.
[10] For a discussion of these criticisms, see David S. Webster, "Meth-ods of Assessing Quality," _Change_, October 1981, pp. 20-24.

ticles have been written on the assessment of graduate programs since the release of the Roose-Andersen report. With the heightening interest in these evaluations, many in the academic community have recognized the need to assess graduate programs, using other criteria in addition to peer judgment.

> Though carefully done and useful in a number of ways, these ratings (Cartter and Roose-Andersen) have been criticized for their failure to reflect the complexity of graduate programs, their tendency to emphasize the traditional values that are highly related to program size and wealth, and their lack of timeliness or currency. Rather than repeat such ratings, many members of the graduate community have voiced a preference for developing ways to assess the quality of graduate programs that would be more comprehensive, sensitive to the different program purposes, and appropriate for use at any time by individual departments or universities.[11]

Several attempts have been made to go beyond the reputational assessment. Clark, Harnett, and Baird, in a pilot study[12] of graduate programs in chemistry, history, and psychology, identified as many as 30 possible measures significant for assessing the quality of graduate education. Glower[13] has ranked engineering schools according to the total amount of research spending and the number of graduates listed in Who's Who in Engineering. House and Yeager[14] rated economics departments on the basis of the total number of pages published by full professors in 45 leading journals in this discipline. Other ratings based on faculty publication records have been compiled for graduate programs in a variety of disciplines, including political science, psychology, and sociology. These and other studies demonstrate the feasibility of a national assessment of graduate programs that is founded on more than reputational standing among faculty peers.

---

[11]Clark, p. 1.

[12]M. J. Clark, R. T. Harnett, and L. L. Baird, Assessing Dimensions of Quality in Doctoral Education: A Technical Report of a National Study in Three Fields, Educational Testing Service, Princeton, New Jersey, 1976.

[13]Donald D. Glower, "A Rational Method for Ranking Engineering Programs," Engineering Education, May 1980.

[14]Donald R. House and James H. Yeager, Jr., "The Distribution of Publication Success Within and Among Top Economics Departments: A Disaggregate View of Recent Evidence," Economic Inquiry, Vol. 16, No. 4, October 1978, pp. 593-598.

DEVELOPMENT OF STUDY PLANS

In September 1976 the Conference Board, with support from the Carnegie Corporation of New York and the Andrew W. Mellon Foundation,
convened a three-day meeting to consider whether a study of programs
in graduate education should be undertaken. The 40 invited participants in this meeting included academic administrators, faculty
members, and agency and foundation officials[15] and represented a
variety of institutions, disciplines, and convictions. In these discussions there was considerable debate concerning whether the potential
benefits of such a study outweighed the possible misrepresentations of
the results. On the one hand, "a substantial majority of the Conference [participants believed] that the earlier assessments of graduate
education have received wide and important use: by students and their
advisors, by the institutions of higher education as aids to planning
and the allocation of educational functions, as a check on unwarranted
claims of excellence, and in social science research."[16] On the
other hand, the conference participants recognized that a new study
assessing the quality of graduate education "would be conducted and
received in a very different atmosphere than were the earlier Cartter
and Roose-Andersen reports. . . . Where ratings were previously used
in deciding where to increase funds and how to balance expanding programs, they might now be used in deciding where to cut off funds and
programs."

After an extended debate of these issues, it was the recommendation
of this conference that a study with particular emphasis on the effectiveness of doctoral programs in educating research personnel be undertaken. The recommendation was based principally on four considerations:

> (1) the importance of the study results to national
>   and state bodies,
> (2) the desire to stimulate continuing emphasis on
>   quality in graduate education,
> (3) the need for current evaluations that take into
>   account the many changes that have occurred in
>   programs since the Roose-Andersen study, and
> (4) the value of extending the range of measures used
>   in evaluative studies of graduate programs.

Although many participants expressed interest in an assessment of master's degree and professional degree programs, insurmountable problems
prohibited the inclusion of these types of programs in this study.

Following this meeting a 13-member committee,[17] co-chaired by
Gardner Lindzey and Harriet A. Zuckerman, was formed to develop a de-

---

[15] See Appendix G for a list of the participants in this conference.
[16] From a summary of the Woods Hole Conference (see Appendix G).
[17] See Appendix H for a list of members of the planning committee.

tailed plan for a study limited to research-doctorate programs and designed to improve upon the methodologies utilized in earlier studies. In its deliberations the planning committee carefully considered the criticisms of the Roose-Andersen study and other national assessments. Particular attention was paid to the feasibility of compiling a variety of specific measures (e.g., faculty publication records, quality of students, program resources) that were judged to be related to the quality of research-doctorate programs. Attention was also given to making improvements in the survey instrument and procedures used in the Cartter and Roose-Andersen studies. In September 1978 the planning group submitted a comprehensive report describing alternative strategies for an evaluation of the quality and effectiveness of research-doctorate programs.

> The proposed study has its own distinctive features. It is characterized by a sharp focus and a multidimensional approach. (1) It will focus only on programs awarding research doctorates; other purposes of doctoral training are acknowledged to be important, but they are outside the scope of the work contemplated. (2) The multidimensional approach represents an explicit recognition of the limitations of studies that make assessments solely in terms of ratings of perceived quality provided by peers--the so-called reputational ratings. Consequently, a variety of quality-related measures will be employed in the proposed study and will be incorporated in the presentation of the results of the study.[18]

This report formed the basis for the decision by the Conference Board to embark on a national assessment of doctorate-level programs in the sciences, engineering, and the humanities.

In June 1980 an 18-member committee was appointed to oversee the study. The committee,[19] made up of individuals from a diverse set of disciplines within the sciences, engineering, and the humanities, includes seven members who had been involved in the planning phase and several members who presently serve or have served as graduate deans in either public or private universities. During the first eight months the committee met three times to review plans for the study activities, make decisions on the selection of disciplines and programs to be covered, and design the survey instruments to be used. Early in the study an effort was made to solicit the views of presidents and graduate deans at more than 250 universities. Their suggestions were most helpful to the committee in drawing up final plans for the assessment. With the assistance of the Council of Graduate Schools in the

---

[18]National Research Council, A Plan to Study the Quality and Effectiveness of Research-Doctorate Programs, 1978 (unpublished report).
[19]See p. vii of this volume for a list of members of the study committee.

United States, the committee and its staff have tried to keep the graduate deans informed about the progress being made in this study. The final section of this chapter describes the procedures followed in determining which research-doctorate programs were to be included in the assessment.

SELECTION OF DISCIPLINES AND PROGRAMS TO BE EVALUATED

One of the most difficult decisions made by the study committee was the selection of disciplines to be covered in the assessment. Early in the planning stage it was recognized that some important areas of graduate education would have to be left out of the study. Limited financial resources required that efforts be concentrated on a total of no more than about 30 disciplines in the biological sciences, engineering, humanities, mathematical and physical sciences, and social sciences. At its initial meeting the committee decided that the selection of disciplines within each of these five areas should be made primarily on the basis of the total number of doctorates awarded nationally in recent years.

At the time the study was undertaken, aggregate counts of doctoral degrees earned during the FY1976-78 period were available from two independent sources--the Educational Testing Service (ETS) and the National Research Council (NRC). Table 1.1 presents doctoral awards data for 19 disciplines within the life sciences (including biological and agricultural sciences). As alluded to in footnote 1 of the table, discrepancies between the ETS and NRC counts may be explained, in part, by differences in the data collection procedures. The ETS counts, derived from information provided by universities, have been categorized according to the discipline of the department/academic unit in which the degree was earned. The NRC counts were tabulated from the survey responses of FY1976-78 Ph.D. recipients, who had been asked to identify their fields of specialty. Since separate totals for research doctorates in anatomy, biophysics, cellular/molecular biology, ecology, genetics, pathology, pharmacology, and physiology were not available from the ETS manual, the committee made its selection of six disciplines primarily on the basis of the NRC data. In the case of cellular/molecular biology, consideration was given to the fact that the NRC count excludes doctoral awards in genetics, anatomy, developmental biology, and other related fields and thus substantially underestimates the total number of doctorates in cellular/molecular biology.[20]

The selection of biological science disciplines to be covered in the assessment was especially difficult since there are differing opinions within the scientific community concerning the most appropri-

---

[20] Evidence for this may be found from the data provided by institutional coordinators, who reported that a total of 1,871 doctoral recipients graduated from 89 cellular/molecular biology programs during the FY1976-80 period. See Table 1.2, p. 13.

TABLE 1.1 Number of Research-Doctorates Awarded in Biological Science
Disciplines, FY1976-78

	Source of Data[1]	
	ETS	NRC
Disciplines Included in the Assessment		
Biochemistry	1,428	1,833
Microbiology	1,094	1,358
Zoology	1,045	743
Botany	869	890
Physiology	N/A	921
Cellular/Molecular Biology[2]	N/A	567
Total		6,312
Disciplines Not Included in the Assessment		
Public Health	647	372
Forestry & Natural Resources Mgmt.	620	416
Agronomy & Soil Sciences	616	642
Animal Sciences	521	321
Entomology	482	443
Agricultural Economics	477	464
Horticulture	197	176
Pharmacology	N/A	614
Ecology	N/A	473
Genetics	N/A	409
Anatomy	N/A	392
Biophysics	N/A	375
Pathology	N/A	282
Other Biological Sciences	N/A	2,671
TOTAL		8,050

[1]Data on FY1976-78 doctoral awards were derived from two independent
sources: Educational Testing Service (ETS), Graduate Programs and Ad-
missions Manual, 1979-81, and the NRC's Survey of Earned Doctorates,
1976-78. Differences in field definitions account for discrepancies
between the ETS and NRC data.
[2]NRC data exclude doctoral awards in genetics, anatomy, developmental
biology, and other related fields and thus substantially underestimate
the number of doctorates in cellular/molecular biology.

ate taxonomy of biological fields in graduate education and research. Several knowledgeable individuals were consulted regarding this matter. The taxonomy the committee decided to use in this assessment, although considered by some to be out of date, reflects the departmental structure commonly found in graduate institutions. Some readers may be surprised not to find biology among the six disciplines selected. Since biology encompasses many different biological science disciplines, members of the committee were concerned that a university coordinator, when asked to identify research-doctorate programs to be included in the assessment, might have considerable difficulty in deciding whether a particular biological science program belonged under "biology" or one of the other disciplinary categories. It should be noted that many programs found in departments of biology have been included in the assessment of programs in cellular/molecular biology. In addition, programs from departments of anatomy, biochemistry, biophysics, cell biology, developmental biology, and genetics have been included in the assessment in cellular and molecular biology (see Table 5.1 in Chapter V).

The selection of the research-doctorate programs to be evaluated in each discipline was made in two stages. Programs meeting either of the following criteria[21] were initially nominated for inclusion in the study:

(1) more than a specified number (see below) of research doctorates awarded during the FY1976-78 period or

(2) more than one-third of that specified number of doctorates awarded in FY1979.

In each discipline the specified number of doctorates required for inclusion in the study was determined in such a way that the programs meeting this criterion accounted for at least 90 percent of the doctorates awarded in that discipline during the FY1976-78 period. In the biological science disciplines the following numbers of FY1976-78 doctoral awards were required to satisfy the first criterion (above):

Biochemistry--5 or more doctorates
Botany--7 or more doctorates
Cellular/Molecular Biology--10 or more doctorates
Microbiology--4 or more doctorates
Physiology--11 or more doctorates
Zoology--8 or more doctorates

A list of the nominated programs at each institution was then sent to a designated individual (usually the graduate dean) who had been ap-

---

[21] In the first three volumes of the committee's study, which pertain to the mathematical and physical sciences, humanities, and engineering, it is mistakenly reported that a third criterion based on results from the Roose-Andersen study was used in the nomination of programs to be included in the assessment. This third criterion, while at one time considered by the committee, was not adopted.

pointed by the university president to serve as study coordinator for
the institution. The coordinator was asked to review the list and
eliminate any programs no longer offering research doctorates or
notbelonging in the designated discipline. The coordinator also was
given an opportunity to nominate additional programs that he or she
believed should be included in the study.[22] Coordinators were asked
to restrict their nominations to programs that they considered to be
"of uncommon distinction" and that had awarded no fewer than two research-doctorates during the past two years. In order to be eligible
for inclusion, of course, programs had to belong in one of the disciplines covered in the study. If the university offered more than one
research-doctorate program in a discipline, the coordinator was instructed to provide information on each of them so that these programs
could be evaluated separately. In each of the six biological science
disciplines it was not unusual for a university to have separate programs from the graduate school of arts and sciences and from the medical school, school of agriculture, or the school of public health. In
such cases the separate programs have been identified according to the
schools in which they reside within the university. In many institutions research-doctorate programs that have been identified as being
located in academic units other than arts and sciences nonetheless are
considered within the academic structure of the graduate school.

The committee received excellent cooperation from the study coordinators at universities. Of the 243 institutions that were identified
as having one or more research-doctorate programs satisfying the criteria (listed earlier) for inclusion in the study, only 7 declined to
participate in the study and another 8 failed to provide the program
information requested within the three-month period allotted (despite
several reminders). None of these 15 institutions had doctoral programs that had received strong or distinguished reputational ratings
in prior national studies. Since the information requested had not
been provided, the committee decided not to include programs from these
institutions in any aspect of the assessment. In each of the six chapters that follows, a list is given of the universities that met the
criteria for inclusion in a particular discipline but that are not
represented in the study.

As a result of nominations by institutional coordinators, some programs were added to the original list and others dropped. Table 1.2
reports the final coverage in each of the six biological science disciplines. The number of programs evaluated varies considerably by discipline. A total of 139 biochemistry and 134 microbiology programs have
been included in the study; in zoology only about half this number have
been included. Although the final determination of whether a program
should be considered in the assessment was left in the hands of the
institutional coordinator, it is entirely possible that a few programs
meeting the criteria for inclusion in the assessment were overlooked

----

[22]See Appendix A for the specific instructions given to the coordinators.

TABLE 1.2 Number of Programs Evaluated in Each Discipline and the Total FY1976-80 Doctoral Awards from These Programs

Discipline	Programs	FY1976-80 Doctorates*
Biochemistry	139	2,753
Botany	83	1,574
Cellular/Molecular Biology	89	1,871
Microbiology	134	2,058
Physiology	101	1,369
Zoology	70	1,753
TOTAL	616	11,378

*The data on doctoral awards were provided by the study coordinator at each of the universities covered in the assessment.

by the coordinators. Of particular concern in this regard is the selection of cellular/molecular biology programs. Because of the diversity of departmental structures within universities, one is likely to find inconsistencies in the identification of research-doctorate programs in this discipline. For example, some coordinators decided to include programs in departments of genetics and anatomy, while others chose to exclude such programs.

In the chapter that follows, a detailed description is given of each of the measures used in the evaluation of research-doctorate programs in the biological sciences. The description includes a discussion of the rationale for using the measure, the source from which data for that measure were derived, and any known limitations that would affect the interpretation of the data reported. The committee wishes to emphasize that there are limitations associated with each of the measures and that none of the measures should be regarded as a precise indicator of the quality of a program in educating scientists for careers in research. The reader is strongly urged to consider the descriptive material presented in Chapter II before attempting to interpret the program evaluations reported in subsequent chapters. In presenting a frank discussion of any shortcomings of each measure, the committee's intent is to reduce the possibility of misuse of the results from this assessment of research-doctorate programs.

II
Methodology

Quality . . . you know what it is, yet you don't know
what it is. But that's self-contradictory. But some
things are better than others, that is, they have more
quality. But when you try to say what the quality is,
apart from the things that have it, it all goes poof!
There's nothing to talk about. But if you can't say
what Quality is, how do you know what it is, or how do
you know that it even exists? If no one knows what it
is, then for all practical purposes it doesn't exist
at all. But for all practical purposes it really does
exist. What else are the grades based on? Why else
would people pay fortunes for some things and throw
others in the trash pile? Obviously some things are
better than others . . . but what's the "betterness"?
. . . So round and round you go, spinning mental wheels
and nowhere finding anyplace to get traction. What the
hell is Quality? What is it?

> Robert M. Pirsig
> Zen and the Art of
> Motorcycle Maintenance

Both the planning committee and our own study committee have given
careful consideration to the types of measures to be employed in the
assessment of research-doctorate programs.[1] The committees recognized that any of the measures that might be used is open to criticism
and that no single measure could be expected to provide an entirely
satisfactory index of the quality of graduate education. With respect
to the use of multiple criteria in educational assessment, one critic
has commented:

---

[1]A description of the measures considered may be found in the third
chapter of the planning committee's report, along with a discussion of
the relative merits of each measure.

> At best each is a partial measure encompassing a frac-
> tion of the large concept. On occasion its link to the
> real [world] is problematic and tenuous. Moreover,
> each measure [may contain] a load of irrelevant super-
> fluities, "extra baggage" unrelated to the outcomes
> under study. By the use of a number of such measures,
> each contributing a different facet of information, we
> can limit the effect of irrelevancies and develop a
> more rounded and truer picture of program outcomes.[2]

Although the use of multiple measures alleviates the criticisms
directed at a single dimension or measure, it certainly will not satisfy those who believe that the quality of graduate programs cannot be
represented by quantitative estimates no matter how many dimensions
they may be intended to represent. Furthermore, the usefulness of the
assessment is dependent on the validity and reliability of the criteria
on which programs are evaluated. The decision concerning which measures to adopt in the study was made primarily on the basis of two factors:

(1) the extent to which a measure was judged to be
     related to the quality of research-doctorate pro-
     grams and
(2) the feasibility of compiling reliable data for
     making national comparisons of programs in par-
     ticular disciplines.

Only measures that were applicable to a majority of the disciplines to
be covered were considered. In reaching a final decision the study
committee found the ETS study,[3] in which 27 separate variables were
examined, especially helpful, even though it was recognized that many
of the measures feasible in institutional self-studies would not be
available in a national study. The committee was aided by the many
suggestions received from university administrators and others within
the academic community.

Although the initial design called for an assessment based on approximately six measures, the committee concluded that it would be
highly desirable to expand this effort. As many as 16 measures (listed
in Table 2.1) have been utilized in the assessment of research-doctorate programs in biochemistry, botany, cellular/molecular biology,
microbiology, physiology, and zoology. For nine of the measures data
are available describing most, if not all, of the biological science
programs included in the assessment. For seven measures the coverage
is less complete but encompasses a large fraction of the programs in

---

[2]C. H. Weiss, _Evaluation Research: Methods of Assessing Program Ef-
fectiveness_, Prentice-Hall, Inc., Englewood Cliffs, New Jersey, 1972,
p. 56.
[3]See M. J. Clark et al. (1976) for a description of these variables.

TABLE 2.1 Measures Compiled on Individual Research-Doctorate Programs in the Biological Sciences

Program Size[1]

01 Reported number of faculty members in the program, December 1980.

02 Reported number of program graduates in last five years (July 1975 through June 1980).

03 Reported total number of full-time and part-time graduate students enrolled in the program who intend to earn doctorates, December 1980.

Characteristics of Graduates[2]

04 Fraction of FY1975-79 program graduates who had received some national fellowship or training grant support during their graduate education.

05 Median number of years from first enrollment in graduate school to receipt of the doctorate--FY1975-79 program graduates.[3]

06 Fraction of FY1975-79 program graduates who at the time they completed requirements for the doctorate reported that they had made definite commitments for postgraduation employment.

07 Fraction of FY1975-79 program graduates who at the time they completed requirements for the doctorate reported that they had made definite commitments for postgraduation employment in Ph.D.-granting universities.

Reputational Survey Results[4]

08 Mean rating of the scholarly quality of program faculty.

09 Mean rating of the effectiveness of the program in educating research scholars/scientists.

10 Mean rating of the improvement in program quality in the last five years.

11 Mean rating of the evaluators' familiarity with the work of the program's faculty.

University Library Size[5]

12 Composite index describing the library size in the university in which the program is located, 1979-80.

Research Support

13 Fraction of program faculty members holding research grants from the National Institutes of Health, the National Science Foundation, or the Alcohol, Drug Abuse, and Mental Health Administration at any time during the FY1978-80 period.[6]

14 Total expenditures (in thousands of dollars) reported by the university for research and development activities in a specified field, FY1979.[7]

Publication Records[8]

15 Number of published articles attributed to the program, 1978-79.

16 Estimated "overall influence" of published articles attributed to the program, 1978-79.

[1]Based on information provided to the committee by the participating universities.
[2]Based on data compiled in the NRC's Survey of Earned Doctorates.
[3]In reporting standardized scores and correlations with other variables, a shorter time-to-Ph.D. is assigned a higher score.
[4]Based on responses to the committee's survey conducted in April 1981.
[5]Based on data compiled by the Association of Research Libraries.
[6]Based on matching faculty names provided by institutional coordinators with the names of research grant awardees from the three federal agencies.
[7]Based on data provided to the National Science Foundation by universities.
[8]Based on data compiled by the Institute for Scientific Information and developed by Computer Horizons, Inc.

every discipline. The actual number of programs evaluated on every measure is reported in the second table in each of the next six chapters.

The 16 measures describe a variety of aspects important to the operation and function of research-doctorate programs--and thus are relevant to the quality and effectiveness of programs in educating scientists for careers in research. However, not all of the measures may be viewed as "global indices of quality." Some, such as those relating to program size, are best characterized as "program descriptors" that, although not dimensions of quality per se, are thought to have a significant influence on the effectiveness of programs. Other measures, such as those relating to university library size and support for research and training, describe some of the resources generally recognized as being important in maintaining a vibrant program in graduate education. Measures derived from surveys of faculty peers or from the publication records of faculty members, on the other hand, have traditionally been regarded as indices of the overall quality of graduate programs. Yet these too are not true measures of quality.

> We often settle for an easy-to-gather statistic, perfectly legitimate for its own limited purposes, and then forget that we haven't measured what we want to talk about. Consider, for instance, the reputation approach of ranking graduate departments: We ask a sample of physics professors (say) which the best physics departments are and then tabulate and report the results. The "best" departments are those that our respondents say are the best. Clearly it is useful to know which are the highly regarded departments in a given field, but prestige (which is what we are measuring here) isn't exactly the same as quality.[4]

To be sure, each of the 16 measures reported in this assessment has its own set of limitations. In the sections that follow an explanation is provided of how each measure has been derived and its particular limitations as a descriptor of research-doctorate programs.

PROGRAM SIZE

Information was collected from the study coordinators at each university on the names and ranks of program faculty, doctoral student enrollment, and number of Ph.D. graduates in each of the past five years (FY1976-80). Each coordinator was instructed to include on the faculty list those individuals who, as of December 1, 1980, held academic appointments (typically at the rank of assistant, associate,

---

[4]John Shelton Reed, "How Not To Measure What a University Does," The Chronicle of Higher Education, Vol. 22, No. 12, May 11, 1981, p. 56.

and full professor) and who participated significantly in doctoral
education. Emeritus and adjunct members generally were not to be included. Measure 01 represents the number of faculty identified in a
program. Measure 02 is the reported number of graduates who earned
Ph.D. or equivalent research doctorates in a program during the period
from July 1, 1975, through June 30, 1980. Measure 03 represents the
total number of full-time and part-time students reported to be enrolled in a program in the fall of 1980, who intended to earn research
doctorates. All three of these measures describe different aspects of
program size. In previous studies program size has been shown to be
highly correlated with the reputational ratings of a program, and this
relationship is examined in detail in this report. It should be noted
that since the information was provided by the institutions participating in the study, the data may be influenced by the subjective decisions made by the individuals completing the forms. For example,
some institutional coordinators may be far less restrictive than others
in deciding who should be included on the list of program faculty. To
minimize variation in interpretation, detailed instructions were provided to those filling out the forms.[5] Measure 03 is of particular
concern in this regard since the coordinators at some institutions may
not have known how many of the students currently enrolled in graduate
study intended to earn doctoral degrees.

CHARACTERISTICS OF GRADUATES

One of the most meaningful measures of the success of a research-
doctorate program is the performance of its graduates. How many go on
to lead productive careers in research and/or teaching? Unfortunately,
reliable information on the subsequent employment and career achievements of the graduates of individual programs is not available. In the
absence of this directly relevant information, the committee has relied
on four indirect measures derived from data compiled in the NRC's Survey of Earned Doctorates.[6] Although each measure has serious limitations (described below), the committee believes it more desirable to
include this information than not to include data about program graduates.
In identifying program graduates who had received their doctorates
in the previous five years (FY1975-79),[7] the faculty lists furnished
by the study coordinators at universities were compared with the names
of dissertation advisers (available from the NRC survey). The latter
source contains records for virtually all individuals who have earned

---

[5] A copy of the survey form with the instructions sent to study coordinators is included in Appendix A.
[6] A copy of the questionnaire used in this survey is found in Appendix B.
[7] Survey data for the FY1980 Ph.D. recipients had not yet been compiled at the time this assessment was undertaken.

research doctorates from U.S. universities since 1920. The institution, year, and specialty field of Ph.D. recipients were also used in determining the identity of program graduates. It is estimated that this matching process provided information on the graduate training and employment plans of more than 80 percent of the FY1975-79 graduates from the biological science programs. In the calculation of each of the four measures derived from the NRC survey, program data are reported only if the survey information is available on at least 10 graduates. Consequently, in a discipline with smaller programs--physiology--slightly less than half the programs are included in these measures, whereas more than 80 percent of the zoology programs are included.

Measure 04 constitutes the fraction of FY1975-79 graduates of a program who had received at least some national fellowship support, including National Institutes of Health fellowships or traineeships, National Science Foundation fellowships, other federal fellowships, Woodrow Wilson fellowships, or fellowships/traineeships from other U.S. national organizations. One might expect the more selective programs to have a greater proportion of students with national fellowship support--especially "portable fellowships." Although the committee considered alternative measures of student ability (e.g., Graduate Record Examination scores, undergraduate grade point averages), reliable information of this sort was unavailable for a national assessment. It should be noted that the relevance of the fellowship measure varies considerably among disciplines. In the biomedical sciences a substantial fraction of the graduate students are supported by training grants and fellowships; in most other sciences and engineering disciplines a majority are supported by research assistantships and teaching assistantships. Even in the biological disciplines, however, differences in the patterns of graduate student support at different universities may sharply affect measure 04. Some departments with sizable undergraduate enrollments, for example, may have large numbers of teaching assistantships paid out of state or institutional funds--thereby reducing the need for federal training grant or fellowship support. Similarly, some departments may have an established policy of supporting graduate students as research assistants rather than seeking federal training grant support for their students.

Measure 05 is the median number of years elapsed from the time program graduates first enrolled in graduate school to the time they received their doctoral degrees. For purposes of analysis the committee has adopted the conventional wisdom that the most talented students are likely to earn their doctoral degrees in the shortest periods of time--hence, the shorter the median time-to-Ph.D., the higher the standardized score that is assigned. Although this measure has frequently been employed in social science research as a proxy for student ability, one must regard its use here with some skepticism. It is quite possible that the length of time it takes a student to complete requirements for a doctorate may be significantly affected by the explicit or implicit policies of a university or department. For example, in certain cases a short time-to-Ph.D. may be indicative of less stringent requirements for the degree. Furthermore, previous studies have demonstrated that women and members of minority groups, for reasons having nothing to do with their abilities, are more likely than male Caucasians to interrupt their graduate education or to be enrolled on a part-time basis.[8] As a consequence, the median time-to-Ph.D. may be longer for programs with larger fractions of women and minority students.

Measure 06 represents the fraction of FY1975-79 program graduates who reported at the time they had completed requirements for the doctorate that they had signed contracts or made firm commitments for postgraduation employment (including postdoctoral appointments as well as other positions in the academic or nonacademic sectors) and who provided the names of their prospective employers. Although this measure is likely to vary discipline by discipline according to the availability of employment opportunities, a program's standing relative to other programs in the same discipline should not be affected by this variation. In theory, the graduates with the greatest promise should have the easiest time in finding jobs. However, the measure is also influenced by a variety of other factors, such as personal job preferences and restrictions in geographic mobility, that are unrelated to the ability of the individual. It also should be noted parenthetically that unemployment rates for doctoral recipients are quite low and that nearly all of the graduates seeking jobs find positions soon after completing their doctoral programs.[9] Furthermore, first employment after graduation is by no means a measure of career achievement, which is what one would like to have if reliable data were available.

Measure 07, a variant of measure 06, constitutes the fraction of FY1975-79 program graduates who indicated that they had made firm commitments for employment in Ph.D.-granting universities and who provided the names of their prospective employers. This measure may be presumed to be an indication of the fraction of graduates likely to pursue careers in academic research, although there is no evidence concerning how many of them remain in academic research in the long term. In many science disciplines the path from Ph.D. to postdoctoral apprenticeship to junior faculty has traditionally been regarded as the road of success for the growth and development of research talent. The committee is well aware, of course, that other paths, such as employment in the major laboratories of industry and government, provide equally attractive opportunities for growth. Indeed, in recent years increasing numbers of graduates are entering the nonacademic sectors. Unfortunately the data compiled from the NRC's Survey of Earned Doctorates do

---

[8] For a detailed analysis of this subject, see Dorothy M. Gilford and Joan Snyder, Women and Minority Ph.D.'s in the 1970's: A Data Book, National Academy of Sciences, Washington, D.C., 1977.
[9] For new Ph.D. recipients in science and engineering the unemployment rate has been less than 2 percent (see National Research Council, Postdoctoral Appointments and Disappointments, National Academy Press, Washington, D.C., 1981, p. 313).

TABLE 2.2   Percentage of FY1975-79 Doctoral Recipients with Definite
Commitments for Employment Outside the Academic Sector*

Biochemistry	22
Botany	28
Cellular/Molecular Biology	22
Microbiology	31
Physiology	16
Zoology	24

*Percentages are based on responses to the NRC's Survey of Earned Doc-
torates by those who indicated that they had made firm commitments for
postgraduation employment and who provided the names of their prospective employers. These percentages may be considered to be lower-bound
estimates of the actual percentages of doctoral recipients employed
outside the academic sector.

not enable one to distinguish between employment in the top-flight
laboratories of industry and government and employment in other areas
of the nonacademic sectors. Accordingly, the committee has relied on
a measure that reflects only the academic side and views this measure
as a useful and interesting program characteristic rather than a dimension of quality. In the biological science disciplines, in which
only about one-fourth of the graduates take jobs outside the academic
environs (see Table 2.2), this limitation is not as serious a concern
as it is in the engineering and physical science disciplines.

The inclusion of measures 06 and 07 in this assessment has been an
issue much debated by members of the committee; the strenuous objections by three committee members regarding the use of these measures
are expressed in the Minority Statement, which follows Chapter IX.

REPUTATIONAL SURVEY RESULTS

In April 1981 survey forms were mailed to a total of 1,848 faculty
members in biochemistry, botany, cellular/molecular biology, microbiology, physiology, and zoology. The evaluators were selected from the
faculty lists furnished by the study coordinators at the 228 universities covered in the assessment. These evaluators constituted approximately 15 percent of the total faculty population--12,167 faculty mem-
bers--in the biological science programs being evaluated (see Table
2.3). The survey sample was chosen on the basis of the number of faculty in a particular program and the number of doctorates awarded in
the previous five years (FY1976-80)--with the stipulation that at least
one evaluator was selected from every program covered in the assessment. In selecting the sample each faculty rank was represented in
proportion to the total number of individuals holding that rank, and
preference was given to those faculty members whom the study coordinators had nominated to serve as evaluators. As shown in Table 2.3,

1,485 individuals, 80 percent of the survey sample in the biological sciences, had been recommended by study coordinators.[10]

Each evaluator was asked to consider a stratified random sample of 50 research-doctorate programs in his or her discipline--with programs stratified by the number of faculty members associated with each program. Every program was included on 150 survey forms. The 50 programs to be evaluated appeared on each survey form in random sequence, preceded by an alphabetized list of all programs in that discipline that were being included in the study. No evaluator was asked to consider a program at his or her own institution. Ninety percent of the survey sample group were provided the names of faculty members in each of the 50 programs to be evaluated, along with data on the total number of doctorates awarded in the last five years.[11] The inclusion of this information represents a significant departure from the procedures used in earlier reputational assessments. For purposes of comparison with previous studies, 10 percent (randomly selected in each discipline) were not furnished any information other than the names of the programs.

The survey items were adapted from the form used in the Roose-Andersen study. Prior to mailing, the instrument was pretested using a small sample of faculty members in chemistry and psychology. As a result, two significant improvements were made in the original survey design. A question was added on the extent to which the evaluator was familiar with the work of the faculty in each program. Responses to this question, reported as measure 11, provide some insight into the relationship between faculty recognition and the reputational standing of a program.[12] Also added was a question on the evaluator's field of specialization--thereby making it possible to compare program evaluations in different specialty areas within a particular discipline.

A total of 1,026 faculty members in the biological sciences--56 percent of those asked to participate--completed and returned survey forms (see Table 2.3). Two factors probably have contributed to this response rate being approximately 15 percentage points below the rates reported in the Cartter and Roose-Andersen studies. First, because of the considerable expense of printing individualized survey forms (each 25-30 pages), second copies were not sent to sample members not responding to the first mailing[13]--as was done in the Cartter and Roose-Andersen efforts. Second, it is quite apparent that within the

---

[10]A detailed analysis of the survey participants in each discipline is given in subsequent chapters.

[11]This information was furnished to the committee by the study coordinators at the universities participating in the study.

[12]Evidence of the strength of the relationship is provided by correlations presented in Chapters III-VIII, and an analysis of the relationship is provided in Chapter IX.

[13]A follow-up letter was sent to those not responding to the first mailing, and a second copy was distributed to those few evaluators who specifically requested another form.

TABLE 2.3   Survey Response by Discipline and Characteristics
of Evaluator

	Total Program Faculty N		Survey Sample	
			Total N	Respondents
				N	%
Discipline of Evaluator					
Biochemistry	2,658		417	234	56
Botany	1,589		249	153	61
Cellular/Molecular Biology	2,271		267	139	52
Microbiology	2,195		402	231	58
Physiology	1,964		303	146	48
Zoology	1,490		210	123	59
Faculty Rank					
Professor	6,188		956	510	53
Associate Professor	3,334		597	334	56
Assistant Professor	2,389		292	181	62
Other	256		3	1	33
Evaluator Selection					
Nominated by Institution	3,467		1,485	856	58
Other	8,700		363	170	47
Survey Form					
With Faculty Names	N/A*		1,662	935	56
Without Names	N/A*		186	91	49
Total All Fields	12,167		1,848	1,026	56

*Not applicable.

academic community there has been a growing dissatisfaction in recent years
with educational assessments based on reputational measures. Indeed, this
dissatisfaction was an important factor in the Conference Board's decision
to undertake a multidimensional assessment, and some faculty members
included in the sample made known to the committee their strong objections
to the reputational survey.

As can be seen in Table 2.3, there is some variation in the response
rates in the six biological science disciplines. Of particular interest

is the relatively high rate of response from botanists and the low
rate from physiologists--a result consistent with the findings in the
Cartter and Roose-Andersen surveys.[14] It is not surprising to find
that the evaluators nominated by study coordinators responded more
often than did those who had been selected at random. No appreciable
differences were found among the response rates of assistant, associate, and full professors or between the rates of those evaluators who
were furnished the abbreviated survey form (without lists of program
faculty) and those who were given the longer version.

Each program was considered by an average of approximately 85
survey respondents from other programs in the same discipline. The
evaluators were asked to judge programs in terms of scholarly quality
of program faculty, effectiveness of the program in educating research
scholars/scientists, and change in program quality in the last five
years.[15] The mean ratings of a program on these three survey items
constitute measures 08, 09, and 10. Evaluators were also asked to indicate the extent to which they were familiar with the work of the
program faculty. The average of responses to this item constitutes
measure 11.

In making judgments about the quality of faculty, evaluators were
instructed to consider the scholarly competence and achievements of the
individuals. The ratings were furnished on the following scale:

> 5 Distinguished
> 4 Strong
> 3 Good
> 2 Adequate
> 1 Marginal
> 0 Not sufficient for doctoral education
> X Don't know well enough to evaluate

In assessing the effectiveness of a program, evaluators were asked to
consider the accessibility of faculty, the curricula, the instructional
and research facilities, the quality of the graduate students, the
performance of graduates, and other factors that contribute to a program's effectiveness. This measure was rated accordingly:

> 3 Extremely effective
> 2 Reasonably effective
> 1 Minimally effective
> 0 Not effective
> X Don't know well enough to evaluate

---

[14]To compare the response rates obtained in the earlier surveys, see
Roose and Andersen, Table 28, p. 29.

[15]A copy of the survey instrument with its accompanying instructions
is included in Appendix C.

Evaluators were instructed to assess change in program quality on the basis of whether there has been improvement in the last five years in both the scholarly quality of faculty and the effectiveness in educating research scholars/scientists. The following alternatives were provided:

2 Better than five years ago
1 Little or no change in last five years
0 Poorer than five years ago
X Don't know well enough to evaluate

Evaluators were asked to indicate their familiarity with the work of the program faculty according to the following scale:

2 Considerable familiarity
1 Some familiarity
0 Little or no familiarity

In the computation of mean ratings on measures 08, 09, and 10, the "don't know" responses were ignored. An average program rating based on fewer than 15 responses (excluding the "don't know" responses) is not reported.

Measures 08, 09, and 10 are subject to many of the same criticisms that have been directed at previous reputational surveys. Although care has been taken to improve the sampling design and to provide evaluators with some essential information about each program, the survey results merely reflect a consensus of faculty opinions. As discussed in Chapter I, these opinions may well be based on out of date information or be influenced by a variety of factors unrelated to the quality of the program. In Chapter IX a number of factors that may possibly affect the survey results are examined. In addition to these limitations, it should be pointed out that evaluators, on the average, were unfamiliar with almost half of the programs they were asked to consider.[16] As might be expected, the smaller and less prestigious programs were not as well known, and for this reason one might have less confidence in the average ratings of these programs. For all four survey measures, standard errors of the mean ratings are reported; they tend to be larger for the lesser known programs. The frequency of response to each of the survey items is discussed in Chapter IX.

Two additional comments should be made regarding the survey activity. First, it should be emphasized that the ratings derived from the survey reflect a program's standing relative to other programs in the same discipline and provide no basis for making cross-disciplinary comparisons. For example, the fact that a larger number of microbiology programs received "distinguished" ratings on measure 08 than did zoology programs indicates nothing about the relative quality of faculty in these two disciplines. It may depend, in part, on the total numbers of programs evaluated in these disciplines; in the survey in-

---

[16] See Table 9.6 in Chapter IX.

structions it was suggested to evaluators that no more than 10 percent of the programs listed be designated as "distinguished." Nor is it advisable to compare the rating of a program in one discipline with that of a program in another discipline because the ratings are based on the opinions of different groups of evaluators who were asked to judge entirely different sets of programs. Second, early in the committee's deliberations a decision was made to supplement the ratings obtained from faculty members with ratings from evaluators who hold research-oriented positions in institutions outside the academic sector. These institutions include industrial research laboratories, government research laboratories, and a variety of other research establishments. Over the past 10 years increasing numbers of doctoral recipients have taken positions outside the academic setting. The extensive involvement of these graduates in nonacademic employment is reflected in the percentages reported in Table 2.2: An average of 24 percent of the recent graduates in the biological science disciplines who had definite employment plans indicated that they planned to take positions in nonacademic settings. Data from another NRC survey suggest that the actual fraction employed outside academia may be significantly higher. The committee recognized that the inclusion of nonacademic evaluators would furnish information valuable for assessing nontraditional dimensions of doctoral education and would provide an important new measure not assessed in earlier studies. Results from a survey of this group would provide an interesting comparison with the results obtained from the survey of faculty members. A concentrated effort was made to obtain supplemental funding for adding nonacademic evaluators in selected disciplines to the survey sample, but this effort was unsuccessful. The committee nevertheless remains convinced of the importance of including evaluators from nonacademic research institutions. These institutions are likely to employ increasing numbers of graduates in many disciplines, and it is urged that this group not be overlooked in future assessments of graduate programs.

UNIVERSITY LIBRARY SIZE

University library holdings are generally regarded as an important resource for students in graduate (and undergraduate) education. The Association of Research Libraries (ARL) has compiled data from its academic member institutions and developed a composite measure of a university library's size relative to those of other ARL members. The ARL Library Index, as it is called, is based on 10 characteristics: volumes held, volumes added (gross), microform units held, current serials received, expenditures for library materials, expenditures for binding, total salary and wage expenditures, other operating expenditures, number of professional staff, and number of nonprofessional staff.[17] The 1979-80 index, which constitutes measure 12, is available for 89 of the 228 universities included in the assessment. (These

---

[17]See Appendix D for a description of the calculation of this index.

89 tend to be among the largest institutions.) The limited coverage
of this measure is a major shortcoming. It should be noted that the
ARL index is a composite description of library size and not a qualitative evaluation of the collections, services, or operations of the
library. Also, it is a measure of aggregate size and does not take
into account the library holdings in a particular department or discipline. Finally, although universities with more than one campus were
instructed to include figures for the main campus only, some in fact
may have reported library size for the entire university system.
Whether this misreporting occurred is not known.

RESEARCH SUPPORT

Using computerized data files[18] provided by the National Science
Foundation (NSF) and the National Institutes of Health (NIH), it was
possible to identify which faculty members in each program had been
awarded research grants during the FY1978-80 period by either of these
agencies or by the Alcohol, Drug Abuse, and Mental Health Administration (ADAMHA). The fraction of faculty members in a program who had
received any research grants from these agencies during this three-year
period constitutes measure 13. Since these awards have been made on
the basis of peer judgment, this measure is considered to reflect the
perceived research competence of program faculty. However, it should
be noted that significant amounts of support for research in the biological sciences come from other federal agencies as well, but it was
not feasible to compile data from these other sources. It is estimated[19] that 57 percent of the university faculty members in these
disciplines who received federal R&D funding obtained their support
from NIH and another 24 percent from NSF. The remaining 19 percent
received support from the U.S. Department of Agriculture and other
federal agencies. It should be pointed out that only those faculty
members who served as principal investigators or coinvestigators are
counted in the computation of this measure.

Measure 14 describes the total FY1979 expenditures by a university
for R&D in the biological disciplines. These data have been furnished
to the NSF[20] by universities and include expenditures of funds from
both federal and nonfederal sources. If an institution has more than
one program being evaluated in the same discipline, the aggregate university expenditures for research in that discipline are reported for
each of the programs. In each discipline data are recorded for the 100
universities with the largest R&D expenditures. Unfortunately, these
data are available only for aggregate expenditures in the biological

---

[18] A description of these files is provided in Appendix E.
[19] Based on special tabulations of data from the NRC's Survey of
Doctorate Recipients, 1979.
[20] A copy of the survey instrument used to collect these data appears
in Appendix E.

sciences and are not for expenditures in the individual biological disciplines; thus the value reported for an individual program represents the total university expenditures in the biological sciences.

This measure has several other limitations related to the procedures by which the data have been collected. The committee notes that there is evidence within the source document[21] that universities use different practices for categorizing and reporting expenditures. Apparently, institutional support of research, industrial support of research, and expenditure of indirect costs are reported by different institutions in different categories (or not reported at all). Since measure 14 is based on total expenditures from all sources, the data used here are perturbed only when these types of expenditures are not subsumed under any reporting category. In contrast with measure 13, measure 14 is not reported on a scale relative to the number of faculty members and thus reflects the overall level of research activity at an institution in a particular discipline. Although research grants in the sciences and engineering provide some support for graduate students as well, these measures should not be confused with measure 04, which pertains to fellowships and training grants.

PUBLICATION RECORDS

Data from the 1978 and the 1979 Science Citation Index have been compiled[22] on published articles associated with research-doctorate programs in the biological sciences. Publication counts were associated with programs on the basis of the discipline of the journal in which an article appeared and the institution with which the author was affiliated. Coauthored articles were proportionately attributed to the institutions of the individual authors. Articles appearing in multi-disciplinary journals (e.g., Science, Nature) were apportioned according to the characteristic mix of subject matter in those journals. For the purposes of assigning publication counts, this mix can be estimated with reasonable accuracy.[23]

Two measures have been derived from the publication records: measure 15--the total number of articles published in the 1978-79 period that have been associated with a research-doctorate program; and measure 16--an estimation of the "influence" of these articles. The latter is a product of the number of articles attributed to a program

---

[21]National Science Foundation, Academic Science: R and D Funds, Fiscal Year 1979, Government Printing Office, Washington, D.C., NSF 81-301, 1981.

[22]The publication data have been generated for the committee's use by Computer Horizons, Inc., using source files provided by the Institute for Scientific Information.

[23]Francis Narin, Evaluative Bibliometrics: The Use of Publications and Citations Analysis in the Evaluation of Scientific Activity, Report to the National Science Foundation, March 1976, p. 203.

and the estimated influence of the journals in which these articles appeared. The influence of a journal is determined from the weighted number of times, on the average, an article in that journal is cited--with references from frequently cited journals counting more heavily. A more detailed explanation of the derivation of these measures is given in Appendix F. Neither measure 15 nor measure 16 is based on actual counts of articles written only by program faculty. However, extensive analysis of the "influence" index in the fields of physics, chemistry, and biochemistry has demonstrated the stability of this index and the reliability associated with its use.[24] Of course, this does not imply that the measure captures subtle aspects of publication "influence." It is of interest to note that indices similar to measures 15 and 16 have been shown to be highly correlated with the peer ratings of graduate departments compiled in the Roose-Andersen study.[25]

It must be emphasized that these measures encompass articles (published in selected journals) by _all_ authors affiliated with a given university. Included therefore are articles by program faculty members, students and research personnel, and even members of other departments in that university who publish in those journals. Moreover, these measures do not take into account the differing sizes of programs, and the measures clearly do depend on faculty size. Although consideration was given to reporting the number of published articles _per_ _faculty_ _member_, the committee concluded that since the measure included articles by other individuals besides program faculty members, the aggregate number of articles would be a more reliable measure of overall program quality. It should be noted that if a university had more than one program being evaluated in the same discipline, it was not possible to distinguish the relative contribution of each program. In such cases the aggregate university data in that discipline were assigned to each program.

Since the data are confined to 1978-79, they do not take into account institutional mobility of authors after that period. Thus, articles by authors who have moved from one institution to another since 1979 are credited to the former institution. Also, the publication counts fail to include the contributions of faculty members' publications in journals outside their primary discipline. This point may be especially important for those programs with faculty members whose research is at the intersection of several different disciplines.

The reader should be aware of two additional caveats with regard to the interpretation of measures 15 and 16. First, both measures are based on counts of published articles and do not include books. Since

---

[24]Narin, pp. 283-307.
[25]Richard C. Anderson, Francis Narin, and Paul McAllister, "Publication Ratings Versus Peer Ratings of Universities," _Journal of the American Society for Information Science_, March 1978, pp. 91-103; and Lyle V. Jones, "The Assessment of Scholarship," _New Directions for Program Evaluation_, No. 6, 1980, pp. 1-20.

in the biological sciences most scholarly contributions are published as journal articles, this may not be a serious limitation. Second, the "influence" measure should <u>not</u> be interpreted as an indicator of the impact of articles by individual authors. Rather it is a measure of the impact of the <u>journals</u> in which articles associated with a particular program have been published. Citation counts, with all their difficulties, would have been preferable since they are attributable to individual authors and they register the impact of books as well as journal articles. However, the difficulty and cost of assembling reliable counts of articles by individual authors made their use infeasible.

ANALYSIS AND PRESENTATION OF THE DATA

The next six chapters present all of the information that has been compiled on individual research-doctorate programs in biochemistry, botany, cellular/molecular biology, microbiology, physiology, and zoology. Each chapter follows a similar format, designed to assist the reader in the interpretation of program data. The first table in a chapter provides a list of the programs evaluated in a discipline—including the names of the universities and departments or academic units in which programs reside—along with the full set of data compiled for individual programs. Programs are listed alphabetically according to name of institution, and both raw and standardized values are given for all but one measure.[26] For the reader's convenience an insert of information from Table 2.1 is provided that identifies each of the 16 measures reported in the table and indicates the raw scale used in reporting values for a particular measure. Standardized values, converted from raw values to have a mean of 50 and a standard deviation of 10,[27] are computed for every measure so that comparisons can easily be made of a program's relative standing on different measures. Thus, a standardized value of 30 corresponds with a raw value that is two standard deviations below the mean for that measure, and a standardized value of 70 represents a raw value two standard deviations above the mean. While the reporting of values in standardized form is convenient for comparing a particular program's standing on different measures, it may be misleading in interpreting actual differences in the values reported for two or more programs—especially when the distribution of the measure being examined is highly skewed. For example, the numbers of published articles (measure 15) associated with four biochemistry programs are reported in Table 3.1 as follows:

---

[26] Since the scale used to compute measure 16—the estimated "influence" of published articles—is entirely arbitrary, only standardized values are reported for this measure.

[27] The conversion was made from the precise raw value rather than from the rounded value reported for each program. Thus, two programs may have the same reported raw value for a particular measure but different standardized values.

Program	Raw Value	Standardized Value
A	1	40
B	6	40
C	21	42
D	38	44

Although programs C and D have many times the number of articles as have programs A and B, the differences reported on a standardized scale appear to be small. Thus, the reader is urged to take note of the raw values before attempting to interpret differences in the standardized values given for two or more programs.

The initial table in each chapter also presents estimated standard errors of mean ratings derived from the four survey items (measures 08-11). A standard error is an estimated standard deviation of the sample mean rating and may be used to assess the stability of a mean rating reported for a particular program.[28] For example, one may assert (with .95 confidence) that the population mean rating would lie within two standard errors of the sample mean rating reported in this assessment.

No attempt has been made to establish a composite ranking of programs in a discipline. Indeed, the committee is convinced that no single measure adequately reflects the quality of a research-doctorate program and wishes to emphasize the importance of viewing individual programs from the perspective of multiple indices or dimensions.

The second table in each chapter presents summary statistics (i.e., number of programs evaluated, mean, standard deviation, and decile values) for each of the program measures.[29] The reader should find these statistics helpful in interpreting the data reported on individual programs. Next is a table of the intercorrelations among the various measures for that discipline. This table should be of particular interest to those desiring information about the interrelations of the various measures.

The remainder of each chapter is devoted to an examination of results from the reputational survey. Included are an analysis of the characteristics of survey participants and graphical portrayals of the relationship of the mean rating of scholarly quality of faculty (measure 08) with the number of faculty (measure 01) and the relationship

---

[28]The standard error estimate has been computed by dividing the standard deviation of a program's ratings by the square root of the number of ratings. For a more extensive discussion of this topic, see Fred N. Kerlinger, Foundations of Behavioral Research, Holt, Reinhart, and Winston, Inc., New York, 1973, Chapter 12. Readers should note that the estimate is a measure of the variation in response and by no means includes all possible sources of error.

[29]Standardized scores have been computed from precise values of the mean and standard deviation of each measure and not the rounded values reported in the second table of a chapter.

of the mean rating of program effectiveness (measure 09) with the number of graduates (measure 02). A frequently mentioned criticism of the Roose-Andersen and Cartter studies is that small but distinguished programs have been penalized in the reputational ratings because they are not as highly visible as larger programs of comparable quality. The comparisons of survey ratings with measures of program size are presented as the first two figures in each chapter and provide evidence about the number of small programs in each discipline that have received high reputational ratings. Since in each case the reputational rating is more highly correlated with the square root of program size than with the size measure itself, measures 01 and 02 are plotted on a square root scale.[30] To assist the reader in interpreting results of the survey evaluations, each chapter concludes with a graphical presentation of the mean rating for every program of the scholarly quality of faculty (measure 08) and an associated "confidence interval" of 1.5 standard errors. In comparing the mean ratings of two programs, if their reported confidence intervals of 1.5 standard errors do not overlap, one may safely conclude that the program ratings are significantly different (at the .05 level of significance)--i.e., the observed difference in mean ratings is too large to be plausibly attributable to sampling error.[31]

The final chapter of this report gives an overview of the evaluation process in the six biological science disciplines and includes a summary of general findings. Particular attention is given to some of the extraneous factors that may influence program ratings of individual evaluators and thereby distort the survey results. The chapter concludes with a number of specific suggestions for improving future assessments of research-doctorate programs.

---

[30]For a general discussion of transforming variables to achieve linear fits, see John W. Tukey, Exploring Data Analysis, Addison-Wesley, Reading, Massachusetts, 1977.

[31]This rule for comparing nonoverlapping intervals is valid as long as the ratio of the two estimated standard errors does not exceed 2.41. (The exact statistical significance of this criterion then lies between .050 and .034.) Inspection of the standard errors reported in each discipline shows that for programs with mean ratings differing by less than 1.0 (on measure 08), the standard error of one mean very rarely exceeds twice the standard error of another.

III
Biochemistry Programs

In this chapter 139 research-doctorate programs in biochemistry are assessed. These programs, according to the information supplied by their universities, have accounted for 2,753 doctoral degrees awarded during the FY1976-80 period--approximately 89 percent of the aggregate number of biochemistry doctorates earned from U.S. universities in this five-year span.[1] Because biochemistry transcends the boundaries of many other biological science disciplines and because biochemistry programs may be found in a variety of institutional settings (including biology departments, medical school departments, agricultural school departments, etc.), the committee encountered difficulty in identifying a comprehensive set of research-doctorate programs that have produced graduates in this discipline. On the average, 25 full-time and part-time students intending to earn doctorates were enrolled in a program in December 1980, with an average faculty size of 19 members.[2] Most of the 139 programs, listed in Table 3.1, are located in biochemistry or biological chemistry departments. Approximately 10 percent are found in departments of chemistry. Fourteen programs were initiated since 1970, and each of 10 universities--Boston University, University of California (San Diego), Harvard University, University of Kansas, Ohio State University, Pennsylvania State University, University of Pittsburgh, SUNY at Buffalo, West Virginia University, and University of Wisconsin (Madison)--includes two biochemistry programs in the study. In addition to the 129 institutions represented in this discipline, another 15 were initially identified as meeting the criteria[3] for inclusion in the assessment:

---

[1] Data from the NRC's Survey of Earned Doctorates indicate that 3,109 research doctorates in biochemistry were awarded by U.S. universities between FY1976 and FY1980.

[2] See the reported means for measures 03 and 01 in Table 3.2.

[3] As mentioned in Chapter I, the primary criterion for inclusion was that a university had awarded at least 5 doctorates in biochemistry during the FY1976-78 period.

University of Alabama
California Institute of Technology
Florida State University--Tallahassee
Fordham University
Medical College of Georgia
Indiana University--Bloomington
Ohio University
University of Oregon Health Sciences Center
State University of Rutgers--Newark
University of South Carolina--Columbia
Texas Tech University--Lubbock
University of Texas Health Science Center--Dallas
Tufts University
Utah State University--Logan
Washington University--Saint Louis

Three of these institutions--Medical College of Georgia, University of Oregon Health Sciences Center, and University of Texas Health Sciences Center (Dallas)--chose not to participate in the assessment in _any_ discipline. Biochemistry programs at the other 12 institutions have not been included in the evaluations in this discipline, since in each case the study coordinator either indicated that the institution did not at that time have a research-doctorate program in biochemistry or failed to provide the information requested by the committee.

Before examining individual program results presented in Table 3.1, the reader is urged to refer to Chapter II, in which each of the 16 measures used in the assessment is discussed. Summary statistics describing every measure are given in Table 3.2. For nine of the measures, data are reported for at least 115 of the 139 biochemistry programs. For measures 04-07, which pertain to characteristics of the program graduates, data are presented for only approximately two-thirds of the programs; the other third had too few graduates on which to base statistics.[4] For measure 12, a composite index of the size of a university library, data are available for 88 programs; for measure 14, the total university expenditures for research in the biological sciences, data are available for 104 programs. The programs not evaluated on measures 12 and 14 are typically smaller--in terms of faculty size and graduate student enrollment--than other biochemistry programs. Were data on these two measures available for all 139 programs, it is likely that their reported means would be appreciably lower (and that some of the correlations of these measures with others would be higher). With regard to measure 10, the rated change in program quality, results were not reported for programs with fewer than 15 ratings on the survey item.

Intercorrelations among the 16 measures (Pearson product-moment

---

[4]As mentioned in Chapter II, data for measures 04-07 are not reported if they are based on the survey responses of fewer than 10 FY1975-79 program graduates.

coefficients) are given in Table 3.3. Of particular note are the high positive correlations of the reputational survey ratings (08, 09) with measures of publication records (15, 16) and with measure 04--the fraction of program graduates who had had national fellowship or training grant suppport. Figure 3.1 illustrates the relation between the mean rating of the scholarly quality of faculty (measure 08) and the number of faculty members (measure 01) for each of 138 programs in biochemistry. Figure 3.2 plots the mean rating of program effectiveness (measure 09) against the total number of FY1976-80 program graduates (measure 02). Although in both figures there is a significant positive correlation between program size and reputational rating, it is quite apparent that some of the smaller programs received high mean ratings and that some of the larger programs received low mean ratings.

Table 3.4 describes the 234 faculty members who participated in the evaluation of biochemistry programs. These individuals constituted 56 percent of those asked to respond to the survey in this discipline and 9 percent of the faculty population in the 138 research-doctorate programs being evaluated.[5] Nearly three-fourths of the survey participants had earned their highest degree prior to 1970, and half held the rank of full professor.

One exception should be noted with regard to the survey evaluations in biochemistry. In the program listing on the survey form, New Mexico State University at Las Cruces was identified as being located in Alamogordo, where there is another branch of the same university system not offering the research doctorate. Since a large majority of faculty evaluators indicated that they were unfamiliar with this program, and it is quite possible that some of them were misled by the inaccurate description of this institution, the committee has decided not to report the survey results for this program.

To assist the reader in interpreting results of the survey evaluations, estimated standard errors have been computed for mean ratings of the scholarly quality of faculty in 138 biochemistry programs (and are given in Table 3.1). For each program the mean rating and an associated "confidence interval" of 1.5 standard errors are illustrated in Figure 3.3 (listed in order of highest to lowest mean rating). In comparing two programs, if their confidence intervals do not overlap, one may conclude that there is a significant difference in their mean ratings at a .05 level of significance.[6] From this figure it is also apparent that one should have somewhat more confidence in the accuracy of the mean ratings of higher-rated programs than lower-rated programs. This generalization results primarily from the fact that evaluators are not as likely to be familiar with the less prestigious programs, and consequently the mean ratings of these programs are usually based on fewer survey responses.

---

[5] See Table 2.3 in Chapter II.
[6] See pp. 31-33 for a discussion of the interpretation of mean ratings and associated confidence intervals.

TABLE 3.1 Program Measures (Raw and Standardized Values) in Biochemistry

Prog No.	University - Department/Academic Unit	Program Size			Characteristics of Program Graduates			
		(01)	(02)	(03)	(04)	(05)	(06)	(07)
001.	Alabama, University of-Birmingham	33	15	13	.56	7.5	.78	.56
	Biochemistry	*62*	*47*	*44*	*53*	*28*	*47*	*49*
002.	Albany Medical College	16	6	9	NA	NA	NA	NA
	Biochemistry	*47*	*42*	*42*				
003.	Albert Einstein College of Medicine	21	8	13	NA	NA	NA	NA
	Biochemistry	*52*	*43*	*44*				
004.	Arizona, University of-Tucson	13	21	29	.71	5.4	1.00	.88
	Biochemistry	*45*	*50*	*52*	*58*	*58*	*66*	*73*
005.	Arkansas, Univ of-Medical Sciences Campus	21	6	5	NA	NA	NA	NA
	Biochemistry	*52*	*42*	*40*				
006.	Auburn University	6	14	7	NA	NA	NA	NA
	Chemistry/Animal and Dairy Sciences	*39*	*46*	*41*				
007.	Baylor College of Medicine-Houston	13	15	26	.39	7.0	.83	.67
	Biochemistry	*45*	*47*	*50*	*47*	*35*	*52*	*57*
008.	Boston University	43	24	42	.31	6.7	.66	.52
	Interdepartmental Biochemistry Program	*71*	*52*	*58*	*44*	*39*	*37*	*47*
009.	Boston University	39	9	9	.39	5.7	.67	.50
	Medical and Dental Sciences	*67*	*44*	*42*	*47*	*54*	*38*	*45*
010.	Brandeis University	11	26	45	.93	6.2	.90	.77
	Biochemistry	*43*	*53*	*59*	*66*	*46*	*58*	*65*
011.	Brown University	16	1	1	NA	NA	NA	NA
	Biology and Medicine	*47*	*39*	*38*				
012.	Bryn Mawr College	11	12	13	.46	6.5	.73	.36
	Biology/Chemistry	*43*	*45*	*44*	*49*	*42*	*43*	*36*
013.	CUNY-Graduate School	35	32	64	.04	7.2	.89	.54
	Biochemistry	*64*	*57*	*68*	*34*	*32*	*56*	*48*
014.	California, University of-Berkeley	17	62	72	.89	5.7	.86	.66
	Biochemistry	*48*	*74*	*72*	*65*	*54*	*54*	*57*
015.	California, University of-Davis	55	45	52	.57	5.8	.71	.51
	Biochemistry	*81*	*64*	*63*	*54*	*53*	*42*	*46*
016.	California, University of-Irvine	13	7	10	NA	NA	NA	NA
	Molecular Biol and Biochem/ Biological Chem	*45*	*42*	*43*				
017.	California, University of-Los Angeles	38	45	82	.86	5.7	.79	.53
	Chemistry/Biological Chemistry	*66*	*64*	*77*	*64*	*53*	*48*	*48*
018.	California, University of-Riverside	18	35	44	.09	5.2	.91	.61
	Biochemistry	*49*	*58*	*59*	*36*	*61*	*58*	*53*
019.	California, University of-San Diego	26	32	30	.80	5.5	.93	.73
	Biology	*56*	*57*	*52*	*62*	*57*	*60*	*62*
020.	California, University of-San Diego	23	26	69	.73	5.7	.85	.62
	Chemistry	*53*	*53*	*71*	*59*	*54*	*53*	*54*

* indicates program was initiated since 1970.

NOTE: On the first line of data for every program, raw values for each measure are reported; on the second line values are reported in standardized form, with mean = 50 and standard deviation = 10. "NA" indicates that the value for a measure is not available.

TABLE 3.1 Program Measures (Raw and Standardized Values) in Biochemistry

Prog No.	Survey Results (08)	(09)	(10)	(11)	University Library (12)	Research Support (13)	(14)	Published Articles (15)	(16)	Survey Ratings Standard Error (08)	(09)	(10)	(11)
001.	2.5	1.8	1.6	0.5	NA	.49	4467	90		.14	.10	.13	.07
	49	51	68	46		44	44	50	49				
002.	1.8	NA	NA	0.2	NA	.31	3066	16		.16	NA	NA	.05
	41			39		36	42	42	42				
003.	3.1	1.9	0.8	0.8	NA	.67	9184	177		.12	.08	.11	.07
	54	53	36	52		52	51	59	63				
004.	2.6	1.7	1.2	0.5	0.9	.92	7828	128		.11	.10	.11	.06
	50	49	53	45	57	63	49	54	51				
005.	1.4	NA	NA	0.2	NA	.24	NA	14		.23	NA	NA	.05
	37			39		32		41	42				
006.	1.2	NA	NA	0.1	NA	NA	NA	13		.20	NA	NA	.04
	35			37				41	42				
007.	2.8	1.7	1.2	0.8	NA	.77	14051	174		.12	.08	.12	.07
	51	50	51	53		56	59	59	59				
008.	2.7	1.7	1.4	0.6	-0.4	.61	NA	NA		.13	.09	.11	.08
	50	49	61	48	45	49			NA				
009.	2.5	1.4	1.1	0.5	-0.4	.51	NA	69		.13	.12	.12	.06
	48	44	48	47	45	45		47	48				
010.	4.2	2.5	1.1	1.6	NA	1.00	5487	85		.08	.06	.06	.06
	67	66	46	71		67	45	49	51				
011.	2.8	1.5	1.1	0.6	-1.1	.75	NA	44		.12	.13	.11	.07
	52	45	49	47	38	56		45	46				
012.	1.7	1.3	NA	0.3	NA	.00	NA	2		.29	.24	NA	.06
	40	42		41		22		40	41				
013.	2.7	1.8	1.1	0.4	NA	.54	NA	145		.15	.10	.11	.06
	51	51	46	44		46		56	54				
014.	4.6	2.8	1.1	1.6	2.2	1.00	18977	301		.07	.05	.08	.06
	71	72	47	71	70	67	66	73	71				
015.	3.7	2.3	1.3	1.3	0.6	.73	18053	228		.09	.07	.08	.07
	61	63	57	65	55	54	65	65	59				
016.	3.0	1.8	1.1	0.8	NA	.62	6547	80		.09	.06	.11	.07
	54	51	50	54		49	47	49	50				
017.	4.1	2.3	1.3	1.4	2.0	.84	15581	344		.08	.06	.07	.06
	66	63	58	67	68	60	61	78	75				
018.	2.7	1.8	1.2	0.6	-1.0	.89	6232	71		.13	.11	.14	.07
	50	53	53	48	39	62	47	48	47				
019.	3.8	2.3	1.4	1.2	-0.0	.69	8706	217		.08	.06	.08	.07
	63	61	59	62	48	53	50	64	65				
020.	4.2	2.3	1.4	1.3	-0.0	.83	8706	217		.08	.06	.08	.07
	66	63	63	66	48	59	50	64	65				

NOTE: On the first line of data for every program, raw values for each measure are reported; on the second line values are reported in standardized form, with mean = 50 and standard deviation = 10. "NA" indicates that the value for a measure is not available. Since the scale used to compute measure 16 is entirely arbitrary, only values in standardized form are reported for this measure.

TABLE 3.1 Program Measures (Raw and Standardized Values) in Biochemistry

Prog No.	University – Department/Academic Unit	Program Size			Characteristics of Program Graduates			
		(01)	(02)	(03)	(04)	(05)	(06)	(07)
021.	California, University of–San Francisco	36	22	25	.59	6.0	.82	.59
	Biochemistry	*65*	*51*	*50*	*54*	*50*	*51*	*52*
022.	California, University of–Santa Barbara	6	1	5	NA	NA	NA	NA
	Biochemistry and Molecular Biology*	*39*	*39*	*40*				
023.	Case Western Reserve University	16	20	33	.94	6.0	.87	.47
	Biochemistry	*47*	*50*	*54*	*67*	*50*	*55*	*43*
024.	Chicago, University of	22	35	45	.80	5.5	.70	.60
	Biochemistry	*53*	*58*	*59*	*62*	*57*	*41*	*53*
025.	Cincinnati, University of	15	12	24	.17	6.3	.82	.46
	Biological Chemistry	*46*	*45*	*49*	*39*	*46*	*51*	*42*
026.	Colorado State University–Fort Collins	9	10	26	.09	5.3	.82	.64
	Biochemistry	*41*	*44*	*50*	*36*	*59*	*51*	*55*
027.	Colorado, University of	24	2	6	NA	NA	NA	NA
	Biochemistry/Biophysics/Genetics	*54*	*40*	*41*				
028.	Columbia University	21	15	21	.67	6.1	1.00	.60
	Biochemistry	*52*	*47*	*48*	*57*	*48*	*66*	*53*
029.	Connecticut, University of–Storrs	13	18	6	.25	8.7	.69	.46
	Biological Sciences	*45*	*49*	*41*	*42*	*11*	*40*	*43*
030.	Cornell University–Ithaca	34	40	51	.66	6.0	.94	.71
	Biochemistry, Molecular and Cell Biology	*63*	*61*	*62*	*57*	*50*	*61*	*61*
031.	Cornell University–Medical Center	25	23	21	.76	6.5	.91	.73
	Biochemistry	*55*	*52*	*48*	*60*	*42*	*58*	*62*
032.	Dartmouth College	10	2	17	NA	NA	NA	NA
	Biochemistry*	*42*	*40*	*46*				
033.	Delaware, University of–Newark	8	11	24	.27	5.8	.82	.36
	Chemistry	*40*	*45*	*49*	*43*	*53*	*51*	*36*
034.	Duke University	32	40	59	.93	5.7	.91	.76
	Biochemistry	*61*	*61*	*66*	*66*	*53*	*58*	*64*
035.	Emory University	22	7	9	NA	NA	NA	NA
	Biochemistry	*53*	*42*	*42*				
036.	Florida, University of–Gainesville	20	19	21	.29	4.9	.85	.70
	Biochemistry and Molecular Biology	*51*	*49*	*48*	*43*	*65*	*53*	*60*
037.	George Washington University	12	13	21	.33	6.5	.67	.20
	Biochemistry	*44*	*46*	*48*	*45*	*42*	*38*	*24*
038.	Georgetown University	9	15	20	.25	8.2	.70	.30
	Biochemistry	*41*	*47*	*47*	*42*	*18*	*41*	*31*
039.	Georgia, University of–Athens	16	13	24	.36	6.0	.55	.55
	Biochemistry	*47*	*46*	*49*	*46*	*50*	*28*	*49*
040.	Harvard University	16	52	57	.85	6.0	.94	.65
	Biochemistry & Molecular Biology (Grad Sch)	*47*	*68*	*65*	*64*	*49*	*61*	*56*

* indicates program was initiated since 1970.

NOTE: On the first line of data for every program, raw values for each measure are reported; on the second line values are reported in standardized form, with mean = 50 and standard deviation = 10. "NA" indicates that the value for a measure is not available.

TABLE 3.1 Program Measures (Raw and Standardized Values) in Biochemistry

Prog No.	Survey Results (08)	(09)	(10)	(11)	University Library (12)	Research Support (13)	(14)	Published Articles (15)	(16)	Survey Ratings Standard Error (08)	(09)	(10)	(11)
021.	4.4	2.4	1.7	1.5	NA	.83	13194	369		.08	.07	.08	.06
	69	*64*	*74*	*71*		*59*	*57*	*81*	*78*				
022.	3.0	1.5	1.0	0.8	-0.1	NA	NA	53		.14	.14	.10	.08
	54	*46*	*41*	*54*	*47*			*46*	*47*				
023.	3.2	2.1	0.9	0.9	-1.3	.81	7721	6		.09	.06	.10	.07
	56	*58*	*39*	*56*	*35*	*58*	*49*	*40*	*42*				
024.	3.9	2.3	1.2	1.3	0.9	.86	17589	229		.07	.06	.08	.07
	64	*62*	*51*	*65*	*57*	*61*	*64*	*65*	*67*				
025.	2.4	1.8	1.4	0.6	-0.2	.80	9365	65		.14	.08	.10	.07
	48	*52*	*63*	*48*	*46*	*58*	*51*	*47*	*47*				
026.	2.1	1.5	1.2	0.4	-1.1	NA	8863	53		.13	.13	.14	.07
	44	*44*	*51*	*45*	*37*		*51*	*46*	*46*				
027.	2.9	1.6	1.5	0.8	-0.9	.71	11967	123		.11	.09	.12	.07
	53	*48*	*65*	*53*	*40*	*54*	*55*	*53*	*54*				
028.	3.9	2.1	1.2	1.2	1.7	.86	11090	176		.08	.07	.10	.07
	64	*59*	*52*	*64*	*66*	*60*	*54*	*59*	*59*				
029.	2.6	1.6	0.9	0.7	-0.5	.77	15199	39		.13	.12	.11	.07
	50	*47*	*40*	*50*	*44*	*56*	*60*	*44*	*44*				
030.	4.3	2.5	1.4	1.5	1.6	.74	14597	272		.07	.06	.07	.06
	67	*66*	*59*	*71*	*64*	*55*	*60*	*70*	*66*				
031.	3.6	2.2	1.0	1.0	NA	.24	14597	76		.10	.07	.09	.07
	60	*59*	*42*	*58*		*32*	*60*	*48*	*51*				
032.	2.4	1.4	0.9	0.5	-1.1	.90	4419	34		.16	.16	.15	.07
	47	*44*	*37*	*46*	*37*	*62*	*44*	*44*	*44*				
033.	2.5	1.7	1.5	0.6	NA	NA	NA	35		.11	.13	.13	.08
	48	*49*	*64*	*50*				*44*	*44*				
034.	3.9	2.4	1.3	1.2	0.3	.75	11320	180		.11	.08	.09	.08
	63	*64*	*57*	*63*	*52*	*56*	*54*	*60*	*62*				
035.	2.1	1.2	1.2	0.5	-0.6	.41	2874	47		.15	.13	.16	.07
	45	*40*	*52*	*46*	*42*	*40*	*41*	*45*	*45*				
036.	2.4	1.7	1.4	0.5	0.8	.60	3486	63		.13	.10	.12	.06
	48	*50*	*59*	*47*	*56*	*49*	*42*	*47*	*47*				
037.	2.3	1.5	1.0	0.4	NA	.50	2641	21		.16	.11	.17	.06
	47	*46*	*43*	*44*		*44*	*41*	*42*	*43*				
038.	2.0	1.4	1.0	0.4	-0.6	NA	4200	38		.16	.14	.13	.06
	43	*43*	*43*	*44*	*42*		*43*	*44*	*44*				
039.	2.5	1.7	1.1	0.5	0.4	.88	10714	109		.15	.13	.07	.09
	48	*50*	*48*	*47*	*53*	*61*	*54*	*52*	*49*				
040.	4.9	2.7	1.1	1.8	3.0	1.00	34979	224		.04	.06	.06	.05
	74	*71*	*50*	*76*	*78*	*67*	*91*	*65*	*67*				

NOTE: On the first line of data for every program, raw values for each measure are reported; on the second line values are reported in standardized form, with mean = 50 and standard deviation = 10. "NA" indicates that the value for a measure is not available. Since the scale used to compute measure 16 is entirely arbitrary, only values in standardized form are reported for this measure.

TABLE 3.1 Program Measures (Raw and Standardized Values) in Biochemistry

Prog No.	University - Department/Academic Unit	Program Size (01)	(02)	(03)	Characteristics of Program Graduates (04)	(05)	(06)	(07)
041.	Harvard University	28	22	21	.95	5.7	.83	.72
	Biological Chemistry (Medical School)	*58*	*51*	*48*	*67*	*54*	*52*	*61*
042.	Hawaii, University of	13	16	29	.25	6.8	.50	.33
	Biochemistry and Biophysics	*45*	*48*	*52*	*42*	*39*	*24*	*33*
043.	Health Sciences, Univ of/Chicago Med School	11	3	4	NA	NA	NA	NA
	*Biochemistry**	*43*	*40*	*40*				
044.	Houston, University of	17	20	23	.31	5.5	.69	.63
	Biophysical Sciences	*48*	*50*	*49*	*44*	*57*	*40*	*54*
045.	Howard University	7	4	NA	NA	NA	NA	NA
	*Biochemistry**	*39*	*41*					
046.	Illinois Institute of Technology	10	19	14	.44	6.3	.56	.50
	Biology	*42*	*49*	*45*	*49*	*46*	*30*	*45*
047.	Illinois, University of-Medical Center	18	25	26	.11	6.2	.93	.48
	Biological Chemistry	*49*	*53*	*50*	*37*	*47*	*60*	*44*
048.	Illinois, University-Urbana/Champaign	17	40	83	.92	5.9	.83	.61
	Biochemistry	*48*	*61*	*77*	*66*	*52*	*52*	*53*
049.	Indiana University-Purdue University	18	15	18	.27	6.8	.73	.40
	Biochemistry	*49*	*47*	*47*	*43*	*39*	*44*	*38*
050.	Iowa State University-Ames	20	24	37	.10	5.8	.80	.55
	Biochemistry and Biophysics	*51*	*52*	*56*	*37*	*52*	*49*	*49*
051.	Iowa, University of-Iowa City	23	21	36	.63	5.0	.87	.52
	Biochemistry	*53*	*50*	*55*	*55*	*64*	*55*	*47*
052.	Johns Hopkins University	13	120	28	.93	6.0	.96	.64
	Biochemistry	*45*	*99*	*51*	*67*	*50*	*62*	*56*
053.	Kansas State University-Manhattan	13	7	13	NA	NA	NA	NA
	Biochemistry	*45*	*42*	*44*				
054.	Kansas, University of	13	16	20	.38	5.8	.88	.56
	Biochemistry (Graduate School)	*45*	*48*	*47*	*46*	*52*	*55*	*50*
055.	Kansas, University of	19	17	14	.07	6.0	.50	.43
	Biochemistry (Schl of Medicine-Kansas City)	*50*	*48*	*45*	*35*	*50*	*24*	*40*
056.	Kentucky, University of	12	8	12	NA	NA	NA	NA
	Biochemistry	*44*	*43*	*44*				
057.	Loma Linda University	9	NA	7	NA	NA	NA	NA
	Biochemistry	*41*		*41*				
058.	Louisiana State University-Baton Rouge	9	9	13	NA	NA	NA	NA
	Biochemistry	*41*	*44*	*44*				
059.	Louisville, University of	16	8	22	NA	NA	NA	NA
	Biochemistry	*47*	*43*	*48*				
060.	Loyola University of Chicago	12	12	27	NA	NA	NA	NA
	Biochemistry and Biophysics	*44*	*45*	*51*				

* indicates program was initiated since 1970.

NOTE: On the first line of data for every program, raw values for each measure are reported; on the second line values are reported in standardized form, with mean = 50 and standard deviation = 10. "NA" indicates that the value for a measure is not available.

TABLE 3.1 Program Measures (Raw and Standardized Values) in Biochemistry

Prog No.	Survey Results (08)	(09)	(10)	(11)	University Library (12)	Research Support (13)	(14)	Published Articles (15)	(16)	Survey Ratings Standard Error (08)	(09)	(10)	(11)
041.	4.4	2.5	1.0	1.4	3.0	.39	34979	424		.09	.07	.07	.06
	69	67	45	68	78	39	91	87	90				
042.	2.2	1.5	1.1	0.5	-0.1	.54	4440	20		.14	.10	.09	.07
	46	45	49	47	47	46	44	42	43				
043.	2.0	0.9	NA	0.3	NA	.36	NA	7		.12	.17	NA	.06
	43	34		41		38		41	42				
044.	2.0	NA	NA	0.2	-0.9	.59	NA	27		.17	NA	NA	.04
	43			38	40	48		43	43				
045.	1.1	0.6	NA	0.2	-0.4	NA	NA	16		.16	.13	NA	.05
	34	27		39	44			42	42				
046.	1.6	1.2	NA	0.1	NA	.40	NA	13		.21	.16	NA	.04
	39	39		38		40		41	42				
047.	2.5	1.6	0.9	0.5	NA	.50	4393	170		.14	.11	.16	.06
	48	48	41	46		44	44	59	56				
048.	3.8	2.4	1.2	1.2	2.0	.88	6074	150		.09	.08	.08	.07
	62	64	54	63	68	61	46	56	53				
049.	2.5	1.7	1.0	0.4	NA	.72	2940	NA		.14	.09	.08	.07
	49	51	41	44		54	42		NA				
050.	2.9	1.9	1.0	0.9	-0.5	.50	5287	56		.11	.10	.08	.08
	53	54	42	56	43	44	45	46	45				
051.	3.5	2.0	1.4	1.0	0.3	.74	7088	91		.07	.07	.08	.06
	59	56	63	58	51	55	48	50	48				
052.	3.4	2.2	1.1	0.9	-0.4	.69	19837	223		.10	.08	.09	.08
	58	61	49	56	45	53	68	65	66				
053.	2.0	1.4	1.2	0.4	NA	.39	2496	38		.14	.14	.15	.06
	43	43	50	44		39	41	44	44				
054.	2.0	1.6	1.1	0.3	0.1	.54	3161	26		.16	.10	.10	.06
	44	48	46	42	49	46	42	43	43				
055.	2.5	1.7	1.2	0.7	0.1	.68	3161	62		.11	.09	.12	.07
	48	49	54	50	49	53	42	47	47				
056.	2.2	1.4	1.0	0.6	-0.1	.67	484	33		.14	.11	.11	.07
	46	43	41	48	48	52	38	43	44				
057.	0.7	NA	NA	0.1	NA	NA	NA	1		.18	NA	NA	.04
	30			37				40	41				
058.	1.5	1.0	NA	0.2	-0.3	NA	5116	23		.21	.17	NA	.06
	38	35		40	45		45	42	42				
059.	1.8	1.2	1.2	0.4	NA	.25	NA	32		.15	.12	.20	.06
	41	40	52	43		33		43	44				
060.	1.4	1.0	NA	0.2	NA	.00	NA	15		.16	.14	NA	.05
	36	35		39		22		41	42				

NOTE: On the first line of data for every program, raw values for each measure are reported;
on the second line values are reported in standardized form, with mean = 50 and
standard deviation = 10. "NA" indicates that the value for a measure is not available.
Since the scale used to compute measure 16 is entirely arbitrary, only values in
standardized form are reported for this measure.

TABLE 3.1 Program Measures (Raw and Standardized Values) in Biochemistry

Prog No.	University - Department/Academic Unit	Program Size			Characteristics of Program Graduates			
		(01)	(02)	(03)	(04)	(05)	(06)	(07)
061.	Maryland, University of-Baltimore Prof Schl *Biological Chemistry**	16 *47*	NA	3 *39*	NA	NA	NA	NA
062.	Maryland, University of-College Park *Chemistry**	11 *43*	7 *42*	19 *47*	.40 *47*	6.5 *42*	NA	NA
063.	Massachusetts Institute of Technology *Biology*	24 *54*	35 *58*	43 *58*	.73 *59*	5.5 *57*	.88 *56*	.61 *53*
064.	Massachusetts, University of-Amherst *Biochemistry*	8 *40*	15 *47*	25 *50*	.33 *45*	5.9 *51*	.73 *44*	.33 *33*
065.	Medical University of South Carolina *Biochemistry*	25 *55*	15 *47*	11 *43*	.10 *37*	7.5 *28*	.90 *58*	.60 *53*
066.	Miami, University of-Florida *Biochemistry*	25 *55*	25 *53*	18 *47*	.63 *56*	5.8 *52*	.65 *37*	.46 *43*
067.	Michigan State University-East Lansing *Biochemistry*	37 *66*	34 *58*	69 *71*	.60 *55*	5.2 *61*	.90 *58*	.63 *54*
068.	Michigan, University of-Ann Arbor *Biological Chemistry*	51 *78*	53 *69*	60 *66*	.88 *64*	5.6 *56*	.88 *55*	.67 *57*
069.	Minnesota, University of *Biochemistry (Graduate Schl & Medical Schl)*	41 *69*	49 *66*	50 *62*	.67 *57*	6.2 *47*	.73 *44*	.56 *49*
070.	Missouri, University of-Columbia *Biochemistry*	23 *53*	18 *49*	12 *44*	.25 *42*	5.4 *58*	.90 *58*	.65 *56*
071.	Nebraska, University of-Lincoln *Chemistry/School of Life Sciences*	16 *47*	16 *48*	35 *55*	.21 *41*	7.5 *28*	.72 *43*	.22 *25*
072.	New Hampshire, University of *Biochemistry*	6 *39*	10 *44*	6 *41*	.20 *40*	NA	.90 *58*	.60 *53*
073.	New Jersey, College of Medicine & Dentistry *Biochemistry**	14 *46*	8 *43*	13 *44*	NA	NA	NA	NA
074.	New Mexico State University-Las Cruces *Chemistry*	7 *39*	10 *44*	14 *45*	NA	NA	NA	NA
075.	New York University *Basic Medical Sciences*	25 *55*	14 *46*	26 *50*	.75 *60*	7.0 *35*	.75 *45*	.58 *51*
076.	North Carolina State University-Raleigh *Biochemistry*	12 *44*	16 *48*	25 *50*	.22 *41*	5.9 *51*	.88 *56*	.53 *48*
077.	North Carolina, University of-Chapel Hill *Biochemistry and Nutrition*	33 *62*	39 *61*	57 *65*	.35 *46*	5.3 *59*	.88 *56*	.52 *47*
078.	North Dakota State University-Fargo *Biochemistry*	11 *43*	9 *44*	9 *42*	.27 *43*	4.8 *66*	.82 *51*	.55 *49*
079.	North Dakota, University of-Grand Forks *Biochemistry*	6 *39*	9 *44*	7 *41*	NA	NA	NA	NA
080.	Northern Illinois University-De Kalb *Chemistry*	5 *38*	2 *40*	10 *43*	NA	NA	NA	NA

* indicates program was initiated since 1970.

NOTE: On the first line of data for every program, raw values for each measure are reported; on the second line values are reported in standardized form, with mean = 50 and standard deviation = 10. "NA" indicates that the value for a measure is not available.

TABLE 3.1 Program Measures (Raw and Standardized Values) in Biochemistry

Prog No.	Survey Results (08)	(09)	(10)	(11)	University Library (12)	Research Support (13)	(14)	Published Articles (15)	(16)	Survey Ratings Standard Error (08)	(09)	(10)	(11)
061.	2.2	1.5	1.3	0.5	NA	.63	6061	65		.13	.13	.16	.06
	45	45	56	46		50	46	47	47				
062.	1.8	NA	NA	0.2	0.2	.36	1623	27		.28	NA	NA	.04
	42			39	50	38	39	43	42				
063.	5.0	2.9	1.3	1.7	-0.3	.92	17348	300		.03	.04	.07	.06
	74	74	57	74	45	63	64	73	73				
064.	2.4	1.7	1.2	0.5	-0.7	NA	3022	64		.13	.09	.10	.06
	48	49	54	47	41		42	47	47				
065.	2.0	1.5	NA	0.3	NA	.52	3178	29		.20	.17	NA	.06
	43	45		41		45	42	43	43				
066.	2.7	1.7	1.2	0.8	NA	.64	6101	73		.12	.08	.09	.07
	51	50	51	54		51	46	48	48				
067.	3.3	2.1	1.2	0.9	0.3	.62	10357	153		.09	.06	.10	.07
	57	58	53	56	52	50	53	57	53				
068.	3.7	2.3	1.1	1.3	1.8	.67	15431	126		.09	.06	.07	.07
	62	63	49	65	66	52	61	54	55				
069.	3.4	2.1	1.4	1.1	1.2	.66	13696	250		.09	.05	.08	.07
	58	58	60	60	60	51	58	68	63				
070.	2.5	1.5	1.1	0.5	-0.2	.70	4628	NA		.13	.12	.14	.07
	48	45	48	47	46	53	44		NA				
071.	1.7	1.4	1.2	0.3	-0.5	.50	2965	47		.13	.11	.14	.06
	40	43	52	42	43	44	42	45	44				
072.	1.0	NA	NA	0.1	NA	NA	NA	4		.20	NA	NA	.03
	32			37				40	41				
073.	1.6	1.1	NA	0.3	NA	.43	4529	80		.17	.14	NA	.05
	39	36		40		41	44	49	46				
074.	NA	NA	NA	NA	NA	NA	NA	18		NA	NA	NA	NA
								42	43				
075.	3.4	1.9	0.7	0.8	0.5	.52	9934	117		.09	.06	.11	.06
	58	53	31	53	53	45	52	53	51				
076.	2.2	1.4	1.0	0.5	NA	.50	6741	38		.16	.12	.14	.07
	45	43	43	45		44	47	44	44				
077.	3.2	2.0	1.5	1.0	1.0	.64	9849	94		.09	.08	.09	.08
	56	56	65	57	58	50	52	50	51				
078.	1.0	NA	NA	0.2	NA	.09	5698	8		.15	NA	NA	.04
	33			38		26	46	41	41				
079.	1.7	NA	NA	0.5	NA	NA	NA	8		.19	NA	NA	.07
	41			45				41	41				
080.	1.1	0.8	NA	0.3	NA	NA	NA	15		.15	.17	NA	.06
	34	30		41				41	42				

NOTE: On the first line of data for every program, raw values for each measure are reported;
on the second line values are reported in standardized form, with mean = 50 and
standard deviation = 10. "NA" indicates that the value for a measure is not available.
Since the scale used to compute measure 16 is entirely arbitrary, only values in
standardized form are reported for this measure.

TABLE 3.1 Program Measures (Raw and Standardized Values) in Biochemistry

Prog No.	University - Department/Academic Unit	Program Size (01)	(02)	(03)	Characteristics of Program Graduates (04)	(05)	(06)	(07)
081.	Northwestern University	26	42	28	.62	5.3	.94	.75
	Biochemistry and Molecular Biology/ Biochem	56	62	51	55	59	61	63
082.	Notre Dame, University of	5	14	15	.00	5.3	1.00	.75
	Chemistry	38	46	45	33	60	66	63
083.	Ohio State University-Columbus	16	25	34	.15	5.3	.79	.53
	Biochemistry	47	53	54	38	60	48	47
084.	Ohio State University-Columbus	19	23	18	.26	5.8	.56	.28
	Physiological Chemistry	50	52	47	42	53	29	29
085.	Oklahoma State University-Stillwater	15	27	13	.25	4.9	.81	.57
	Biochemistry	46	54	44	42	65	50	51
086.	Oklahoma, University of-Norman	25	21	30	.36	6.0	.69	.31
	Biochemistry and Molecular Biology	55	50	52	46	50	40	32
087.	Oregon State University-Corvallis	25	20	30	.33	5.8	.90	.53
	Biochemistry and Biophysics	55	50	52	45	53	57	47
088.	Oregon, University of-Eugene	13	9	2	.84	5.9	.84	.68
	Biology/Chemistry	45	44	39	63	51	53	59
089.	Pennsylvania State University	14	22	25	.09	5.2	.73	.64
	Biochemistry (Graduate School)	46	51	50	36	61	43	55
090.	Pennsylvania State University	10	13	16	NA	NA	NA	NA
	Biological Chemistry (Medical Center)	42	46	46				
091.	Pennsylvania, University of	60	27	27	.76	6.3	.72	.56
	Biochemistry	86	54	51	60	45	43	50
092.	Pittsburgh, University of	9	10	18	NA	NA	NA	NA
	Biochemistry (School of Medicine)	41	44	47				
093.	Pittsburgh, University of	27	11	12	.40	6.0	.40	.20
	Biological Sciences (Arts and Sciences)*	57	45	44	47	50	16	24
094.	Princeton University	17	26	31	.82	5.9	.89	.63
	Biochemical Sciences	48	53	53	62	51	57	55
095.	Purdue University-West Lafayette	18	37	52	.51	5.4	.88	.61
	Biological Sciences	49	60	63	51	58	56	53
096.	Rhode Island, University of	6	9	6	.36	6.5	.79	.29
	Biochemistry/Biophysics	39	44	41	46	42	48	30
097.	Rice University	11	19	36	.27	4.6	.93	.73
	Biochemistry	43	49	55	43	70	60	62
098.	Rochester, University of	19	30	23	.70	6.0	1.00	.75
	Biochemistry	50	56	49	58	50	66	63
099.	Rockefeller University	38	17	12	.40	5.9	.78	.50
	Biochemistry	66	48	44	47	51	47	45
100.	Rutgers, The State University-New Brunswick	51	34	94	.27	5.7	.73	.57
	Biochemistry	78	58	83	43	54	44	50

* indicates program was initiated since 1970.

NOTE: On the first line of data for every program, raw values for each measure are reported; on the second line values are reported in standardized form, with mean = 50 and standard deviation = 10. "NA" indicates that the value for a measure is not available.

TABLE 3.1 Program Measures (Raw and Standardized Values) in Biochemistry

Prog No.	Survey Results (08)	(09)	(10)	(11)	University Library (12)	Research Support (13)	(14)	Published Articles (15)	(16)	Survey Ratings Standard Error (08)	(09)	(10)	(11)
081.	3.7	2.1	1.1	1.2	0.3	.96	4760	126		.10	.08	.10	.06
	61	58	48	62	51	65	44	54	53				
082.	1.7	1.1	NA	0.4	−1.3	NA	NA	33		.19	.19	NA	.07
	40	38		43	35			43	45				
083.	2.5	1.5	0.9	0.6	0.9	.63	8330	62		.13	.09	.09	.06
	48	45	39	48	57	50	50	47	46				
084.	2.3	1.4	0.8	0.4	0.9	.58	8330	51		.16	.12	.10	.07
	46	44	34	43	57	48	50	45	45				
085.	2.3	1.6	1.0	0.4	−1.9	.40	3127	24		.13	.10	.09	.07
	47	48	41	44	29	40	42	42	43				
086.	2.3	1.6	1.1	0.5	−0.6	.16	NA	27		.12	.09	.12	.07
	46	48	46	47	43	29		43	43				
087.	3.1	2.0	1.4	0.9	NA	.88	7108	79		.11	.06	.09	.08
	55	57	60	55		61	48	49	47				
088.	3.3	2.1	1.1	0.8	−0.9	.77	NA	70		.10	.08	.07	.07
	57	58	46	53	39	56		48	48				
089.	2.7	1.9	1.2	0.6	0.7	.57	8024	89		.11	.07	.09	.08
	50	54	52	48	55	47	49	50	47				
090.	2.1	1.4	1.1	0.4	0.7	.80	8024	81		.16	.11	.17	.06
	45	43	46	43	55	58	49	49	51				
091.	4.0	2.2	1.2	1.4	0.7	.65	23550	302		.08	.07	.07	.07
	65	60	50	68	55	51	73	73	69				
092.	2.3	1.5	0.6	0.5	0.1	NA	6462	67		.14	.13	.14	.07
	46	45	27	46	49		47	47	47				
093.	2.8	1.8	1.0	0.6	0.1	.78	6462	51		.11	.10	.13	.07
	52	51	45	49	49	57	47	45	46				
094.	3.5	2.0	0.6	1.0	0.9	.82	3574	66		.09	.07	.11	.08
	59	57	25	59	57	59	43	47	48				
095.	3.3	2.0	1.2	1.0	−0.5	.89	10337	204		.09	.05	.10	.07
	57	56	51	58	43	62	53	62	60				
096.	1.4	1.1	NA	0.2	NA	NA	NA	34		.17	.19	NA	.05
	37	36		39				44	43				
097.	3.1	2.0	1.5	0.8	−1.4	.73	NA	45		.10	.08	.09	.07
	55	55	65	54	34	54		45	46				
098.	2.5	1.6	1.2	0.5	−0.6	.84	15969	106		.11	.09	.11	.06
	48	48	53	47	42	60	62	52	50				
099.	4.6	2.5	1.0	1.6	NA	.76	27299	194		.06	.07	.07	.06
	71	66	44	72		56	79	61	65				
100.	3.2	1.9	1.3	0.7	0.8	.33	7505	71		.12	.08	.08	.07
	56	54	57	50	56	37	49	48	46				

NOTE: On the first line of data for every program, raw values for each measure are reported; on the second line values are reported in standardized form, with mean = 50 and standard deviation = 10. "NA" indicates that the value for a measure is not available. Since the scale used to compute measure 16 is entirely arbitrary, only values in standardized form are reported for this measure.

TABLE 3.1 Program Measures (Raw and Standardized Values) in Biochemistry

Prog No.	University - Department/Academic Unit	Program Size			Characteristics of Program Graduates			
		(01)	(02)	(03)	(04)	(05)	(06)	(07)
101.	SUNY Upstate Medical Center *Biochemistry*	11 / 43	10 / 44	12 / 44	NA	NA	NA	NA
102.	SUNY at Albany *Biological Sciences*	6 / 39	NA	NA	.15 / 38	6.0 / 50	.75 / 45	.58 / 51
103.	SUNY at Buffalo *Biochemistry (Roswell Park Graduate Div)*	13 / 45	8 / 43	6 / 41	NA	NA	NA	NA
104.	SUNY at Buffalo *Biochemistry (School of Medicine)*	25 / 55	36 / 59	30 / 52	.27 / 43	6.6 / 40	.77 / 47	.68 / 59
105.	SUNY at Stony Brook *Biochemistry**	26 / 56	15 / 47	48 / 61	.24 / 41	6.6 / 41	.87 / 55	.67 / 57
106.	SUNY-College of Environ Science & Forestry *School of Biology, Chemistry & Ecology**	4 / 37	1 / 39	6 / 41	NA	NA	NA	NA
107.	SUNY-Downstate Medical Center *Biochemistry*	17 / 48	10 / 44	14 / 45	NA	NA	NA	NA
108.	Saint Louis University *Biochemistry*	19 / 50	20 / 50	24 / 49	.94 / 67	5.5 / 57	.88 / 55	.56 / 50
109.	South Dakota, University of-Vermillion *Biochem, Physiology, and Pharmacology*	14 / 46	8 / 43	6 / 41	NA	NA	NA	NA
110.	Southern California, University of *Biochemistry*	18 / 49	14 / 46	15 / 45	.57 / 54	5.7 / 54	1.00 / 66	.62 / 54
111.	Southern Illinois University-Carbondale *Chemistry and Biochemistry*	7 / 39	9 / 44	13 / 44	NA	NA	NA	NA
112.	Stanford University *Biochemistry*	27 / 57	47 / 65	27 / 51	.95 / 67	5.7 / 54	.95 / 62	.67 / 57
113.	Syracuse University *Biology**	6 / 39	21 / 50	10 / 43	.33 / 45	5.2 / 61	.83 / 52	.67 / 57
114.	Temple University *Biochemistry*	18 / 49	11 / 45	11 / 43	NA	NA	NA	NA
115.	Tennessee, Univ of-Ctr for Health Sciences *Biochemistry*	36 / 65	20 / 50	20 / 47	.30 / 44	7.2 / 33	.83 / 52	.58 / 51
116.	Tennessee, University of-Knoxville *Biochemistry*	8 / 40	14 / 46	9 / 42	.59 / 54	5.8 / 53	1.00 / 66	.82 / 69
117.	Texas A & M University *Biochemistry and Biophysics*	23 / 53	26 / 53	22 / 48	.12 / 37	6.0 / 50	.73 / 44	.35 / 34
118.	Texas, U of-Health Science Center, Houston *Biochem & Molecular Biology/Biochemistry*	49 / 76	20 / 50	29 / 52	.35 / 46	5.2 / 62	.74 / 44	.63 / 55
119.	Texas, University of-Austin *Chemistry*	10 / 42	18 / 49	45 / 59	.23 / 41	6.3 / 46	.77 / 47	.55 / 49
120.	Texas, U of-Health Science Ctr, San Antonio *Biochemistry**	23 / 53	9 / 44	18 / 47	NA	NA	NA	NA

* indicates program was initiated since 1970.

NOTE: On the first line of data for every program, raw values for each measure are reported; on the second line values are reported in standardized form, with mean = 50 and standard deviation = 10. "NA" indicates that the value for a measure is not available.

TABLE 3.1 Program Measures (Raw and Standardized Values) in Biochemistry

Prog No.	Survey Results (08)	(09)	(10)	(11)	University Library (12)	Research Support (13)	(14)	Published Articles (15)	(16)	Survey Ratings Standard Error (08)	(09)	(10)	(11)
101.	1.9	1.2	NA	0.3	NA	.55	NA	34		.14	.12	NA	.06
	43	39		41		46		44	44				
102.	2.0	0.9	0.7	0.5	-1.0	NA	NA	56		.14	.19	.21	.07
	43	34	31	45	39			46	47				
103.	2.5	1.4	1.0	0.4	0.3	.00	6799	40		.18	.13	.10	.05
	48	44	43	43	51	22	47	44	44				
104.	2.5	1.6	1.3	0.5	0.3	.48	6799	61		.12	.11	.14	.07
	48	48	55	46	51	43	47	47	45				
105.	3.0	2.0	1.4	0.9	-0.6	.77	5802	104		.12	.07	.09	.08
	54	55	63	56	42	56	46	51	53				
106.	0.7	0.7	NA	0.1	NA	NA	NA	7		.18	.21	NA	.04
	30	29		38				41	42				
107.	2.0	1.2	0.8	0.4	NA	.53	3077	59		.18	.19	.14	.07
	43	38	32	43		46	42	46	45				
108.	2.8	1.7	1.0	0.8	NA	.63	3674	67		.13	.08	.11	.08
	51	51	45	52		50	43	47	47				
109.	1.3	1.0	NA	0.3	NA	.50	NA	7		.16	.13	NA	.05
	36	34		40		44		41	42				
110.	3.0	1.8	1.1	0.8	0.4	.89	2405	80		.10	.09	.10	.07
	54	51	49	54	52	62	41	49	47				
111.	1.6	1.1	1.2	0.3	-0.2	NA	NA	2		.19	.17	.14	.05
	39	37	52	41	46			40	41				
112.	4.9	2.8	1.4	1.7	2.0	.85	12514	290		.03	.05	.08	.05
	74	73	60	76	68	60	56	72	78				
113.	1.8	1.3	0.8	0.4	-0.3	NA	NA	29		.16	.13	.14	.06
	41	42	36	44	45			43	43				
114.	2.9	1.8	1.1	0.7	-0.4	.67	6914	77		.11	.09	.12	.07
	53	51	48	52	44	52	48	48	50				
115.	2.5	1.6	1.1	0.4	NA	.31	2127	59		.13	.10	.10	.05
	49	48	50	43		35	40	46	46				
116.	1.6	1.4	0.9	0.3	-0.4	NA	NA	26		.17	.12	.15	.06
	39	43	40	41	44			43	43				
117.	2.2	NA	NA	0.3	-0.5	.39	3199	70		.16	NA	NA	.06
	45			42	44	39	42	48	45				
118.	2.9	1.8	1.6	0.7	NA	.53	4151	NA		.13	.08	.10	.07
	53	52	71	50		46	43		NA				
119.	3.0	1.9	0.9	0.8	1.6	.70	5757	98		.11	.08	.10	.08
	54	55	37	53	64	53	46	51	50				
120.	2.7	1.7	1.7	0.5	NA	.70	6064	NA		.14	.12	.09	.06
	50	49	77	46		53	46		NA				

NOTE: On the first line of data for every program, raw values for each measure are reported; on the second line values are reported in standardized form, with mean = 50 and standard deviation = 10. "NA" indicates that the value for a measure is not available. Since the scale used to compute measure 16 is entirely arbitrary, only values in standardized form are reported for this measure.

TABLE 3.1 Program Measures (Raw and Standardized Values) in Biochemistry

Prog No.	University - Department/Academic Unit	Program Size			Characteristics of Program Graduates			
		(01)	(02)	(03)	(04)	(05)	(06)	(07)
121.	Texas, University of-Med Branch, Galveston *Human Biological Chemistry & Genetics**	21 *52*	8 *43*	17 *46*	NA	NA	NA	NA
122.	Thomas Jefferson University *Biochemistry*	14 *46*	5 *41*	7 *41*	NA	NA	NA	NA
123.	Tulane University *Biochemistry*	12 *44*	4 *41*	10 *43*	NA	NA	NA	NA
124.	Utah, University of-Salt Lake City *Biochemistry*	14 *46*	8 *43*	8 *42*	NA	NA	NA	NA
125.	Vanderbilt University *Biochemistry*	17 *48*	27 *54*	29 *52*	.75 *60*	6.3 *46*	.75 *45*	.70 *60*
126.	Vermont, University of *Biochemistry*	9 *41*	8 *43*	19 *47*	NA	NA	NA	NA
127.	Virginia Commonwealth University/Medical Col *Biochemistry*	19 *50*	13 *46*	21 *48*	.40 *47*	5.3 *60*	1.00 *66*	.70 *60*
128.	Virginia Polytechnic Institute & State Univ *Biochemistry and Nutrition*	16 *47*	7 *42*	11 *43*	NA	NA	NA	NA
129.	Virginia, University of *Biochemistry*	15 *46*	11 *45*	12 *44*	NA	NA	NA	NA
130.	Wake Forest University *Biochemistry*	15 *46*	5 *41*	9 *42*	NA	NA	NA	NA
131.	Washington State University-Pullman *Biochemistry and Biophysics**	16 *47*	16 *48*	25 *50*	.18 *39*	5.3 *60*	.80 *49*	.30 *31*
132.	Washington, University of-Seattle *Biochemistry*	21 *52*	43 *63*	4 *40*	.90 *65*	5.9 *51*	.84 *53*	.63 *55*
133.	Wayne State University *Biochemistry*	18 *49*	13 *46*	17 *46*	.15 *38*	6.0 *50*	.69 *40*	.54 *48*
134.	West Virginia University *Agricultural Biochemistry*	8 *40*	10 *44*	13 *44*	NA	NA	NA	NA
135.	West Virginia University *Medical Biochemistry*	18 *49*	10 *44*	NA	NA	NA	NA	NA
136.	Wisconsin, University of-Madison *Biochemistry*	30 *59*	102 *96*	99 *85*	.68 *58*	5.7 *54*	.85 *54*	.64 *56*
137.	Wisconsin, University of-Madison *Physiological Chemistry*	15 *46*	16 *48*	10 *43*	.83 *63*	6.5 *42*	.67 *38*	.50 *45*
138.	Wyoming, University of *Biochemistry*	4 *37*	5 *41*	10 *43*	NA	NA	NA	NA
139.	Yale University *Molec Biophysics & Biochem/Pharmacol/Biol*	64 *89*	88 *88*	127 *98*	.83 *63*	5.6 *55*	.83 *51*	.61 *54*

* indicates program was initiated since 1970.

NOTE: On the first line of data for every program, raw values for each measure are reported; on the second line values are reported in standardized form, with mean = 50 and standard deviation = 10. "NA" indicates that the value for a measure is not available.

TABLE 3.1 Program Measures (Raw and Standardized Values) in Biochemistry

Prog No.	Survey Results (08)	(09)	(10)	(11)	University Library (12)	Research Support (13)	(14)	Published Articles (15)	(16)	Survey Ratings Standard Error (08)	(09)	(10)	(11)
121.	2.0	0.9	NA	0.3	NA	.62	4581	NA		.19	.15	NA	.06
	43	33		41		50	44		NA				
122.	1.4	NA	NA	0.2	NA	.50	1851	16		.21	NA	NA	.05
	37			38		44	40	42	42				
123.	2.0	1.1	NA	0.3	-1.0	.42	3690	45		.24	.17	NA	.06
	44	38		41	38	40	43	45	44				
124.	2.8	1.8	0.9	0.5	-0.6	.71	6905	36		.14	.16	.15	.07
	52	51	37	47	42	54	48	44	44				
125.	3.2	2.0	1.2	1.0	-0.7	1.00	5204	151		.10	.06	.09	.07
	56	56	52	57	41	67	45	57	59				
126.	1.8	1.1	1.3	0.4	NA	NA	4628	25		.16	.14	.15	.07
	41	37	57	44			44	43	42				
127.	2.2	1.7	1.7	0.4	NA	.63	6556	79		.15	.14	.15	.06
	45	50	73	43		50	47	49	48				
128.	1.8	1.3	1.2	0.3	-0.0	.56	3108	43		.16	.17	.22	.06
	41	42	52	42	48	47	42	45	43				
129.	3.1	1.9	1.3	0.7	0.7	.87	6224	100		.12	.09	.09	.08
	55	53	57	50	56	61	47	51	53				
130.	1.8	1.0	1.0	0.4	NA	.40	3010	29		.12	.14	.09	.06
	41	35	43	43		40	42	43	43				
131.	2.7	1.8	1.4	0.6	-0.3	.88	998	68		.12	.08	.12	.07
	50	52	63	48	45	61	39	47	45				
132.	3.8	2.2	1.1	1.3	1.5	.86	14164	222		.08	.06	.08	.07
	62	61	48	65	63	60	59	64	67				
133.	2.6	1.6	0.8	0.5	-0.4	.44	6372	51		.12	.11	.12	.06
	49	48	34	47	45	42	47	45	43				
134.	1.1	NA	NA	0.1	NA	NA	NA	9		.15	NA	NA	.03
	34			35				41	41				
135.	2.0	1.4	1.1	0.3	NA	.61	NA	33		.15	.11	.18	.06
	43	43	49	42		49		43	43				
136.	4.6	2.7	1.1	1.7	1.6	.87	19738	290		.06	.05	.07	.05
	71	70	46	74	64	61	68	72	70				
137.	3.5	2.2	1.0	1.0	1.6	.80	19738	157		.11	.07	.08	.07
	59	59	41	58	64	58	68	57	57				
138.	1.2	1.0	NA	0.3	NA	NA	NA	12		.20	.19	NA	.06
	35	35		41				41	42				
139.	4.5	2.6	1.4	1.5	2.1	.78	4337	373		.07	.07	.08	.07
	70	68	63	70	69	57	44	81	87				

NOTE: On the first line of data for every program, raw values for each measure are reported; on the second line values are reported in standardized form, with mean = 50 and standard deviation = 10. "NA" indicates that the value for a measure is not available. Since the scale used to compute measure 16 is entirely arbitrary, only values in standardized form are reported for this measure.

TABLE 3.2 Summary Statistics Describing Each Program Measure--Biochemistry

Measure	Number of Programs Evaluated	Mean	Standard Deviation	DECILES								
				1	2	3	4	5	6	7	8	9
Program Size												
01 Raw Value	139	19	11	7	10	13	15	16	18	21	25	35
Std Value	139	50	10	39	42	45	46	47	49	52	55	64
02 Raw Value	136	20	18	6	8	10	13	15	19	22	27	40
Std Value	136	50	10	42	43	44	46	47	49	51	54	61
03 Raw Value	136	25	21	6	10	13	15	20	24	27	35	52
Std Value	136	50	10	41	43	44	45	47	49	51	55	63
Program Graduates												
04 Raw Value	95	.47	.28	.11	.23	.27	.33	.39	.57	.67	.76	.88
Std Value	95	50	10	37	41	43	45	47	54	57	60	65
05 Raw Value	94	6.0	.7	6.9	6.5	6.2	6.0	5.9	5.8	5.7	5.4	5.2
Std Value	94	50	10	37	42	47	50	51	52	54	58	61
06 Raw Value	94	.81	.12	.67	.72	.74	.79	.83	.85	.88	.90	.94
Std Value	94	50	10	38	43	44	48	52	53	56	58	61
07 Raw Value	94	.56	.14	.33	.47	.52	.55	.58	.61	.64	.67	.73
Std Value	94	50	10	34	44	47	49	51	54	56	58	62
Survey Results												
08 Raw Value	138	2.6	1.0	1.4	1.8	2.0	2.3	2.5	2.7	3.0	3.4	4.0
Std Value	138	50	10	37	41	43	47	49	51	54	58	64
09 Raw Value	126	1.7	.5	1.1	1.3	1.5	1.6	1.7	1.8	2.0	2.1	2.4
Std Value	126	50	10	37	41	45	48	50	52	56	58	64
10 Raw Value	109	1.2	.2	.9	1.0	1.0	1.1	1.1	1.2	1.2	1.3	1.4
Std Value	109	50	10	39	43	43	48	48	52	52	57	61
11 Raw Value	138	.7	.4	.2	.3	.4	.5	.5	.6	.8	1.0	1.3
Std Value	138	50	10	39	41	44	46	46	49	53	58	65
University Library												
12 Raw Value	88	.2	1.0	-1.0	-.6	-.5	-.3	.0	.3	.7	.9	1.6
Std Value	88	50	10	38	42	43	45	48	51	55	57	64
Research Support												
13 Raw Value	115	.63	.22	.35	.44	.52	.60	.65	.70	.77	.83	.88
Std Value	115	50	10	37	41	45	49	51	53	56	59	61
14 Raw Value	104	8419	6463	2950	3195	4445	5614	6462	7267	9120	12650	16796
Std Value	104	50	10	42	42	44	46	47	48	51	57	63
Publication Records												
15 Raw Value	133	92	90	13	26	34	47	63	73	94	152	224
Std Value	133	50	10	41	43	44	45	47	48	50	57	65
16 Std Value	133	50	10	42	43	44	45	46	47	51	55	65

NOTE: Standardized values reported in the preceding table have been computed from exact values of the mean and standard deviation and not the rounded values reported here. Since the scale used to compute measure 16 is entirely arbitrary, only data in standardized form are reported for this measure.

TABLE 3.3   Intercorrelations Among Program Measures on 139 Programs in Biochemistry

	01	02	03	04	05	06	07	08	09	10	11	12	13	14	15	16
Program Size																
01		.48	.57	.26	.03	-.07	.09	.58	.54	.38	.53	.40	.08	.33	.62	.58
02			.72	.47	.16	.23	.27	.63	.67	.14	.63	.46	.35	.46	.66	.65
03				.29	.17	.15	.18	.60	.61	.26	.59	.48	.32	.27	.59	.55
Program Graduates																
04					.11	.27	.39	.70	.70	.04	.70	.54	.42	.50	.59	.62
05						.28	.34	.15	.21	.22	.17	.02	.16	.03	.11	.12
06							.66	.24	.27	.18	.25	.09	.28	.12	.20	.22
07								.35	.36	.14	.34	.16	.33	.29	.33	.34
Survey Results																
08									.96	.21	.96	.63	.62	.69	.83	.83
09										.27	.92	.61	.58	.64	.79	.79
10											.21	.10	.17	.03	.31	.28
11												.64	.60	.69	.84	.85
University Library																
12													.21	.56	.67	.66
Research Support																
13														.30	.48	.47
14															.71	.71
Publication Records																
15																.98
16																

NOTE: Since in computing correlation coefficients program data must be available for both of the measures being correlated, the actual number of programs on which each coefficient is based varies.

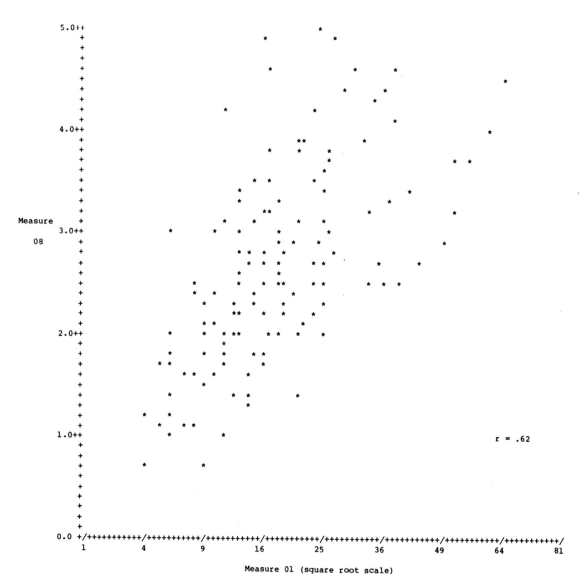

FIGURE 3.1 Mean rating of scholarly quality of faculty (measure 08) versus number of faculty members (measure 01)--138 programs in biochemistry.

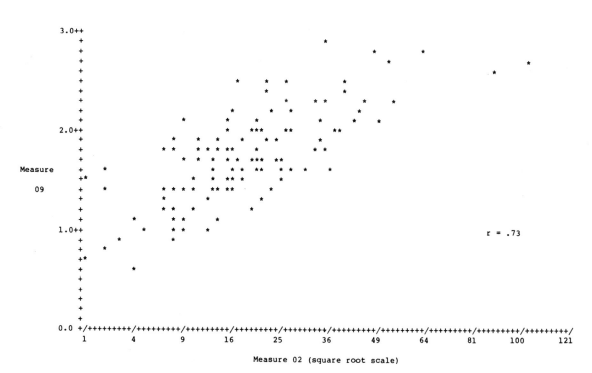

FIGURE 3.2 Mean rating of program effectiveness in educating research scholars/scientists (measure 09) versus number of graduates in last five years (measure 02)--124 programs in biochemistry.

TABLE 3.4   Characteristics of Survey Participants in Biochemistry

	Respondents	
	N	%
Field of Specialization		
Biochemistry	179	77
Molecular Biology	33	14
Other/Unknown	22	9
Faculty Rank		
Professor	118	50
Associate Professor	82	35
Assistant Professor	34	15
Year of Highest Degree		
Pre-1950	21	9
1950-59	40	17
1960-69	108	46
Post-1969	60	26
Unknown	5	2
Evaluator Selection		
Nominated by Institution	191	82
Other	43	18
Survey Form		
With Faculty Names	210	90
Without Names	24	10
Total Evaluators	234	100

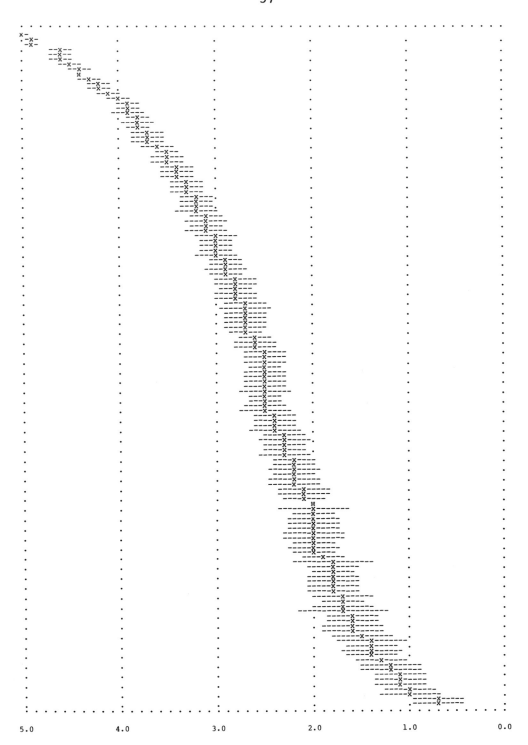

Mean Survey Rating (measure 08)

FIGURE 3.3 Mean rating of scholarly quality of faculty in 138 programs in biochemistry.

NOTE: Programs are listed in sequence of mean rating, with the highest-rated program appearing at the top of the page. The broken lines (---) indicate a confidence interval of ±1.5 standard errors around the reported mean (x) of each program.

IV
Botany Programs

In this chapter 83 research-doctorate programs in botany are assessed. These programs, according to the information supplied by their
universities, have accounted for 1,574 doctoral degrees awarded during
the FY1976-80 period.[1] On the average, 20 full-time and part-time
students intending to earn doctorates were enrolled in a program in
December 1980, with an average faculty size of 19 members.[2] A majority of the 83 programs, listed in Table 4.1, are located in botany or
botanical science departments. Approximately one-third are found in
departments of plant pathology or plant physiology. Four programs were
initiated since 1970. Each of 11 institutions--Clemson University,
University of Georgia, University of Illinois, Iowa State University,
University of Missouri, North Carolina State University, Ohio State
University, Oklahoma State University, Pennsylvania State University,
Virginia Polytechnic Institute and State University, and University of
Wisconsin (Madison)--has two botany programs evaluated in this study.
Each of five institutions--University of California (Berkeley), Uni-
versity of California (Davis), University of Kentucky, University of
Minnesota, and Texas A&M University--has three botany programs evalu-
ated. In addition to the 62 institutions represented in this disci-
pline, another 2 were initially identified as meeting the criteria[3]
for inclusion in the assessment:

> Brandeis University
> Harvard University

---

[1] Data from the NRC's Survey of Earned Doctorates indicate that 1,488
research doctorates in botany, phytopathology, and plant physiology
were awarded by U.S. universities between FY1976 and FY1980. Since the
NRC figure is based on field of degree and not department, it may exclude some doctorates included in the numbers reported by the institutional coordinators.

[2] See the reported means for measures 03 and 01 in Table 4.2.

[3] As mentioned in Chapter I, the primary criterion for inclusion was
that a university had awarded at least 7 doctorates in botany during
the FY1976-78 period.

Botany programs at these two institutions have not been included in the evaluations in this discipline, since in each case the study coordinator indicated that the institution did not at that time have a research-doctorate program in botany.

Before examining individual program results presented in Table 4.1, the reader is urged to refer to Chapter II, in which each of the 16 measures used in the assessment is discussed. Summary statistics describing every measure are given in Table 4.2. For nine of the measures, data are reported for at least 78 of the 83 botany programs. For measures 04-07, which pertain to characteristics of the program graduates, data are presented for only approximately two-thirds of the programs; the other third had too few graduates on which to base statistics.[4] For measure 12, a composite index of the size of a university library, data are available for 68 programs. With respect to measure 13--the fraction of faculty with research grants from the National Institutes of Health, the National Science Foundation, or the Alcohol, Drug Abuse, and Mental Health Administration--data are reported for 45 programs that had at least 10 faculty members; for measure 14, the total university expenditures for research in the biological sciences, data are available for 69 programs. The programs not evaluated on measures 12, 13, and 14 are typically smaller--in terms of faculty size and graduate student enrollment--than other botany programs. Were data on these two measures available for all 83 programs, it is likely that their reported means would be appreciably lower (and that some of the correlations of these measures with others would be higher).

Intercorrelations among the 16 measures (Pearson product-moment coefficients) are given in Table 4.3. Of particular note are the moderately high positive correlations of the measures of the numbers of faculty (01) and students (03) with reputational survey ratings (08, 09). Figure 4.1 illustrates the relation between the mean rating of the scholarly quality of faculty (measure 08) and the number of faculty members (measure 01) for each of 83 programs in botany. Figure 4.2 plots the mean rating of program effectiveness (measure 09) against the total number of FY1976-80 program graduates (measure 02). Although in both figures there is a significant positive correlation between program size and reputational rating, it is quite apparent that some of the smaller programs received high mean ratings.

Table 4.4 describes the 153 faculty members who participated in the evaluation of botany programs. These individuals constituted 61 percent of those asked to respond to the survey in this discipline and 10 percent of the faculty population in the 83 research-doctorate programs being evaluated.[5] Approximately three-fourths of the survey participants were botanists, plant physiologists, or phytopathologists; the

---

[4] As mentioned in Chapter II, data for measures 04-07 are not reported if they are based on the survey responses of fewer than 10 FY1975-79 program graduates.
[5] See Table 2.3 in Chapter II.

remainder were in ecology or other biological science fields. More
than two-thirds of the survey participants had earned their highest
degree prior to 1970, and a majority held the rank of full professor.

To assist the reader in interpreting results of the survey evaluations, estimated standard errors have been computed for mean ratings
of the scholarly quality of faculty in 83 botany programs (and are
given in Table 4.1). For each program the mean rating and an associated "confidence interval" of 1.5 standard errors are illustrated in
Figure 4.3 (listed in order of highest to lowest mean rating). In
comparing two programs, if their confidence intervals do not overlap,
one may conclude that there is a significant difference in their mean
ratings at a .05 level of significance.[6] From this figure it is also
apparent that one should have somewhat more confidence in the accuracy
of the mean ratings of higher-rated programs than lower-rated programs.
This generalization results primarily from the fact that evaluators are
not as likely to be familiar with the less prestigious programs, and
consequently the mean ratings of these programs are usually based on
fewer survey responses.

---

[6] See pp. 31-33 for a discussion of the interpretation of mean ratings
and associated confidence intervals.

TABLE 4.1 Program Measures (Raw and Standardized Values) in Botany

Prog No.	University - Department/Academic Unit	Program Size (01)	(02)	(03)	Characteristics of Program Graduates (04)	(05)	(06)	(07)
001.	Arizona, University of-Tucson	9	10	11	NA	NA	NA	NA
	Botany	43	46	44				
002.	Auburn University	15	9	3	NA	NA	NA	NA
	Botany, Plant Pathology, and Microbiology	47	46	38				
003.	Brigham Young University	12	18	16	.08	5.5	.58	.25
	Botany and Range Science	45	49	47	40	63	44	45
004.	California, University of-Irvine	9	9	8	NA	NA	NA	NA
	Dev & Cell Bio/Ecol & Evolut Bio/Molec Bio	43	46	42				
005.	California, University of-Berkeley	15	42	40	.34	5.8	.86	.60
	Botany	47	60	64	60	58	62	70
006.	California, University of-Berkeley	16	14	19	.13	5.2	.83	.17
	Plant Pathology	48	48	49	44	67	61	39
007.	California, University of-Berkeley	35	4	7	.19	6.6	.85	.60
	Plant Physiology	62	43	41	48	48	62	70
008.	California, University of-Davis	55	38	20	.21	6.8	.61	.34
	Botany	76	58	50	50	45	46	52
009.	California, University of-Davis	20	29	NA	.15	5.4	.81	.46
	Plant Pathology	51	54		45	64	59	60
010.	California, University of-Davis	85	41	NA	.09	6.4	.64	.34
	Plant Physiology	98	60		41	50	48	52
011.	California, University of-Los Angeles	20	28	21	.31	5.5	.54	.46
	Biology	51	54	51	58	63	41	60
012.	California, University of-Riverside	15	31	37	.04	6.2	.70	.30
	Plant Pathology	47	55	61	37	54	52	49
013.	Chicago, University of	5	8	13	NA	NA	NA	NA
	Biology	40	45	45				
014.	Claremont Graduate School	5	4	4	NA	NA	NA	NA
	Botany	40	43	39				
015.	Clemson University	12	8	3	NA	NA	NA	NA
	Plant Pathology	45	45	38				
016.	Clemson University	11	6	16	NA	NA	NA	NA
	Plant Physiology	44	44	47				
017.	Colorado State University-Fort Collins	27	8	11	.00	5.5	.70	.30
	Botany and Plant Pathology	56	45	44	34	63	52	49
018.	Colorado, University of	10	11	14	.14	8.0	.36	.14
	Environmental, Population & Organismic Bio	43	46	46	45	29	29	37
019.	Connecticut, University of-Storrs	13	9	20	NA	NA	NA	NA
	Biological Sciences	45	46	50				
020.	Cornell University-Ithaca	26	59	38	.18	6.5	.78	.42
	Botany	55	67	62	47	50	57	58

* indicates program was initiated since 1970.

NOTE: On the first line of data for every program, raw values for each measure are reported; on the second line values are reported in standardized form, with mean = 50 and standard deviation = 10. "NA" indicates that the value for a measure is not available.

TABLE 4.1 Program Measures (Raw and Standardized Values) in Botany

Prog No.	Survey Results (08)	(09)	(10)	(11)	University Library (12)	Research Support (13)	(14)	Published Articles (15)	(16)	Survey Ratings Standard Error (08)	(09)	(10)	(11)
001.	2.2	1.6	1.0	0.4	0.9	NA	7828	32		.13	.11	.10	.06
	40	45	38	40	55		49	45	45				
002.	2.3	1.5	1.2	0.6	NA	.00	NA	28		.15	.09	.11	.07
	41	42	54	46		37		44	44				
003.	2.4	1.7	1.2	0.5	-0.6	.08	NA	10		.12	.08	.09	.06
	43	47	49	44	41	41		40	42				
004.	3.0	1.8	1.1	0.7	NA	NA	6547	16		.13	.07	.11	.07
	50	50	44	49			47	41	43				
005.	4.3	2.5	0.9	1.1	2.2	.73	18977	101		.08	.06	.09	.08
	65	65	34	66	69	71	69	58	56				
006.	3.8	2.1	1.2	0.7	2.2	.06	18977	101		.12	.06	.12	.09
	59	56	50	49	69	40	69	58	56				
007.	4.2	2.3	1.1	0.9	2.2	.31	18977	101		.08	.08	.10	.08
	64	60	44	57	69	52	69	58	56				
008.	4.5	2.6	1.4	1.4	0.6	.26	18053	208		.07	.06	.08	.08
	68	67	63	74	53	49	67	79	86				
009.	4.3	2.5	1.2	0.6	0.6	.20	18053	208		.11	.08	.10	.09
	66	66	52	48	53	47	67	79	86				
010.	4.5	2.6	1.5	1.2	0.6	.24	18053	208		.07	.06	.08	.08
	68	68	65	66	53	48	67	79	86				
011.	3.8	2.1	1.2	1.0	2.0	.65	15581	25		.09	.06	.08	.08
	60	57	51	62	66	67	63	43	49				
012.	3.9	2.3	1.3	0.8	-1.0	.40	6232	117		.13	.07	.09	.09
	61	61	58	54	37	56	46	61	59				
013.	2.6	1.7	0.9	0.6	0.9	NA	17589	14		.15	.10	.12	.06
	45	48	37	48	55		66	41	43				
014.	3.4	1.7	0.8	0.7	NA	NA	NA	1		.15	.12	.07	.08
	55	47	27	52				38	40				
015.	1.9	1.3	NA	0.2	NA	.00	1275	13		.18	.11	NA	.05
	36	39		35		37	37	41	41				
016.	1.3	0.8	NA	0.2	NA	.00	1275	13		.26	.17	NA	.04
	29	27		32		37	37	41	41				
017.	3.0	1.8	1.3	0.9	-1.1	.04	8863	47		.12	.07	.08	.07
	49	50	55	57	36	39	51	48	48				
018.	2.4	1.7	1.4	0.4	-0.9	.40	11967	12		.18	.14	.15	.07
	42	46	63	40	38	56	56	41	44				
019.	2.6	1.7	1.3	0.7	-0.5	.39	15199	14		.09	.07	.09	.07
	45	47	55	49	42	55	62	41	43				
020.	4.2	2.5	1.2	1.1	1.6	.31	14597	169		.07	.06	.09	.08
	65	65	51	66	63	51	61	71	68				

NOTE: On the first line of data for every program, raw values for each measure are reported; on the second line values are reported in standardized form, with mean = 50 and standard deviation = 10. "NA" indicates that the value for a measure is not available. Since the scale used to compute measure 16 is entirely arbitrary, only values in standardized form are reported for this measure.

TABLE 4.1 Program Measures (Raw and Standardized Values) in Botany

Prog No.	University - Department/Academic Unit	Program Size			Characteristics of Program Graduates			
		(01)	(02)	(03)	(04)	(05)	(06)	(07)
021.	Duke University	19	35	59	.43	6.0	.59	.41
	Botany	*50*	*57*	*77*	*66*	*56*	*44*	*57*
022.	Florida, University of-Gainesville	42	28	60	.12	7.7	.74	.32
	Botany/Plant Pathology	*67*	*54*	*77*	*43*	*34*	*55*	*50*
023.	Georgia, University of-Athens	19	23	33	.36	7.0	.77	.41
	Botany	*50*	*52*	*59*	*61*	*43*	*57*	*57*
024.	Georgia, University of-Athens	19	10	7	.36	6.0	.36	.09
	Plant Pathology	*50*	*46*	*41*	*61*	*56*	*29*	*34*
025.	Hawaii, University of	41	20	21	.29	7.5	.71	.18
	*Botanical Sciences**	*66*	*50*	*51*	*56*	*36*	*52*	*40*
026.	Illinois, University-Urbana/Champaign	27	16	28	.25	5.9	.81	.50
	Botany	*56*	*49*	*55*	*53*	*57*	*59*	*63*
027.	Illinois, University-Urbana/Champaign	39	29	6	.05	5.7	.74	.26
	Plant Pathology and Plant Physiology	*65*	*54*	*40*	*37*	*61*	*54*	*46*
028.	Indiana University-Bloomington	14	23	22	.44	5.8	.50	.31
	Biology	*46*	*52*	*51*	*67*	*58*	*38*	*50*
029.	Iowa State University-Ames	20	20	23	.11	6.5	.83	.33
	Botany	*51*	*50*	*52*	*42*	*49*	*61*	*51*
030.	Iowa State University-Ames	16	11	12	NA	NA	NA	NA
	Plant Pathology, Seed and Weed Sciences	*48*	*46*	*44*				
031.	Iowa, University of-Iowa City	12	14	18	.19	6.0	.81	.44
	Botany	*45*	*48*	*48*	*48*	*56*	*59*	*59*
032.	Kansas State University-Manhattan	13	4	10	NA	NA	NA	NA
	Plant Pathology	*45*	*43*	*43*				
033.	Kansas, University of	11	7	9	NA	NA	NA	NA
	Botany	*44*	*45*	*42*				
034.	Kentucky, University of	7	3	4	NA	NA	NA	NA
	Biological Sciences	*41*	*43*	*39*				
035.	Kentucky, University of	14	9	11	NA	NA	NA	NA
	Plant Pathology (College of Agriculture)	*46*	*46*	*44*				
036.	Kentucky, University of	10	5	9	NA	NA	NA	NA
	Plant Physiology (College of Agriculture)	*43*	*44*	*42*				
037.	Louisiana State University-Baton Rouge	7	5	6	NA	NA	NA	NA
	Botany	*41*	*44*	*40*				
038.	Maryland, University of-College Park	21	31	59	.08	6.8	.54	.19
	Botany	*51*	*55*	*77*	*40*	*45*	*41*	*41*
039.	Massachusetts, University of-Amherst	18	20	27	.44	6.5	.72	.33
	Botany	*49*	*50*	*55*	*68*	*49*	*53*	*51*
040.	Miami University-Ohio	14	12	15	.08	5.5	.91	.46
	Botany	*46*	*47*	*46*	*40*	*63*	*66*	*60*

* indicates program was initiated since 1970.

NOTE: On the first line of data for every program, raw values for each measure are reported; on the second line values are reported in standardized form, with mean = 50 and standard deviation = 10. "NA" indicates that the value for a measure is not available.

TABLE 4.1 Program Measures (Raw and Standardized Values) in Botany

Prog No.	Survey Results (08)	(09)	(10)	(11)	University Library (12)	Research Support (13)	(14)	Published Articles (15)	(16)	Survey Ratings Standard Error (08)	(09)	(10)	(11)
021.	4.0	2.5	1.2	1.0	0.3	.84	11320	22		.10	.07	.09	.09
	62	65	50	62	50	76	55	43	44				
022.	3.1	1.9	1.3	1.0	0.8	.10	3486	94		.09	.05	.09	.07
	51	52	58	62	54	42	41	57	50				
023.	3.7	2.1	1.5	1.0	0.4	.63	10714	126		.08	.06	.09	.08
	58	56	69	62	51	66	54	63	59				
024.	3.0	1.9	1.4	0.5	0.4	.05	10714	126		.16	.11	.10	.08
	50	52	65	44	51	40	54	63	59				
025.	3.0	1.8	1.3	0.6	-0.1	.20	4440	63		.13	.09	.09	.07
	49	48	59	48	45	46	43	51	46				
026.	3.8	2.2	1.2	1.0	2.0	.41	6074	134		.07	.05	.09	.08
	60	58	52	63	66	56	46	65	66				
027.	3.9	2.3	1.4	1.0	2.0	.28	6074	134		.10	.07	.09	.08
	60	61	62	62	66	50	46	65	66				
028.	3.7	2.1	1.0	1.0	0.9	.57	NA	24		.09	.06	.08	.09
	58	57	40	62	56	64		43	46				
029.	3.2	1.9	1.1	0.6	-0.5	.10	5287	57		.10	.06	.07	.08
	52	52	46	46	42	42	45	49	48				
030.	3.0	1.9	1.0	0.6	-0.5	.00	5287	57		.15	.06	.11	.08
	50	51	38	45	42	37	45	49	48				
031.	2.6	1.7	0.9	0.5	0.3	.25	7088	10		.13	.09	.13	.07
	45	47	37	45	50	49	48	40	43				
032.	2.7	1.6	1.5	0.5	NA	.15	2496	22		.16	.12	.13	.07
	46	44	69	42		44	40	43	42				
033.	2.7	1.8	1.1	0.6	0.1	.55	3161	9		.12	.11	.10	.07
	46	49	40	46	40	62	41	40	42				
034.	1.9	1.0	NA	0.4	-0.1	NA	484	46		.18	.15	NA	.07
	36	31		39	46		36	47	46				
035.	3.3	2.0	1.6	0.6	-0.1	.00	484	46		.11	.07	.09	.08
	53	54	72	48	46	37	36	47	46				
036.	2.7	1.6	1.3	0.4	-0.1	.30	484	46		.15	.10	.12	.07
	45	45	55	41	46	51	36	47	46				
037.	1.9	1.3	1.1	0.4	-0.3	NA	5116	38		.17	.13	.12	.06
	36	38	46	40	43		44	46	44				
038.	2.7	1.7	1.2	0.8	0.2	.24	1623	20		.12	.08	.11	.07
	47	48	53	52	48	48	38	42	43				
039.	3.4	1.8	1.1	0.9	-0.7	.33	3022	36		.11	.07	.08	.08
	54	50	43	56	40	53	41	45	46				
040.	3.1	1.8	1.3	0.6	-0.8	.43	NA	14		.13	.09	.09	.07
	51	50	55	49	39	57		41	43				

NOTE: On the first line of data for every program, raw values for each measure are reported; on the second line values are reported in standardized form, with mean = 50 and standard deviation = 10. "NA" indicates that the value for a measure is not available. Since the scale used to compute measure 16 is entirely arbitrary, only values in standardized form are reported for this measure.

TABLE 4.1 Program Measures (Raw and Standardized Values) in Botany

Prog No.	University - Department/Academic Unit	Program Size			Characteristics of Program Graduates			
		(01)	(02)	(03)	(04)	(05)	(06)	(07)
041.	Michigan State University-East Lansing	28	46	53	.19	6.6	.63	.31
	Botany and Plant Pathology	*56*	*62*	*72*	*48*	*48*	*47*	*50*
042.	Michigan, University of-Ann Arbor	74	31	41	.41	6.3	.57	.32
	Biological Sciences	*90*	*55*	*64*	*65*	*52*	*43*	*51*
043.	Minnesota, University of	26	8	12	.40	8.0	.54	.15
	Agriculture/ Biological Sciences/ Forestry	*55*	*45*	*44*	*64*	*29*	*41*	*38*
044.	Minnesota, University of	18	20	6	.32	7.5	.43	.10
	Botany	*49*	*50*	*40*	*58*	*36*	*34*	*34*
045.	Minnesota, University of	18	22	17	.20	7.5	.64	.36
	Plant Pathology	*49*	*51*	*48*	*49*	*36*	*48*	*53*
046.	Missouri, University of-Columbia	8	7	11	NA	NA	NA	NA
	Biological Sciences	*42*	*45*	*44*				
047.	Missouri, University of-Columbia	10	8	14	NA	NA	NA	NA
	*Plant Pathology**	*43*	*45*	*46*				
048.	Montana, University of-Missoula	10	10	10	.27	7.0	.50	.10
	Botany	*43*	*46*	*43*	*55*	*43*	*38*	*34*
049.	Nebraska, University of-Lincoln	24	17	27	.18	6.1	.80	.50
	Life Sciences	*54*	*49*	*55*	*48*	*54*	*59*	*63*
050.	North Carolina State University-Raleigh	20	20	26	.17	7.4	.89	.33
	Botany	*51*	*50*	*54*	*46*	*38*	*64*	*51*
051.	North Carolina State University-Raleigh	36	19	36	.21	6.8	.95	.32
	Plant Pathology	*62*	*50*	*61*	*50*	*46*	*68*	*50*
052.	North Carolina, University of-Chapel Hill	19	15	27	.25	6.2	.65	.40
	Botany	*50*	*48*	*55*	*53*	*54*	*48*	*56*
053.	North Dakota State University-Fargo	8	13	10	NA	NA	NA	NA
	Botany	*42*	*47*	*43*				
054.	North Dakota, University of-Grand Forks	2	4	10	NA	NA	NA	NA
	Biology	*37*	*43*	*43*				
055.	Ohio State University-Columbus	21	22	19	.13	5.5	.83	.30
	Botany	*51*	*51*	*49*	*44*	*63*	*60*	*49*
056.	Ohio State University-Columbus	22	8	19	.20	5.0	.60	.20
	Plant Pathology	*52*	*45*	*49*	*49*	*70*	*45*	*42*
057.	Oklahoma State University-Stillwater	7	4	4	NA	NA	NA	NA
	Botany	*41*	*43*	*39*				
058.	Oklahoma State University-Stillwater	40	194	42	.03	6.5	.50	.08
	Plant Sciences	*65*	*99*	*65*	*36*	*49*	*38*	*33*
059.	Oklahoma, University of-Norman	12	12	10	.17	6.9	.67	.08
	Botany/Microbiology	*45*	*47*	*43*	*46*	*44*	*50*	*33*
060.	Oregon State University-Corvallis	27	30	41	.16	6.6	.63	.27
	Botany and Plant Pathology	*56*	*55*	*64*	*46*	*48*	*47*	*46*

* indicates program was initiated since 1970.

NOTE: On the first line of data for every program, raw values for each measure are reported; on the second line values are reported in standardized form, with mean = 50 and standard deviation = 10. "NA" indicates that the value for a measure is not available.

TABLE 4.1 Program Measures (Raw and Standardized Values) in Botany

Prog No.	Survey Results (08)	(09)	(10)	(11)	University Library (12)	Research Support (13)	(14)	Published Articles (15)	(16)	Survey Ratings Standard Error (08)	(09)	(10)	(11)
041.	3.8	2.3	1.1	1.4	0.3	.25	10357	151		.08	.05	.08	.07
	60	60	46	75	50	49	53	68	71				
042.	4.2	2.5	1.1	1.0	1.8	.61	15431	52		.13	.09	.10	.09
	64	65	43	62	64	65	62	48	49				
043.	3.3	1.9	1.3	0.5	1.2	.35	13696	98		.12	.09	.10	.07
	54	52	57	43	58	53	59	58	53				
044.	3.3	1.9	1.1	0.6	1.2	.39	13696	98		.11	.06	.10	.07
	54	52	48	46	58	55	59	58	53				
045.	3.5	2.3	1.2	0.7	1.2	.11	13696	98		.18	.10	.11	.09
	55	60	49	50	58	42	59	58	53				
046.	2.2	1.4	0.9	0.4	-0.2	NA	4628	35		.17	.11	.10	.06
	39	39	36	41	45		43	45	45				
047.	2.9	1.7	1.1	0.6	-0.2	.20	4628	35		.12	.08	.08	.08
	48	47	46	45	45	47	43	45	45				
048.	1.8	1.2	0.9	0.4	NA	.10	NA	0		.14	.09	.08	.07
	35	35	36	42		42		38	40				
049.	3.1	1.9	1.4	0.9	-0.5	.25	2965	42		.14	.09	.09	.08
	51	51	62	57	42	49	40	47	47				
050.	2.8	1.9	1.2	0.5	NA	.05	6741	115		.13	.08	.10	.07
	47	52	52	45		40	47	61	55				
051.	3.8	2.3	1.4	0.7	NA	.00	6741	115		.13	.10	.12	.09
	59	60	60	49		37	47	61	55				
052.	3.7	2.2	1.3	0.9	1.0	.53	9849	15		.09	.06	.08	.08
	58	57	59	59	56	61	53	41	42				
053.	1.6	1.0	NA	0.3	NA	NA	5698	27		.16	.12	NA	.05
	33	30		35			45	44	43				
054.	0.6	0.4	NA	0.2	NA	NA	NA	2		.18	.15	NA	.04
	20	17		31				39	40				
055.	3.3	2.0	1.4	1.1	0.9	.29	8330	61		.11	.07	.10	.09
	53	54	64	63	55	50	50	50	52				
056.	2.8	1.8	1.2	0.5	0.9	.00	8330	61		.17	.09	.12	.08
	48	49	52	43	55	37	50	50	52				
057.	1.6	1.0	0.9	0.3	-1.9	NA	3127	22		.15	.11	.07	.05
	32	31	33	37	27		41	43	43				
058.	2.5	1.7	1.3	0.3	-1.9	.00	3127	22		.13	.12	.09	.05
	43	48	55	37	27	37	41	43	43				
059.	3.1	1.9	1.3	0.8	-0.6	.33	NA	15		.11	.08	.07	.08
	51	50	57	55	41	53		41	45				
060.	3.3	2.0	1.2	1.2	NA	.33	7108	112		.09	.05	.07	.07
	54	54	49	67		53	48	60	56				

NOTE: On the first line of data for every program, raw values for each measure are reported; on the second line values are reported in standardized form, with mean = 50 and standard deviation = 10. "NA" indicates that the value for a measure is not available. Since the scale used to compute measure 16 is entirely arbitrary, only values in standardized form are reported for this measure.

TABLE 4.1 Program Measures (Raw and Standardized Values) in Botany

Prog No.	University - Department/Academic Unit	Program Size			Characteristics of Program Graduates			
		(01)	(02)	(03)	(04)	(05)	(06)	(07)
061.	Oregon, University of-Eugene	10	2	1	NA	NA	NA	NA
	Biology	*43*	*42*	*37*				
062.	Pennsylvania State University	13	6	8	NA	NA	NA	NA
	Botany	*45*	*44*	*42*				
063.	Pennsylvania State University	33	19	19	.19	7.0	.88	.50
	Plant Pathology	*60*	*50*	*49*	*48*	*43*	*64*	*63*
064.	Purdue University-West Lafayette	9	18	21	.46	5.7	.54	.25
	Biological Sciences	*43*	*49*	*51*	*69*	*60*	*41*	*45*
065.	Rhode Island, University of	13	10	10	NA	7.2	.40	.30
	Botany	*45*	*46*	*43*		*40*	*32*	*49*
066.	Rutgers, The State University-New Brunswick	30	17	33	.13	7.5	.44	.19
	Botany/Plant Physiology	*58*	*49*	*59*	*43*	*36*	*34*	*41*
067.	SUNY-College of Environ Science & Forestry	11	6	7	NA	NA	NA	NA
	Environmental and Forest Biology	*44*	*44*	*41*				
068.	Southern Illinois University-Carbondale	15	17	23	.14	7.8	.71	.21
	Botany	*47*	*49*	*52*	*45*	*33*	*53*	*43*
069.	Tennessee, University of-Knoxville	16	19	19	.29	6.3	.69	.06
	Botany	*48*	*50*	*49*	*56*	*53*	*51*	*32*
070.	Texas A & M University	7	6	14	NA	NA	NA	NA
	Biology	*41*	*44*	*46*				
071.	Texas A & M University	11	8	14	NA	NA	NA	NA
	Plant Pathology	*44*	*45*	*46*				
072.	Texas A & M University	11	7	6	NA	NA	NA	NA
	Plant Physiology	*44*	*45*	*40*				
073.	Texas, University of-Austin	23	34	33	.50	6.2	.60	.43
	Botany	*53*	*56*	*59*	*72*	*53*	*45*	*58*
074.	Vanderbilt University	6	7	5	NA	NA	NA	NA
	General Biology	*40*	*45*	*40*				
075.	Virginia Polytechnic Institute & State Univ	27	18	24	.00	6.1	.57	.14
	Plant Pathology & Physiology	*56*	*49*	*53*	*34*	*54*	*43*	*37*
076.	Virginia Polytechnic Institute & State Univ	12	8	13	NA	NA	NA	NA
	Biology	*45*	*45*	*45*				
077.	Washington State University-Pullman	12	15	15	.00	6.8	.58	.42
	Botany	*45*	*48*	*46*	*34*	*46*	*44*	*57*
078.	Washington University-Saint Louis	11	6	11	NA	NA	NA	NA
	*Plant Biology**	*44*	*44*	*44*				
079.	Washington, University of-Seattle	17	19	19	.41	7.5	.65	.47
	Botany	*48*	*50*	*49*	*65*	*36*	*48*	*61*
080.	Wisconsin, University of-Madison	17	38	46	.17	6.1	.86	.57
	Botany	*48*	*58*	*68*	*47*	*55*	*62*	*68*

* indicates program was initiated since 1970.

NOTE: On the first line of data for every program, raw values for each measure are reported; on the second line values are reported in standardized form, with mean = 50 and standard deviation = 10. "NA" indicates that the value for a measure is not available.

TABLE 4.1 Program Measures (Raw and Standardized Values) in Botany

Prog No.	Survey Results (08)	(09)	(10)	(11)	University Library (12)	Research Support (13)	(14)	Published Articles (15)	(16)	Survey Ratings Standard Error (08)	(09)	(10)	(11)
061.	2.5	1.5	1.0	0.6	-0.9	.50	NA	6		.15	.09	.08	.08
	43	43	39	45	37	60		39	40				
062.	2.3	1.4	1.0	0.4	0.7	.39	8024	78		.16	.12	.11	.05
	42	41	38	41	54	55	49	54	48				
063.	3.7	2.2	1.3	0.6	0.7	.00	8024	78		.13	.11	.12	.09
	58	59	56	46	54	37	49	54	48				
064.	3.4	2.0	0.9	0.8	-0.5	NA	10337	106		.13	.07	.07	.08
	54	54	35	55	41		53	59	60				
065.	2.3	1.5	1.1	0.4	NA	.23	NA	22		.17	.13	.07	.06
	41	42	47	41		48		43	42				
066.	3.0	1.8	1.2	0.7	0.8	.13	7505	48		.10	.08	.08	.06
	50	50	52	50	55	43	48	48	48				
067.	3.1	1.9	1.0	0.3	NA	.27	NA	15		.16	.08	.10	.06
	51	51	41	37		50		41	42				
068.	2.3	1.3	0.9	0.5	-0.2	.00	NA	19		.14	.09	.10	.06
	41	38	37	43	45	37		42	42				
069.	2.7	1.8	1.0	0.5	-0.4	.06	NA	35		.13	.10	.09	.07
	46	50	43	45	43	40		45	44				
070.	2.0	1.4	0.9	0.5	-0.5	NA	3199	56		.18	.16	.11	.07
	37	39	36	43	42		41	49	51				
071.	2.2	1.5	1.2	0.5	-0.5	.00	3199	56		.15	.11	.10	.07
	40	42	50	43	42	37	41	49	51				
072.	2.6	1.7	1.0	0.4	-0.5	.18	3199	56		.20	.13	.10	.07
	45	47	38	41	42	46	41	49	51				
073.	4.5	2.6	1.4	1.2	1.6	.74	5757	36		.08	.06	.08	.08
	68	67	60	69	63	71	45	45	46				
074.	1.8	1.3	1.0	0.5	-0.7	NA	5204	11		.21	.13	.08	.08
	35	37	38	42	39		44	40	43				
075.	2.4	1.4	1.3	0.6	-0.0	.00	3108	42		.13	.10	.12	.08
	43	40	56	45	46	37	41	47	45				
076.	2.6	1.6	1.3	0.6	-0.0	.33	3108	42		.17	.11	.16	.08
	45	45	59	47	46	53	41	47	45				
077.	2.9	1.9	1.4	0.6	-0.3	.50	998	107		.11	.07	.11	.07
	48	52	63	48	44	60	37	59	56				
078.	3.6	2.0	1.5	0.8	-0.4	.55	16825	12		.14	.08	.11	.08
	56	53	66	55	43	62	65	41	43				
079.	3.7	2.1	1.3	1.0	1.5	.53	14164	40		.08	.04	.08	.08
	58	55	59	62	61	62	60	46	49				
080.	3.8	2.3	1.0	1.1	1.6	.65	19738	132		.08	.06	.09	.08
	60	60	38	66	62	67	70	64	64				

NOTE: On the first line of data for every program, raw values for each measure are reported; on the second line values are reported in standardized form, with mean = 50 and standard deviation = 10. "NA" indicates that the value for a measure is not available. Since the scale used to compute measure 16 is entirely arbitrary, only values in standardized form are reported for this measure.

TABLE 4.1 Program Measures (Raw and Standardized Values) in Botany

Prog No.	University – Department/Academic Unit	Program Size (01)	(02)	(03)	Characteristics of Program Graduates (04)	(05)	(06)	(07)
081.	Wisconsin, University of–Madison	27	24	45	.13	6.1	.73	.37
	Plant Pathology	56	52	67	44	54	54	54
082.	Wisconsin, University of–Milwaukee	9	NA	NA	NA	NA	NA	NA
	Botany*	43						
083.	Yale University	21	49	57	.32	6.1	.92	.41
	Biology/Forestry and Environmental Studies	51	63	75	58	54	66	56

* indicates program was initiated since 1970.

NOTE: On the first line of data for every program, raw values for each measure are reported; on the second line values are reported in standardized form, with mean = 50 and standard deviation = 10. "NA" indicates that the value for a measure is not available.

TABLE 4.1 Program Measures (Raw and Standardized Values) in Botany

Prog No.	Survey Results (08)	(09)	(10)	(11)	University Library (12)	Research Support (13)	(14)	Published Articles (15)	(16)	Survey Ratings Standard Error (08)	(09)	(10)	(11)
081.	4.3	2.6	1.1	0.9	1.6	.22	19738	132		.12	.08	.08	.10
	65	66	45	57	62	48	70	64	64				
082.	2.1	1.2	1.1	0.4	NA	NA	NA	NA		.17	.13	.13	.06
	38	36	44	38					NA				
083.	4.1	2.3	1.1	1.0	2.1	.48	4337	25		.09	.07	.08	.07
	63	61	43	60	68	59	43	43	46				

NOTE: On the first line of data for every program, raw values for each measure are reported; on the second line values are reported in standardized form, with mean = 50 and standard deviation = 10. "NA" indicates that the value for a measure is not available. Since the scale used to compute measure 16 is entirely arbitrary, only values in standardized form are reported for this measure.

TABLE 4.2 Summary Statistics Describing Each Program Measure--Botany

Measure	Number of Programs Evaluated	Mean	Standard Deviation	DECILES								
				1	2	3	4	5	6	7	8	9
Program Size												
01 Raw Value	83	19	14	7	10	11	13	15	18	20	26	34
Std Value	83	50	10	41	43	44	46	47	49	51	55	61
02 Raw Value	82	19	23	5	7	8	10	14	18	20	28	35
Std Value	82	50	10	44	45	45	46	48	49	50	54	57
03 Raw Value	80	20	15	6	8	10	13	16	19	23	33	41
Std Value	80	50	10	40	42	43	45	47	49	52	59	64
Program Graduates												
04 Raw Value	52	.21	.13	.04	.10	.13	.17	.19	.20	.28	.34	.41
Std Value	52	50	10	37	42	44	47	48	49	55	60	65
05 Raw Value	53	6.5	.8	7.5	7.3	6.8	6.6	6.4	6.2	6.1	5.8	5.5
Std Value	53	50	10	36	39	45	48	51	53	55	59	63
06 Raw Value	53	.67	.15	.46	.54	.58	.63	.66	.71	.77	.82	.86
Std Value	53	50	10	36	41	44	47	49	53	57	60	63
07 Raw Value	53	.32	.14	.10	.17	.25	.30	.32	.34	.41	.43	.49
Std Value	53	50	10	34	39	45	49	50	51	56	58	62
Survey Results												
08 Raw Value	83	3.0	.8	1.9	2.3	2.6	2.8	3.0	3.3	3.5	3.8	4.1
Std Value	83	50	10	36	41	45	47	50	53	56	59	63
09 Raw Value	83	1.8	.4	1.3	1.5	1.7	1.7	1.8	1.9	2.0	2.2	2.4
Std Value	83	50	10	38	43	47	47	49	52	54	58	63
10 Raw Value	78	1.2	.2	.9	1.0	1.1	1.1	1.2	1.2	1.3	1.3	1.4
Std Value	78	50	10	35	41	46	46	52	52	57	57	63
11 Raw Value	83	.7	.3	.4	.4	.5	.6	.6	.7	.8	1.0	1.1
Std Value	83	50	10	40	40	44	47	47	51	54	61	64
University Library												
12 Raw Value	68	.3	1.0	-.9	-.5	-.4	-.1	.2	.6	.9	1.2	1.8
Std Value	68	50	10	37	42	43	46	49	53	56	59	65
Research Support												
13 Raw Value	69	.28	.22	.00	.05	.10	.20	.25	.31	.39	.48	.58
Std Value	69	50	10	37	40	42	46	49	51	55	59	64
14 Raw Value	69	8406	5704	1588	3127	4409	5534	6741	8146	10714	14251	18053
Std Value	69	50	10	38	41	43	45	47	50	54	60	67
Publication Records												
15 Raw Value	82	60	51	11	15	22	34	42	56	78	104	131
Std Value	82	50	10	40	41	43	45	47	49	54	59	64
16 Std Value	82	50	10	42	43	44	45	46	48	52	56	63

NOTE: Standardized values reported in the preceding table have been computed from exact values of the mean and standard deviation and not the rounded values reported here. Since the scale used to compute measure 16 is entirely arbitrary, only data in standardized form are reported for this measure.

TABLE 4.3 Intercorrelations Among Program Measures on 83 Programs in Botany

Measure

	01	02	03	04	05	06	07	08	09	10	11	12	13	14	15	16
Program Size																
01		.42	.48	-.10	-.08	.04	.04	.56	.57	.36	.52	.31	-.04	.31	.55	.55
02			.55	-.14	.04	-.06	-.07	.29	.34	.11	.27	-.01	.03	.09	.23	.24
03				.04	.02	.21	.24	.51	.54	.09	.60	.29	.26	.17	.33	.32
Program Graduates																
04					-.07	-.18	.11	.31	.23	-.24	.25	.34	.54	.20	-.12	-.11
05						.25	.24	.26	.25	-.13	.21	.11	.12	.12	.04	.16
06							.58	.36	.32	-.07	.23	.24	-.03	.04	.24	.18
07								.59	.56	-.09	.51	.43	.50	.28	.24	.26
Survey Results																
08									.97	.29	.83	.66	.49	.62	.60	.62
09										.32	.80	.62	.45	.61	.61	.63
10											.24	.02	-.05	-.07	.26	.24
11												.54	.54	.48	.51	.56
University Library																
12													.34	.55	.40	.37
Research Support																
13														.36	-.02	.04
14															.47	.52
Publication Records																
15																.96
16																

NOTE: Since in computing correlation coefficients program data must be available for both of the measures being correlated, the actual number of programs on which each coefficient is based varies.

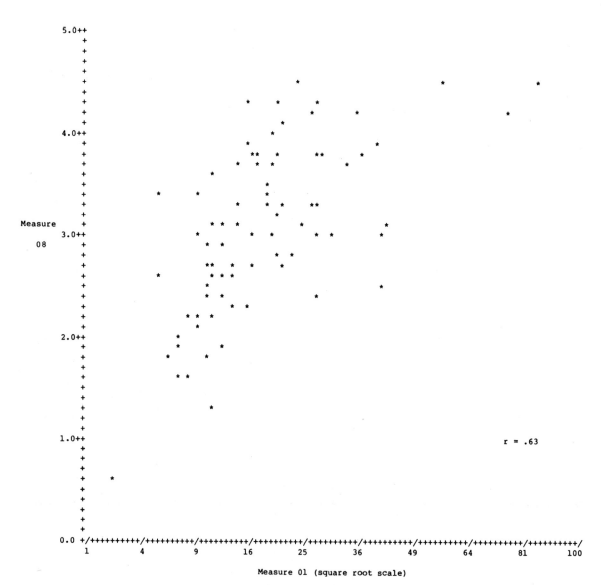

FIGURE 4.1 Mean rating of scholarly quality of faculty (measure 08) versus number of faculty members (measure 01)--83 programs in botany.

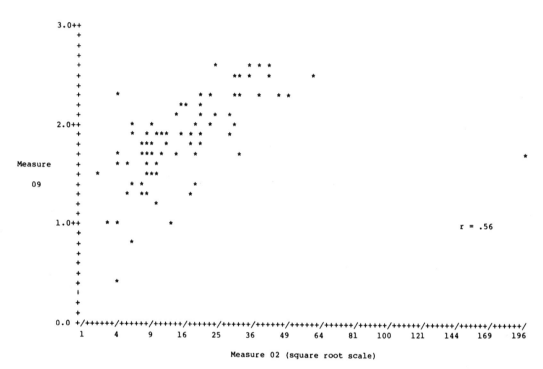

FIGURE 4.2 Mean rating of program effectiveness in educating research scholars/scientists
(measure 09) versus number of graduates in last five years (measure 02)--82 programs
in botany.

TABLE 4.4 Characteristics of Survey Participants in Botany

	Respondents	
	N	%
Field of Specialization		
Botany	45	29
Ecology	16	11
Plant Physiology	35	23
Phytopathology	35	23
Other/Unknown	22	14
Faculty Rank		
Professor	85	56
Associate Professor	51	33
Assistant Professor	16	11
Other/Unknown	1	1
Year of Highest Degree		
Pre-1950	9	6
1950-59	25	16
1960-69	79	52
Post-1969	39	26
Unknown	1	1
Evaluator Selection		
Nominated by Institution	131	86
Other	22	14
Survey Form		
With Faculty Names	136	89
Without Names	17	11
Total Evaluators	153	100

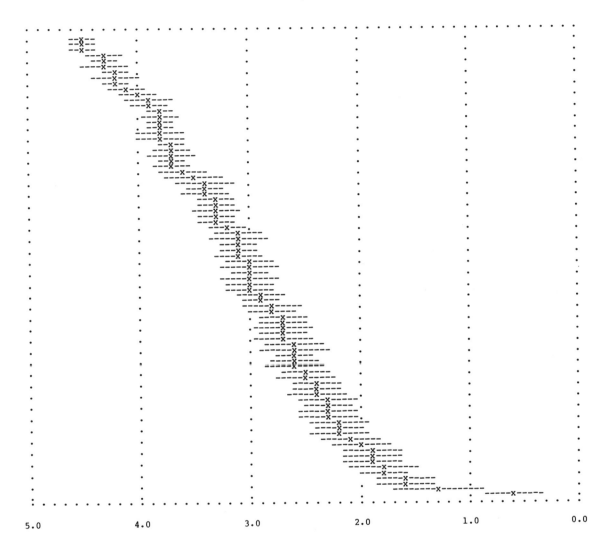

5.0   4.0   3.0   2.0   1.0   0.0

Mean Survey Rating (measure 08)

FIGURE 4.3 Mean rating of scholarly quality of faculty in 83 programs in botany.

NOTE: Programs are listed in sequence of mean rating, with the highest-rated program appearing at the top of the page. The broken lines (---) indicate a confidence interval of ±1.5 standard errors around the reported mean (x) of each program.

V
Cellular/Molecular Biology Programs

In this chapter 89 research-doctorate programs in cellular/molecular biology are assessed. These programs, according to the information supplied by their universities, have accounted for 1,871 doctoral degrees awarded during the FY1976-80 period.[1] Because cellular and molecular biology programs transcend the boundaries of many other biological science disciplines and because these programs may be found in a variety of different institutional settings (including biology departments, medical school departments, etc.), the committee encountered difficulty in identifying a comprehensive set of research-doctorate programs that have produced graduates in this discipline. On the average, 34 full-time and part-time students intending to earn doctorates were enrolled in a program in December 1980, with an average faculty size of 26 members.[2] Roughly half of the 89 programs, listed in Table 5.1, are located in departments of biology or biological sciences and one-fourth in departments of cellular or molecular biology. The remainder are in departments of anatomy, genetics, and other biological sciences. Eighteen programs were initiated since 1970. Each of six institutions--Florida State University, University of Pittsburgh, SUNY at Buffalo, Tufts University, University of Utah, and Washington University (St. Louis)--has two cellular/molecular biology programs included in the assessment. The Albert Einstein College of Medicine has three programs evaluated and the University of Chicago has four. In addition to the 78 institutions represented in this discipline, another 17 were initially identified as meeting the criteria[3] for inclusion in the assessment:

---

[1]Data from the NRC's Survey of Earned Doctorates indicate that 199 research doctorates in cytology, 773 in molecular biology, and 952 in general biology were awarded by U.S. universities between FY1976 and FY1980. Since the NRC figure is based on field of degree and not department, it may exclude some doctorates included in the numbers reported by the institutional coordinators.

[2]See the reported means for measures 03 and 01 in Table 5.2.

[3]As mentioned in Chapter I, the primary criterion for inclusion was that a university had awarded at least 10 doctorates in cellular/molecular biology during the FY1976-78 period.

University of California--Davis
University of California--San Francisco
Colorado State University--Fort Collins
Cornell University--Ithaca
Dartmouth College
University of Florida--Gainesville
Fordham University
Idaho State University--Pocatello
Illinois Institute of Technology
University of Iowa--Iowa City
University of Kentucky
University of Louisville
University of Miami--Florida
University of New Mexico--Albuquerque
New York University
Saint John's University
College of William and Mary

Saint John's University chose not to participate in the assessment in _any_ discipline. Cellular/molecular biology programs at the other 16 institutions have not been included in the evaluations in this discipline, since in each case the study coordinator either indicated that the institution did not at that time have a research-doctorate program in cellular/molecular biology or failed to provide the information requested by the committee.

Before examining the individual program results presented in Table 5.1, the reader is urged to refer to Chapter II, in which each of the 16 measures used in the assessment is discussed. Summary statistics describing every measure are given in Table 5.2. For eight of the measures, data are reported for at least 77 of the 89 cellular/molecular biology programs. For measures 04-07, which pertain to characteristics of the program graduates, data are presented for only approximately two-thirds of the programs; the other third had too few graduates on which to base statistics.[4] For measure 12, a composite index of the size of a university library, data are available for 63 programs; for measure 14, the total university expenditures for research in the biological sciences, data are available for 67 programs. The programs not evaluated on measures 12 and 14 are typically smaller--in terms of faculty size and graduate student enrollment--than other cellular/ molecular biology programs. Were data on these two measures available for all 89 programs, it is likely that their reported means would be appreciably lower (and that some of the correlations of these measures with others would be higher). With regard to reputational survey measures 09 and 10, results were not reported for any programs with fewer than 15 ratings.

Intercorrelations among the 16 measures (Pearson product-moment

---

[4]As mentioned in Chapter II, data for measures 04-07 are not reported if they are based on the survey responses of fewer than 10 FY1975-79 program graduates.

coefficients) are given in Table 5.3. Of particular note are the high positive correlations of the reputational survey ratings (08, 09) with measures of publication records (15, 16) and total research expenditures (14). Figure 5.1 illustrates the relation between the mean rating of the scholarly quality of faculty (measure 08) and the number of faculty members (measure 01) for each of 86 programs in cellular/molecular biology. Figure 5.2 plots the mean rating of program effectiveness (measure 09) against the total number of FY1976-80 program graduates (measure 02). Although in both figures there is a significant positive correlation between program size and reputational rating, it is quite apparent that many of the smaller programs received high mean ratings.

Table 5.4 describes the 139 faculty members who participated in the evaluation of cellular/molecular biology programs. These individuals constituted 52 percent of those asked to respond to the survey in this discipline and 6 percent of the faculty population in the 89 research-doctorate programs being evaluated.[5] Approximately two-thirds of the evaluators identified themselves as cellular or molecular biologists, with the remainder split among biochemistry, genetics, and other biological science disciplines. A majority of the survey participants had earned their highest degree prior to 1970, and almost half held the rank of full professor.

One exception should be noted with regard to the survey evaluations in this discipline. In the program listing on the survey form, New Mexico State University at Las Cruces was identified as being located in Alamogordo, where there is another branch of the same university system not offering the research doctorate. Since a large majority of faculty evaluators indicated that they were unfamiliar with this program and it is quite possible that some of them were misled by the inaccurate identification of this institution, the committee has decided not to report the survey results for this program.

To assist the reader in interpreting results of the survey evaluations, estimated standard errors have been computed for mean ratings of the scholarly quality of faculty in 86 cellular/molecular biology programs (and are given in Table 5.1). For each program the mean rating and an associated "confidence interval" of 1.5 standard errors are illustrated in Figure 5.3 (listed in order of highest to lowest mean rating). In comparing two programs, if their confidence intervals do not overlap, one may conclude that there is a significant difference in their mean ratings at a .05 level of significance.[6] From this figure it is also apparent that one should have somewhat more confidence in the accuracy of the mean ratings of higher-rated programs than lower-rated programs. This generalization results primarily from the fact that evaluators are not as likely to be familiar with the less prestigious programs, and consequently the mean ratings of these programs are usually based on fewer survey responses.

---

[5] See Table 2.3 in Chapter II.

[6] See pp. 31-33 for a discussion of the interpretation of mean ratings and associated confidence intervals.

TABLE 5.1 Program Measures (Raw and Standardized Values) in Cellular/Molecular Biol.

Prog No.	University - Department/Academic Unit	Program Size			Characteristics of Program Graduates			
		(01)	(02)	(03)	(04)	(05)	(06)	(07)
001.	Albert Einstein College of Medicine *Anatomy*	8	2	11	NA	NA	NA	NA
		42	40	43				
002.	Albert Einstein College of Medicine *Cell Biology*	18	10	19	.80	NA	NA	NA
		47	44	45	58			
003.	Albert Einstein College of Medicine *Molecular Biology*	8	11	16	NA	NA	NA	NA
		42	44	44				
004.	Arizona, University of-Tucson *Cellular and Developmental Biology**	11	1	10	NA	NA	NA	NA
		43	40	43				
005.	Atlanta University *Biology*	10	29	26	.83	6.0	.83	.17
		43	53	48	59	52	53	24
006.	Baylor College of Medicine-Houston *Cell Biology**	30	21	30	.46	5.3	.85	.54
		52	49	49	45	61	54	48
007.	Boston University *Biology*	18	18	35	.27	7.3	.46	.27
		47	48	50	38	34	18	31
008.	Bowling Green State University *Biological Sciences*	29	18	32	.31	7.0	.60	.07
		52	48	49	39	38	32	17
009.	Brandeis University *Biology*	16	19	44	.69	6.1	.88	.69
		46	48	53	54	50	57	58
010.	Brown University *Biology and Medicine*	24	18	25	.67	6.0	.88	.69
		49	48	47	53	52	57	58
011.	CUNY-Graduate School *Biology*	111	85	114	.25	8.5	.77	.43
		89	80	75	37	18	47	41
012.	California, University of-Irvine *Molec & Biochem/Biol Chem/Dev & Cell/Micro*	26	16	43	.60	4.5	.87	.67
		50	47	53	50	72	56	57
013.	California Institute of Technology *Biology*	23	48	47	.81	6.1	.90	.63
		49	62	54	58	50	59	55
014.	California, University of-Berkeley *Molecular Biology*	14	41	33	.77	5.7	.86	.57
		45	59	50	57	56	55	50
015.	California, University of-Los Angeles *Molecular Biology*	42	27	35	.69	5.4	.74	.58
		58	52	50	54	60	45	51
016.	California, University of-Riverside *Biology*	21	21	19	.40	7.8	.80	.50
		48	49	45	43	28	50	46
017.	California, University of-San Diego *Biology*	46	74	50	.91	6.2	.83	.73
		59	74	55	62	49	·53	61
018.	California, University of-Santa Barbara *Biological Sciences*	49	75	98	.18	6.8	.70	.30
		61	75	70	34	41 ·	41	33
019.	Case Western Reserve University *Anatomy/Biochem/Biol/Micro/Pathol/Physiol**	33	3	24	NA	NA	NA	NA
		53	41	47				
020.	Chicago, University of *Biology*	8	18	14	NA	NA	NA	NA
		42	48	44				

* indicates program was initiated since 1970.

NOTE: On the first line of data for every program, raw values for each measure are reported; on the second line values are reported in standardized form, with mean = 50 and standard deviation = 10. "NA" indicates that the value for a measure is not available.

TABLE 5.1 Program Measures (Raw and Standardized Values) in Cellular/Molecular Biol.

Prog No.	Survey Results (08)	(09)	(10)	(11)	University Library (12)	Research Support (13)	(14)	Published Articles (15)	(16)	Survey Ratings Standard Error (08)	(09)	(10)	(11)
001.	2.8	1.3	1.5	0.7	NA	NA	9184	234		.17	.17	.16	.08
	49	36	62	49			48	58	61				
002.	3.5	2.0	1.0	1.0	NA	.78	9184	234		.10	.07	.08	.08
	56	53	42	56		56	48	58	61				
003.	2.9	1.7	1.1	0.7	NA	NA	9184	234		.15	.12	.15	.09
	50	45	46	50			48	58	61				
004.	2.0	1.1	1.2	0.4	0.9	.55	7828	82		.17	.16	.18	.07
	40	30	49	42	56	46	46	46	45				
005.	NA	NA	NA	0.1	NA	.30	NA	5		NA	NA	NA	.04
				36		35		40	40				
006.	3.6	2.1	1.5	1.1	NA	.77	14051	225		.09	.06	.08	.08
	57	56	62	59		56	56	57	57				
007.	2.6	1.4	0.9	0.4	-0.4	.50	NA	26		.15	.13	.11	.07
	46	38	36	43	44	44		42	41				
008.	1.5	NA	NA	0.1	NA	.21	NA	17		.26	NA	NA	.04
	35			36		31		41	41				
009.	3.6	2.2	1.1	1.2	NA	.88	5487	98		.10	.08	.09	.08
	57	59	44	60		61	43	47	49				
010.	3.1	1.9	1.2	0.9	-1.1	.63	NA	75		.10	.06	.10	.08
	52	50	51	53	37	49		45	45				
011.	2.4	1.5	1.0	0.4	NA	.24	NA	74		.18	.23	.17	.07
	44	41	41	42		32		45	44				
012.	3.2	1.9	1.2	0.9	NA	.85	6547	144		.11	.09	.11	.08
	53	51	51	55		59	44	51	50				
013.	4.8	2.8	1.1	1.6	NA	.91	5446	187		.05	.06	.08	.07
	70	72	47	71		62	43	54	55				
014.	4.2	2.3	1.2	1.5	2.2	.86	18977	387		.08	.07	.10	.07
	64	61	48	68	69	60	63	70	68				
015.	3.8	2.2	1.6	1.2	2.0	.86	15581	444		.09	.07	.08	.07
	60	57	66	62	67	60	58	74	72				
016.	2.6	1.6	1.1	0.4	-1.0	.38	6232	96		.18	.12	.13	.06
	47	42	44	42	38	38	44	47	46				
017.	4.3	2.5	1.5	1.4	-0.0	.74	8706	304		.08	.07	.10	.08
	64	66	60	66	47	54	48	63	63				
018.	3.2	2.0	1.1	0.7	-0.1	.59	NA	86		.10	.08	.14	.07
	52	52	46	50	47	48		46	47				
019.	2.7	1.5	0.8	0.5	-1.3	.70	7721	143		.17	.16	.14	.07
	47	40	31	44	35	53	46	51	51				
020.	3.4	1.9	1.0	0.9	0.9	NA	17589	325		.11	.08	.11	.09
	55	51	41	53	56		61	65	64				

NOTE: On the first line of data for every program, raw values for each measure are reported; on the second line values are reported in standardized form, with mean = 50 and standard deviation = 10. "NA" indicates that the value for a measure is not available. Since the scale used to compute measure 16 is entirely arbitrary, only values in standardized form are reported for this measure.

TABLE 5.1 Program Measures (Raw and Standardized Values) in Cellular/Molecular Biol.

Prog No.	University - Department/Academic Unit	Program Size			Characteristics of Program Graduates			
		(01)	(02)	(03)	(04)	(05)	(06)	(07)
021.	Chicago, University of	15	35	28	NA	NA	NA	NA
	Biophysics and Theoretical Biology	45	56	48				
022.	Chicago, University of	18	1	11	NA	NA	NA	NA
	Developmental Biology*	47	40	43				
023.	Chicago, University of	33	11	11	1.00	6.3	.83	.75
	Genetics	53	44	43	66	48	53	62
024.	Cincinnati, University of	9	10	4	.10	5.2	.80	.70
	Biological Sciences	42	44	41	31	63	50	59
025.	Colorado, University of	22	24	57	.68	5.8	.84	.72
	Molecular, Cellular, and Developmental Biol	48	51	57	53	54	54	60
026.	Columbia University	26	27	61	.75	6.3	.90	.62
	Biological Sciences	50	52	58	56	48	59	54
027.	Connecticut, University of-Storrs	15	9	19	.85	6.7	.77	.54
	Biological Sciences	45	43	45	60	42	47	48
028.	Cornell University-Medical Center	17	24	39	.42	5.4	1.00	.58
	Biological Structure/Cell Biology	46	51	52	43	60	69	51
029.	Delaware, University of-Newark	8	5	5	NA	NA	NA	NA
	Life and Health Sciences	42	41	41				
030.	Duke University	134	NA	32	.73	6.1	.66	.55
	Cell and Molecular Biology*	99		49	55	50	37	49
031.	Florida State University-Tallahassee	36	63	64	.46	6.9	.75	.37
	Biological Science	55	69	59	45	40	46	37
032.	Florida State University-Tallahassee	22	17	9	.57	5.5	.89	.51
	Molecular Biophysics*	48	47	42	49	59	59	47
033.	Harvard University	19	35	53	.89	5.7	.92	.58
	Biology (Cellular & Developmental)	47	56	56	62	56	61	51
034.	Houston, University of	12	7	6	NA	NA	NA	NA
	Biology	44	42	41				
035.	Illinois, University-Urbana/Champaign	40	NA	9	.60	6.2	.80	.56
	Cell Biology	57		42	50	49	50	50
036.	Indiana University-Bloomington	18	9	33	.78	5.9	.91	.61
	Biology*	47	43	50	57	53	61	53
037.	Iowa State University-Ames	24	11	25	NA	NA	NA	NA
	Molecular, Cellular, and Developmental Biol	49	44	47				
038.	Johns Hopkins University	12	60	79	.96	6.3	.91	.65
	Biology	44	68	64	64	47	61	56
039.	Kansas, University of	10	12	7	.22	6.5	.77	.53
	Physiology and Cell Biology	43	45	42	36	45	47	48
040.	Loma Linda University	6	NA	4	NA	NA	NA	NA
	Biology	41		41				

* indicates program was initiated since 1970.

NOTE: On the first line of data for every program, raw values for each measure are reported; on the second line values are reported in standardized form, with mean = 50 and standard deviation = 10. "NA" indicates that the value for a measure is not available.

TABLE 5.1 Program Measures (Raw and Standardized Values) in Cellular/Molecular Biol.

Prog No.	Survey Results				University Library	Research Support		Published Articles		Survey Ratings Standard Error			
	(08)	(09)	(10)	(11)	(12)	(13)	(14)	(15)	(16)	(08)	(09)	(10)	(11)
021.	3.7	2.3	1.0	0.8	0.9	.67	17589	325		.11	.09	.11	.08
	58	59	42	51	56	51	61	65	64				
022.	3.4	1.8	0.8	1.0	0.9	.78	17589	325		.10	.12	.11	.07
	54	47	33	57	56	56	61	65	64				
023.	3.9	2.2	1.3	1.1	0.9	.76	17589	325		.10	.08	.10	.09
	61	57	52	58	56	55	61	65	64				
024.	1.7	NA	NA	0.3	-0.2	NA	9365	14		.19	NA	NA	.07
	37			40	45		49	41	41				
025.	4.1	2.4	1.5	1.5	-0.9	.91	11967	125		.09	.07	.07	.07
	62	63	64	67	39	62	53	49	49				
026.	4.1	2.4	1.4	1.4	1.7	.89	11090	94		.08	.07	.10	.08
	63	62	59	65	65	61	51	47	48				
027.	2.7	1.6	1.0	0.7	-0.5	.53	15199	56		.11	.10	.13	.09
	48	42	41	50	43	45	58	44	43				
028.	3.2	1.9	1.1	0.6	NA	.18	14597	102		.15	.14	.14	.08
	52	50	45	46		29	57	48	49				
029.	2.0	1.4	0.9	0.3	NA	NA	NA	39		.19	.13	.13	.06
	40	38	36	40				43	43				
030.	3.7	2.1	1.5	1.0	0.3	.69	11320	203		.09	.08	.09	.08
	58	57	61	57	51	52	52	56	57				
031.	2.8	1.9	1.2	0.4	-0.4	.81	3196	42		.15	.13	.14	.07
	48	51	51	43	43	57	39	43	42				
032.	2.7	1.8	NA	0.5	-0.4	.91	3196	42		.17	.10	NA	.07
	48	47		45	43	62	39	43	42				
033.	4.3	2.6	0.9	1.5	3.0	.90	34979	281		.07	.06	.07	.08
	65	67	36	67	77	61	88	62	64				
034.	1.4	NA	NA	0.3	-0.9	.42	NA	44		.21	NA	NA	.05
	34			39	39	40		43	42				
035.	3.1	1.8	1.2	0.6	2.0	.73	6074	142		.13	.10	.13	.08
	52	48	49	48	67	54	44	51	50				
036.	3.5	2.0	1.3	1.1	0.9	.83	NA	119		.11	.09	.09	.09
	56	53	55	58	57	59		49	48				
037.	2.6	1.6	NA	0.4	-0.5	.58	5287	62		.15	.12	NA	.07
	46	42		43	43	48	42	44	44				
038.	3.3	2.0	0.8	1.0	-0.4	.83	19837	62		.09	.08	.10	.07
	54	53	32	57	44	59	65	44	45				
039.	1.9	1.2	0.9	0.3	0.1	.50	3161	51		.23	.18	.09	.06
	39	32	36	41	49	44	39	44	43				
040.	0.4	NA	NA	0.1	NA	NA	NA	0		.16	NA	NA	.03
	23			35				39	40				

NOTE: On the first line of data for every program, raw values for each measure are reported;
on the second line values are reported in standardized form, with mean = 50 and
standard deviation = 10. "NA" indicates that the value for a measure is not available.
Since the scale used to compute measure 16 is entirely arbitrary, only values in
standardized form are reported for this measure.

TABLE 5.1 Program Measures (Raw and Standardized Values) in Cellular/Molecular Biol.

Prog No.	University – Department/Academic Unit	Program Size			Characteristics of Program Graduates			
		(01)	(02)	(03)	(04)	(05)	(06)	(07)
041.	Marquette University	17	15	16	.40	6.2	NA	NA
	Biology	*46*	*46*	*44*	*43*	*49*		
042.	Massachusetts Institute of Technology	20	35	49	.88	5.2	.82	.61
	Biology	*47*	*56*	*55*	*61*	*62*	*52*	*53*
043.	Michigan State University-East Lansing	33	42	70	NA	NA	NA	NA
	Microbiology and Biochemistry	*53*	*59*	*61*				
044.	Michigan, University of-Ann Arbor	63	3	24	NA	NA	NA	NA
	Cellular and Molecular Biology	*67*	*41*	*47*				
045.	Minnesota, University of	21	9	18	NA	NA	NA	NA
	Genetics and Cell Biology	*48*	*43*	*45*				
046.	Missouri, University of-Columbia	11	2	10	NA	NA	NA	NA
	*Biological Sciences**	*43*	*40*	*43*				
047.	Nebraska, University of-Lincoln	12	15	23	NA	NA	NA	NA
	*Life Sciences**	*44*	*46*	*47*				
048.	New Mexico State University-Las Cruces	19	15	20	.29	6.0	.71	.43
	Biology	*47*	*46*	*46*	*38*	*52*	*42*	*41*
049.	North Carolina, University of-Chapel Hill	51	NA	NA	.55	4.7	1.00	.63
	Cellular Biology/Molecular Biology	*62*			*48*	*70*	*69*	*54*
050.	North Dakota, University of-Grand Forks	9	11	8	NA	NA	NA	NA
	Anatomy	*42*	*44*	*42*				
051.	North Texas State University-Denton	6	8	18	NA	NA	NA	NA
	*Biological Sciences**	*41*	*43*	*45*				
052.	Northwestern University	45	44	93	.46	5.5	.68	.64
	Biochem & Molec/Pharmacol/Anat/Path/Physiol	*59*	*60*	*68*	*45*	*59*	*39*	*55*
053.	Ohio State University-Columbus	11	9	6	NA	NA	NA	NA
	Molecular, Cellular, and Developmental Biol	*43*	*43*	*41*				
054.	Oregon, University of-Eugene	21	4	10	.69	6.7	.58	.42
	Biology	*48*	*41*	*43*	*54*	*43*	*30*	*40*
055.	Pennsylvania, University of	46	27	33	.85	5.9	.78	.56
	Molecular Biology	*59*	*52*	*50*	*60*	*53*	*48*	*50*
056.	Pittsburgh, University of	5	8	19	NA	NA	NA	NA
	Anatomy and Cell Biology (Schl of Medicine)	*41*	*43*	*45*				
057.	Pittsburgh, University of	28	8	26	.25	7.0	.56	.25
	*Biological Sciences (Arts and Sciences)**	*51*	*43*	*48*	*37*	*38*	*28*	*29*
058.	Princeton University	15	39	36	.77	6.2	.69	.62
	Biology	*45*	*58*	*51*	*57*	*49*	*40*	*53*
059.	Purdue University-West Lafayette	38	79	119	.68	6.1	.76	.54
	Biological Sciences	*56*	*77*	*76*	*54*	*51*	*46*	*48*
060.	Rensselaer Polytechnic Institute	10	9	6	NA	NA	NA	NA
	Biology	*43*	*43*	*41*				

* indicates program was initiated since 1970.

NOTE: On the first line of data for every program, raw values for each measure are reported; on the second line values are reported in standardized form, with mean = 50 and standard deviation = 10. "NA" indicates that the value for a measure is not available.

TABLE 5.1 Program Measures (Raw and Standardized Values) in Cellular/Molecular Biol.

Prog No.	Survey Results				University Library	Research Support		Published Articles		Survey Ratings Standard Error			
	(08)	(09)	(10)	(11)	(12)	(13)	(14)	(15)	(16)	(08)	(09)	(10)	(11)
041.	1.8	NA	NA	0.2	NA	.35	NA	5		.18	NA	NA	.05
	38			37		37		40	40				
042.	4.9	2.8	1.3	1.7	−0.3	.85	17348	360		.04	.05	.07	.06
	70	74	56	72	44	59	61	68	72				
043.	2.7	1.7	1.3	0.8	0.3	.70	10357	145		.13	.09	.14	.09
	48	45	53	51	51	53	50	51	49				
044.	3.3	1.7	1.2	0.9	1.8	.14	15431	324		.11	.11	.12	.08
	54	46	49	54	65	28	58	65	64				
045.	2.8	1.7	1.0	0.6	1.2	.86	13696	309		.11	.10	.09	.07
	49	45	39	47	59	60	55	64	60				
046.	1.6	0.9	NA	0.3	−0.2	.64	4628	35		.21	.17	NA	.05
	36	26		39	46	50	41	42	42				
047.	2.1	1.6	NA	0.2	−0.5	.67	2965	44		.23	.18	NA	.06
	41	42		39	43	51	39	43	43				
048.	NA	NA	NA	NA	NA	.32	NA	20		NA	NA	NA	NA
						36		41	42				
049.	3.3	2.0	1.6	0.9	1.0	.73	9849	NA		.09	.05	.11	.08
	54	54	67	55	57	54	49		NA				
050.	1.0	NA	NA	0.1	NA	NA	NA	15		.28	NA	NA	.04
	30			35				41	41				
051.	1.3	1.1	NA	0.2	NA	NA	NA	9		.24	.17	NA	.06
	32	29		39				40	41				
052.	3.2	2.0	1.4	0.8	0.3	.89	4760	147		.11	.10	.13	.08
	53	54	59	53	51	61	42	51	50				
053.	2.1	1.5	1.1	0.4	0.9	.73	8330	91		.16	.15	.17	.07
	41	40	44	42	56	54	47	47	46				
054.	3.7	2.1	1.1	1.1	−0.9	.86	NA	87		.08	.07	.08	.08
	58	56	46	60	38	60		46	47				
055.	3.5	2.0	1.1	1.1	0.7	.61	23550	396		.11	.07	.11	.08
	56	54	44	59	54	49	71	71	68				
056.	2.0	NA	NA	0.2	0.1	NA	6462	89		.19	NA	NA	.05
	40			36	48		44	47	46				
057.	2.8	1.8	1.4	0.7	0.1	.75	6462	63		.10	.10	.14	.07
	49	49	57	49	48	55	44	44	45				
058.	3.3	2.0	0.8	1.1	0.9	.73	3574	98		.12	.08	.12	.08
	53	53	32	58	56	54	40	47	47				
059.	3.4	2.1	1.2	1.0	−0.5	.82	10337	226		.09	.07	.10	.08
	55	55	49	57	42	58	50	57	56				
060.	1.5	NA	NA	0.1	NA	.40	NA	20		.24	NA	NA	.04
	35			36		39		41	41				

NOTE: On the first line of data for every program, raw values for each measure are reported; on the second line values are reported in standardized form, with mean = 50 and standard deviation = 10. "NA" indicates that the value for a measure is not available. Since the scale used to compute measure 16 is entirely arbitrary, only values in standardized form are reported for this measure.

TABLE 5.1 Program Measures (Raw and Standardized Values) in Cellular/Molecular Biol.

Prog No.	University - Department/Academic Unit	Program Size			Characteristics of Program Graduates			
		(01)	(02)	(03)	(04)	(05)	(06)	(07)
061.	Rice University	13	16	16	.74	6.3	.68	.53
	Biology	44	47	44	56	47	39	48
062.	Rochester, University of	27	29	42	.86	7.0	.76	.38
	Biology, Radiation Biol & Biology Trng Prog	51	53	52	60	38	47	38
063.	Rockefeller University	42	19	41	.18	5.4	.82	.71
	Cellular Biology/Molecular Biology	58	48	52	34	60	52	59
064.	SUNY at Albany	16	NA	NA	.54	5.8	.77	.62
	Biological Sciences	46			48	54	47	53
065.	SUNY at Buffalo	17	13	36	NA	NA	NA	NA
	Biological Sciences (Div of Grad & Prof Ed)	46	45	51				
066.	SUNY at Buffalo	13	13	17	NA	NA	NA	NA
	Biology (Roswell Park Graduate Division)	44	45	45				
067.	SUNY at Stony Brook	26	21	29	.31	6.2	.94	.75
	Biology	50	49	48	39	49	63	62
068.	SUNY-Downstate Medical Center	18	10	23	.50	6.3	.91	.36
	Anatomy and Cell Biology/ Biophysics	47	44	47	46	48	60	37
069.	Southern California, University of	37	28	114	.38	6.4	.81	.52
	Biological Sciences	55	52	75	42	47	51	47
070.	Southern Mississippi, Univ of-Hattiesburg	3	3	1	NA	NA	NA	NA
	Biology	40	41	40				
071.	Stanford University	7	NA	2	NA	NA	NA	NA
	Structural Biology*	41		40				
072.	Syracuse University	10	15	10	.30	NA	.80	.70
	Biology*	43	46	43	39		50	59
073.	Texas Woman's University-Denton	10	11	18	.00	5.5	.70	.50
	Biology*	43	44	45	27	58	41	46
074.	Texas, U of-Health Science Center, Houston	21	18	26	.54	6.6	.77	.62
	Cellular and Molec Bio (M D Anderson Hosp)	48	48	48	48	43	47	53
075.	Texas, University of-Austin	29	32	11	.79	6.5	.64	.50
	Biological Sciences*	52	54	43	58	45	36	46
076.	Texas, University of-Dallas	12	17	37	.11	5.5	.79	.74
	Biology*	44	47	51	31	58	49	61
077.	Tufts University	15	10	13	NA	NA	NA	NA
	Biology	45	44	43				
078.	Tufts University	9	13	18	1.00	6.7	.92	.77
	Molecular Biology	42	45	45	66	42	61	63
079.	Tulane University	19	26	36	.42	7.8	.80	.50
	Biology	47	52	51	43	28	50	46
080.	Utah, University of-Salt Lake City	51	23	62	NA	NA	NA	NA
	Biology	62	50	59				

* indicates program was initiated since 1970.

NOTE: On the first line of data for every program, raw values for each measure are reported; on the second line values are reported in standardized form, with mean = 50 and standard deviation = 10. "NA" indicates that the value for a measure is not available.

TABLE 5.1 Program Measures (Raw and Standardized Values) in Cellular/Molecular Biol.

Prog No.	Survey Results (08)	(09)	(10)	(11)	University Library (12)	Research Support (13)	(14)	Published Articles (15)	(16)	Survey Ratings Standard Error (08)	(09)	(10)	(11)
061.	2.7	1.6	1.0	0.4	-1.4	.46	NA	50		.16	.16	.17	.06
	47	42	41	42	33	42		43	45				
062.	3.0	1.9	1.4	0.7	-0.6	.74	15969	233		.10	.11	.11	.08
	51	51	57	50	41	55	59	58	55				
063.	4.8	2.6	1.3	1.7	NA	.81	27299	252		.05	.07	.08	.06
	70	67	53	72		58	76	59	64				
064.	2.7	1.5	1.5	0.6	-1.0	.75	NA	72		.10	.12	.14	.08
	48	40	61	47	38	55		45	46				
065.	2.6	1.6	NA	0.5	0.3	.59	6799	43		.12	.14	NA	.06
	47	42		44	50	48	45	43	42				
066.	2.8	1.7	1.1	0.7	0.3	.00	6799	43		.13	.12	.10	.07
	49	45	45	48	50	21	45	43	42				
067.	2.9	1.8	1.4	0.7	-0.6	.62	5802	149		.10	.09	.10	.07
	50	47	58	50	41	49	43	51	52				
068.	2.5	1.6	1.5	0.4	NA	.39	3077	78		.15	.14	.14	.07
	45	42	64	43		39	39	46	44				
069.	2.8	1.6	1.2	0.4	0.4	.35	2405	48		.18	.16	.13	.07
	49	44	51	43	51	37	38	43	44				
070.	0.2	NA	NA	0.0	NA	NA	NA	24		.09	NA	NA	.02
	21			34				41	41				
071.	4.0	2.3	1.6	1.1	2.0	NA	12514	243		.10	.11	.10	.09
	61	60	67	58	68		54	59	62				
072.	2.3	1.5	0.8	0.4	-0.3	.70	NA	45		.18	.11	.13	.07
	43	40	33	41	44	53		43	43				
073.	NA	NA	NA	0.1	NA	.10	NA	6		NA	NA	NA	.04
				36		26		40	40				
074.	2.8	1.6	1.3	0.7	NA	.76	4151	NA		.13	.13	.15	.07
	48	43	54	49		56	41		NA				
075.	3.0	1.6	1.1	0.6	1.6	.79	5757	143		.14	.11	.16	.07
	51	43	46	47	64	57	43	51	49				
076.	2.3	1.5	1.1	0.5	NA	.50	NA	NA		.16	.16	.12	.07
	44	41	43	44		44			NA				
077.	1.6	NA	NA	0.2	NA	.40	3518	9		.18	NA	NA	.06
	36			38		39	40	40	41				
078.	2.8	1.9	1.2	0.6	NA	NA	3518	86		.15	.11	.13	.08
	48	49	49	46			40	46	47				
079.	2.3	NA	NA	0.3	-1.0	.16	3690	6		.15	NA	NA	.07
	44			40	37	29	40	40	41				
080.	3.5	2.0	1.8	0.9	-0.6	.61	6905	60		.10	.08	.07	.08
	56	52	74	54	42	49	45	44	45				

NOTE: On the first line of data for every program, raw values for each measure are reported; on the second line values are reported in standardized form, with mean = 50 and standard deviation = 10. "NA" indicates that the value for a measure is not available. Since the scale used to compute measure 16 is entirely arbitrary, only values in standardized form are reported for this measure.

TABLE 5.1 Program Measures (Raw and Standardized Values) in Cellular/Molecular Biol.

Prog No.	University - Department/Academic Unit	Program Size			Characteristics of Program Graduates			
		(01)	(02)	(03)	(04)	(05)	(06)	(07)
081.	Utah, University of-Salt Lake City	10	11	12	NA	NA	NA	NA
	Cellular, Viral, and Molecular Biology	*43*	*44*	*43*				
082.	Vanderbilt University	13	21	26	.60	5.4	.86	.71
	Molecular Biology	*44*	*49*	*48*	*50*	*60*	*55*	*60*
083.	Virginia, University of	20	22	49	.85	6.3	.70	.55
	Biology	*47*	*50*	*55*	*60*	*48*	*41*	*49*
084.	Washington University-Saint Louis	53	19	57	.82	6.0	.82	.82
	*Biology and Biomed Sci (Molecular Biology)**	*63*	*48*	*57*	*59*	*52*	*52*	*67*
085.	Washington University-Saint Louis	82	9	39	NA	NA	NA	NA
	Biology and Biomedical Sci (Cell Biology	*76*	*43*	*52*				
086.	Washington, University of-Seattle	17	28	8	.96	5.0	.96	.74
	Genetics	*46*	*52*	*42*	*64*	*66*	*65*	*62*
087.	Wayne State University	16	NA	NA	NA	NA	NA	NA
	Biological Sciences	*46*						
088.	Wisconsin, University of-Madison	67	27	91	.71	6.5	.87	.68
	Molecular Biology	*69*	*52*	*68*	*55*	*45*	*57*	*57*
089.	Yale University	76	120	205	.86	5.4	.92	.65
	Biol/Cell Bio/Molec Biophys & Biochem/Genet	*73*	*97*	*99*	*60*	*59*	*62*	*55*

* indicates program was initiated since 1970.

NOTE: On the first line of data for every program, raw values for each measure are reported; on the second line values are reported in standardized form, with mean = 50 and standard deviation = 10. "NA" indicates that the value for a measure is not available.

TABLE 5.1 Program Measures (Raw and Standardized Values) in Cellular/Molecular Biol.

Prog No.	Survey Results				University Library	Research Support		Published Articles		Survey Ratings Standard Error			
	(08)	(09)	(10)	(11)	(12)	(13)	(14)	(15)	(16)	(08)	(09)	(10)	(11)
081.	2.9	1.9	1.5	0.7	−0.6	.70	6905	50		.15	.10	.12	.09
	50	50	64	48	42	53	45	43	43				
082.	2.8	1.7	1.0	0.8	−0.7	.77	5204	25		.11	.09	.11	.08
	48	46	43	52	41	56	42	41	43				
083.	3.1	2.0	1.6	0.9	0.7	.85	6224	50		.12	.06	.10	.09
	52	52	66	53	55	59	44	43	43				
084.	3.8	2.2	1.4	1.2	−0.4	.85	16825	48		.08	.09	.08	.08
	60	57	58	62	44	59	60	43	46				
085.	3.7	2.1	1.3	1.1	−0.4	.73	16825	NA		.10	.10	.13	.08
	58	54	52	59	44	54	60		NA				
086.	4.0	2.5	1.2	1.0	1.5	.82	14164	85		.11	.08	.08	.09
	61	64	48	55	62	58	56	46	45				
087.	2.0	NA	NA	0.3	−0.4	.50	6372	48		.18	NA	NA	.06
	40			40	44	44	44	43	43				
088.	4.6	2.5	1.4	1.5	1.6	.79	19738	561		.07	.06	.07	.07
	67	66	58	67	63	57	65	84	82				
089.	4.7	2.7	1.4	1.7	2.1	.78	4337	511		.07	.07	.08	.06
	69	70	59	72	68	56	41	80	84				

NOTE: On the first line of data for every program, raw values for each measure are reported; on the second line values are reported in standardized form, with mean = 50 and standard deviation = 10. "NA" indicates that the value for a measure is not available. Since the scale used to compute measure 16 is entirely arbitrary, only values in standardized form are reported for this measure.

TABLE 5.2 Summary Statistics Describing Each Program Measure--Cellular/Molecular Biology

Measure	Number of Programs Evaluated	Mean	Standard Deviation	DECILES								
				1	2	3	4	5	6	7	8	9
Program Size												
01 Raw Value	89	26	22	8	10	13	16	18	21	26	36	49
Std Value	89	50	10	42	43	44	46	47	48	50	55	61
02 Raw Value	82	23	21	4	9	11	13	17	19	25	29	44
Std Value	82	50	10	41	43	44	45	47	48	51	53	60
03 Raw Value	86	34	32	7	10	16	19	25	32	36	49	66
Std Value	86	50	10	42	43	44	45	47	49	51	55	60
Program Graduates												
04 Raw Value	59	.59	.26	.22	.31	.42	.54	.63	.70	.78	.84	.88
Std Value	59	50	10	36	39	43	48	52	54	57	60	61
05 Raw Value	57	6.1	.7	7.0	6.7	6.4	6.3	6.2	6.0	5.8	5.5	5.4
Std Value	57	50	10	38	42	46	48	49	52	54	59	60
06 Raw Value	57	.80	.11	.65	.70	.76	.78	.80	.83	.86	.90	.92
Std Value	57	50	10	36	41	46	48	50	53	55	59	61
07 Raw Value	57	.56	.15	.35	.46	.52	.55	.58	.62	.65	.70	.73
Std Value	57	50	10	36	43	47	49	51	54	56	59	61
Survey Results												
08 Raw Value	86	2.9	1.0	1.6	2.1	2.6	2.8	2.9	3.2	3.4	3.7	4.1
Std Value	86	50	10	36	41	47	49	50	53	55	58	62
09 Raw Value	74	1.9	.4	1.4	1.6	1.6	1.8	1.9	2.0	2.0	2.2	2.4
Std Value	74	50	10	38	43	43	48	51	53	53	58	63
10 Raw Value	68	1.2	.2	.9	1.0	1.1	1.1	1.2	1.3	1.4	1.4	1.5
Std Value	68	50	10	37	41	45	45	50	54	58	58	63
11 Raw Value	88	.7	.4	.2	.3	.4	.6	.7	.8	1.0	1.1	1.4
Std Value	88	50	10	38	40	42	47	49	52	56	59	66
University Library												
12 Raw Value	63	.3	1.0	-1.0	-.6	-.5	-.4	.0	.3	.9	1.0	1.8
Std Value	63	50	10	38	42	43	44	48	50	56	57	65
Research Support												
13 Raw Value	77	.64	.22	.28	.41	.55	.63	.71	.75	.78	.83	.86
Std Value	77	50	10	34	40	46	50	53	55	56	59	60
14 Raw Value	67	10243	6479	3421	4681	5829	6530	8079	9947	13578	15814	17589
Std Value	67	50	10	39	41	43	44	47	50	55	59	61
Publication Records												
15 Raw Value	85	133	127	15	39	48	62	86	98	146	234	325
Std Value	85	50	10	41	43	43	44	46	47	51	58	65
16 Std Value	85	50	10	41	42	43	45	46	48	51	61	64

NOTE: Standardized values reported in the preceding table have been computed from exact values of the mean and standard deviation and not the rounded values reported here. Since the scale used to compute measure 16 is entirely arbitrary, only data in standardized form are reported for this measure.

TABLE 5.3 Intercorrelations Among Program Measures on 89 Programs in Cellular/Molecular Biology

Measure

	01	02	03	04	05	06	07	08	09	10	11	12	13	14	15	16
Program Size																
01		.54	.55	.03	-.16	-.09	-.01	.39	.29	.28	.37	.16	.06	.16	.37	.37
02			.83	.16	-.11	.12	-.02	.42	.47	.09	.40	.19	.18	.02	.32	.34
03				.07	-.06	.12	.02	.43	.39	.20	.43	.12	.16	.02	.32	.35
Program Graduates																
04					.13	.32	.29	.58	.51	.10	.54	.34	.55	.30	.42	.42
05						.44	.48	.38	.42	.31	.37	.36	.39	.25	.26	.29
06							.57	.33	.34	.16	.32	.26	.18	.18	.23	.26
07								.41	.35	.10	.48	.13	.48	.20	.29	.32
Survey Results																
08									.96	.33	.94	.47	.58	.57	.69	.71
09										.33	.91	.37	.51	.47	.56	.61
10											.31	.06	.19	-.16	.15	.17
11												.45	.65	.58	.70	.74
University Library																
12													.24	.42	.59	.59
Research Support																
13														.24	.40	.40
14															.58	.59
Publication Records																
15																.99
16																

NOTE: Since in computing correlation coefficients program data must be available for both of the measures being correlated, the actual number of programs on which each coefficient is based varies.

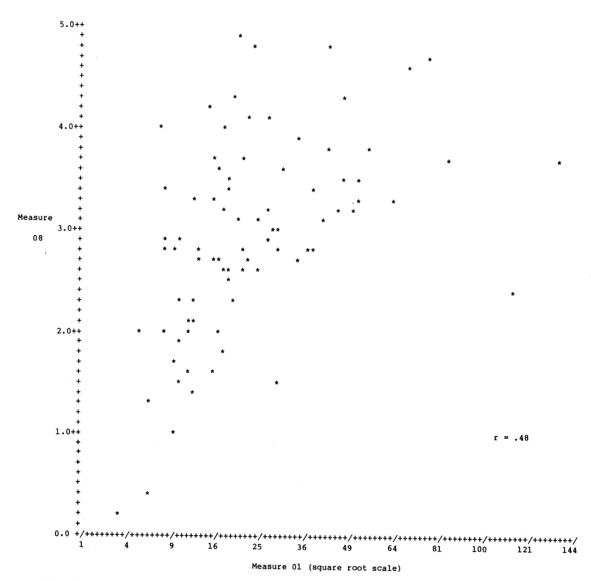

FIGURE 5.1 Mean rating of scholarly quality of faculty (measure 08) versus number of faculty members (measure 01)--86 programs in cellular/molecular biology.

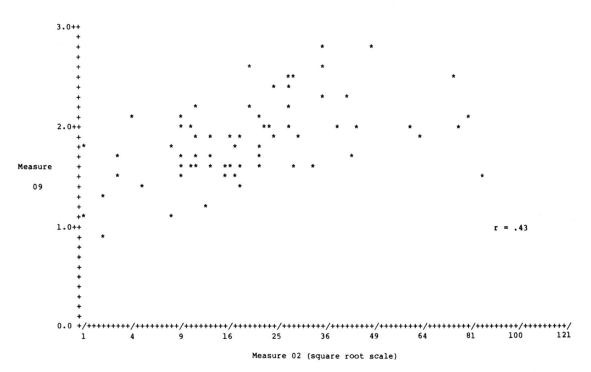

FIGURE 5.2 Mean rating of program effectiveness in educating research scholars/scientists (measure 09) versus number of graduates in last five years (measure 02)--69 programs in cellular/molecular biology.

TABLE 5.4   Characteristics of Survey Participants in Cellular/
Molecular Biology

	Respondents	
	N	%
Field of Specialization		
Biochemistry	17	12
Cell Biology	32	23
Genetics	22	16
Molecular Biology	34	25
Other/Unknown	34	25
Faculty Rank		
Professor	63	45
Associate Professor	46	33
Assistant Professor	30	22
Year of Highest Degree		
Pre-1950	6	4
1950-59	29	21
1960-69	45	32
Post-1969	58	42
Unknown	1	1
Evaluator Selection		
Nominated by Institution	113	81
Other	26	19
Survey Form		
With Faculty Names	130	94
Without Names	9	7
Total Evaluators	139	100

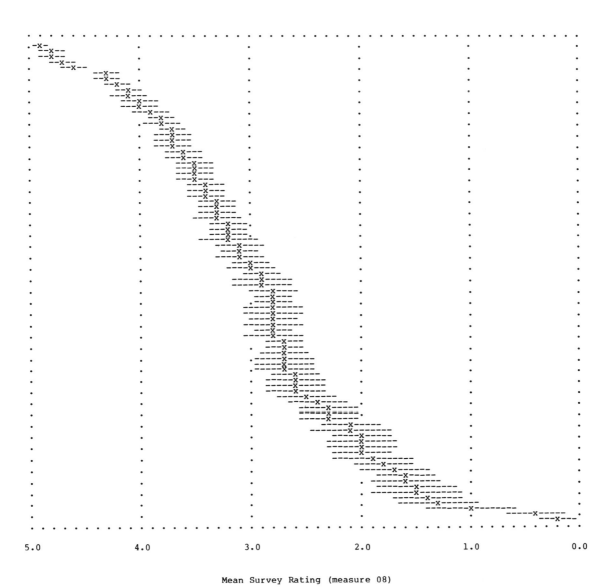

Mean Survey Rating (measure 08)

FIGURE 5.3 Mean rating of scholarly quality of faculty in 86 programs in cellular/molecular biology.

NOTE: Programs are listed in sequence of mean rating, with the highest-rated program appearing at the top of the page. The broken lines (---) indicate a confidence interval of +1.5 standard errors around the reported mean (x) of each program.

VI
Microbiology Programs

In this chapter 134 research-doctorate programs in microbiology are assessed. These programs, according to the information supplied by their universities, have accounted for 2,058 doctoral degrees awarded during the FY1976-80 period--approximately 87 percent of the aggregate number of microbiology, immunology, parasitology, and bacteriology doctorates earned from U.S. universities in this five-year span.[1] On the average, 20 full-time and part-time students intending to earn doctorates were enrolled in a program in December 1980, with an average faculty size of 16 members.[2] Most of the 134 programs, listed in Table 6.1, are located in departments of microbiology; a few are found in departments of biology, immunology, and other related fields. Eighteen programs were initiated since 1970. Each of eight institutions--Auburn University, University of California (San Francisco), University of Kansas, University of Maryland (Baltimore Professional School), University of Oklahoma, Pennsylvania State University, SUNY at Buffalo, and Tulane University has two microbiology programs included in the assessment. Each of five other universities--University of California (Berkeley), University of Chicago, Ohio State University, University of Pennsylvania, and University of Pittsburgh--has three programs evaluated. In addition to the 116 institutions represented in this discipline, another 13 were initially identified as meeting the criteria[3] for inclusion in the assessment:

> CUNY--Graduate School
> University of California--Santa Barbara

---

[1] Data from the NRC's Survey of Earned Doctorates indicate that 2,367 research doctorates in microbiology, immunology, parasitology, and bacteriology were awarded by U.S. universities between FY1976 and FY1980.

[2] See the reported means for measures 03 and 01 in Table 6.2.

[3] As mentioned in Chapter I, the primary criterion for inclusion was that a university had awarded at least 4 doctorates in microbiology during the FY1976-78 period.

University of Colorado
Harvard University
Illinois Institute of Technology
University of Utah--Salt Lake City
Washington University--Saint Louis
Medical College of Georgia
University of Mississippi--Medical Center
University of Oregon--Health Sciences Center
Saint John's University
University of Southwestern Louisiana
University of Texas--Health Science Center, Dallas

The last six institutions chose not to participate in the assessment in any discipline. Microbiology programs at the other seven institutions have not been included in the evaluations in this discipline, since in each case the study coordinator either indicated that the institution did not at that time have a research-doctorate program in microbiology or failed to provide the information requested by the committee.

Before examining individual program results presented in Table 6.1, the reader is urged to refer to Chapter II, in which each of the 16 measures used in the assessment is discussed. Summary statistics describing every measure are given in Table 6.2. For nine of the measures, data are reported for at least 116 of the 134 microbiology programs. For measures 04-07, which pertain to characteristics of the program graduates, data are presented for only approximately half of the programs; the other half had too few graduates on which to base statistics.[4] For measure 12, a composite index of the size of a university library, data are available for 85 programs. With respect to measure 13, the fraction of faculty with research grants from the National Institutes of Health, the National Science Foundation, or the Alcohol, Drug Abuse, and Mental Health Administration, data are reported for 102 programs that had at least 10 faculty members. For measure 14, total university expenditures for research in the biological sciences, data are available for 108 programs. The programs not evaluated on measures 12, 13, and 14 are typically smaller--in terms of faculty size and graduate student enrollment--than other microbiology programs. Were data on these three measures available for all 134 programs, it is likely that their reported means would be appreciably lower (and that some of the correlations of these measures with others would be higher).

Intercorrelations among the 16 measures (Pearson product-moment coefficients) are given in Table 6.3. Of particular note are the high positive correlations of reputational survey ratings (08, 09) with measures of publication records (15, 16) and research expenditures

---

[4]As mentioned in Chapter II, data for measures 04-07 are not reported if they are based on the survey responses of fewer than 10 FY1975-79 program graduates.

(14). Figure 6.1 illustrates the relation between the mean rating of the scholarly quality of faculty (measure 08) and the number of faculty members (measure 01) for each of 131 programs in microbiology. Figure 6.2 plots the mean rating of program effectiveness (measure 09) against the total number of FY1976-80 program graduates (measure 02). Although in both figures there is a significant positive correlation between program size and reputational rating, it is quite apparent that some of the smaller programs received high mean ratings.

Table 6.4 describes the 231 faculty members who participated in the evaluation of microbiology programs. These individuals constituted 58 percent of those asked to respond to the survey in this discipline and 11 percent of the faculty population in the 134 research-doctorate programs being evaluated.[5] About half of the evaluators identified their specialty field as microbiology/bacteriology; others were split among immunology, molecular biology, and other biological sciences. Two-thirds of the survey participants had earned their highest degree prior to 1970, and exactly half held the rank of full professor.

To assist the reader in interpreting results of the survey evaluations, estimated standard errors have been computed for mean ratings of the scholarly quality of faculty in 131 microbiology programs (and are given in Table 6.1). For each program the mean rating and an associated "confidence interval" of 1.5 standard errors are illustrated in Figure 6.3 (listed in order of highest to lowest mean rating). In comparing two programs, if their confidence intervals do not overlap, one may conclude that there is a significant difference in their mean ratings at a .05 level of significance.[6] From this figure it is also apparent that one should have somewhat more confidence in the accuracy of the mean ratings of higher-rated programs than lower-rated programs. This generalization results primarily from the fact that evaluators are not as likely to be familiar with the less prestigious programs, and consequently the mean ratings of these programs are usually based on fewer survey responses.

---

[5] See Table 2.3 in Chapter II.
[6] See pp. 31-33 for a discussion of the interpretation of mean ratings and associated confidence intervals.

TABLE 6.1 Program Measures (Raw and Standardized Values) in Microbiology

Prog No.	University - Department/Academic Unit	Program Size			Characteristics of Program Graduates			
		(01)	(02)	(03)	(04)	(05)	(06)	(07)
001.	Alabama, University of-Birmingham	36	21	35	.53	5.9	.81	.44
	Microbiology	68	55	57	52	53	51	47
002.	Albert Einstein College of Medicine	14	3	3	NA	NA	NA	NA
	Microbiology and Immunology	48	39	42				
003.	Arizona, University of-Tucson	12	9	7	NA	NA	NA	NA
	Microbiology and Medical Technology	46	44	44				
004.	Auburn University	7	3	1	NA	NA	NA	NA
	Botany, Plant Pathology, and Microbiology*	42	39	41				
005.	Auburn University	9	1	3	NA	NA	NA	NA
	Microbiology (School of Veterinary Med)*	43	37	42				
006.	Baylor College of Medicine-Houston	11	12	15	NA	NA	NA	NA
	Microbiology and Immunology	45	47	48				
007.	Boston University	9	NA	11	.23	7.1	.62	.62
	Biology	43		46	41	37	34	57
008.	Brigham Young University	10	3	9	NA	NA	NA	NA
	Microbiology	44	39	45				
009.	California, University of-Irvine	13	15	20	NA	NA	NA	NA
	Microbiol/Molec Biol & Biochem/Biol Chem*	47	49	50				
010.	California, University of-Berkeley	5	7	3	1.00	5.9	.82	.64
	Bacteriology	40	43	42	68	53	52	59
011.	California, University of-Berkeley	5	12	16	1.00	6.5	.80	.67
	Immunology	40	47	48	68	45	50	60
012.	California, University of-Berkeley	5	1	12	NA	NA	NA	NA
	Microbiology	40	37	46				
013.	California, University of-Berkeley	17	6	6	.75	6.2	.69	.31
	Parasitology*	51	42	43	59	49	40	40
014.	California, University of-Davis	78	44	56	.41	6.5	.71	.43
	Microbiology	99	75	67	48	45	43	47
015.	California, University of-Los Angeles	34	59	59	.67	6.1	.80	.57
	Microbiology/Immunology	66	88	69	57	50	50	55
016.	California, University of-San Diego	18	46	50	.86	5.8	.93	.64
	Biology	51	77	65	63	54	61	59
017.	California, University of-San Francisco	4	3	6	NA	NA	NA	NA
	Immunology*	39	39	43				
018.	California, University of-San Francisco	19	5	9	NA	NA	NA	NA
	Microbiology	52	41	45				
019.	Case Western Reserve University	7	15	15	NA	NA	NA	NA
	Microbiology	42	49	48				
020.	Catholic University of America	6	9	10	.20	NA	.90	.00
	Biology	41	44	45	40		59	23

* indicates program was initiated since 1970.

NOTE: On the first line of data for every program, raw values for each measure are reported; on the second line values are reported in standardized form, with mean = 50 and standard deviation = 10. "NA" indicates that the value for a measure is not available.

TABLE 6.1 Program Measures (Raw and Standardized Values) in Microbiology

Prog No.	Survey Results				University Library	Research Support		Published Articles		Survey Ratings Standard Error			
	(08)	(09)	(10)	(11)	(12)	(13)	(14)	(15)	(16)	(08)	(09)	(10)	(11)
001.	3.8	2.3	1.8	1.2	NA	.83	4467	83		.09	.07	.07	.08
	62	62	73	68		67	43	59	60				
002.	3.7	2.0	1.2	0.8	NA	.64	9184	47		.13	.10	.11	.08
	60	55	52	54		58	51	50	58				
003.	2.2	1.4	1.0	0.4	0.9	.17	7828	7		.18	.12	.19	.07
	42	40	43	42	56	38	49	40	41				
004.	1.7	1.1	NA	0.2	NA	NA	NA	7		.24	.15	NA	.04
	35	32		36				40	42				
005.	1.8	1.3	NA	0.2	NA	NA	NA	7		.25	.15	NA	.05
	36	37		37				40	42				
006.	3.1	1.9	1.1	0.7	NA	.36	14051	108		.10	.05	.09	.07
	53	53	46	52		46	59	65	60				
007.	1.7	1.3	NA	0.2	-0.4	NA	NA	4		.26	.21	NA	.05
	36	38		37	43			39	41				
008.	2.0	1.2	NA	0.3	-0.6	.00	NA	8		.20	.16	NA	.06
	40	36		40	41	31		40	42				
009.	3.5	2.0	1.5	0.9	NA	.92	6547	53		.09	.06	.10	.07
	58	55	64	57		71	47	52	54				
010.	3.2	2.0	0.8	0.7	2.2	NA	18977	100		.18	.10	.12	.08
	55	56	35	50	70		68	63	60				
011.	3.5	2.2	1.0	0.7	2.2	NA	18977	100		.14	.11	.06	.08
	58	60	43	53	70		68	63	60				
012.	3.3	1.8	0.8	0.7	2.2	NA	18977	100		.14	.12	.12	.08
	56	50	37	51	70		68	63	60				
013.	NA	NA	NA	0.2	2.2	.06	18977	100		NA	NA	NA	.06
				37	70	33	68	63	60				
014.	4.0	2.4	1.3	1.1	0.6	.40	18053	126		.10	.07	.09	.08
	64	65	54	64	54	48	66	70	57				
015.	4.1	2.5	1.4	1.4	2.0	.71	15581	226		.08	.06	.07	.07
	66	67	60	73	68	61	62	95	76				
016.	4.3	2.5	1.5	1.3	-0.0	.78	8706	44		.09	.08	.09	.08
	68	67	61	69	47	64	50	49	55				
017.	2.6	1.5	0.9	0.4	NA	NA	13194	85		.20	.17	.16	.08
	47	44	38	44			58	60	64				
018.	3.8	2.2	1.4	1.0	NA	.58	13194	85		.12	.09	.10	.08
	62	60	60	60		56	58	60	64				
019.	2.6	1.7	0.6	0.6	-1.3	NA	7721	7		.14	.10	.11	.07
	47	47	27	50	33		49	40	42				
020.	0.8	NA	NA	0.2	NA	NA	NA	1		.18	NA	NA	.05
	25			37				39	41				

NOTE: On the first line of data for every program, raw values for each measure are reported; on the second line values are reported in standardized form, with mean = 50 and standard deviation = 10. "NA" indicates that the value for a measure is not available. Since the scale used to compute measure 16 is entirely arbitrary, only values in standardized form are reported for this measure.

TABLE 6.1 Program Measures (Raw and Standardized Values) in Microbiology

Prog No.	University - Department/Academic Unit	Program Size (01)	(02)	(03)	Characteristics of Program Graduates (04)	(05)	(06)	(07)
021.	Chicago, University of *Immunology**	15 *49*	11 *46*	19 *50*	NA	NA	NA	NA
022.	Chicago, University of *Microbiology*	8 *42*	20 *54*	30 *55*	NA	NA	NA	NA
023.	Chicago, University of *Virology**	13 *47*	9 *44*	12 *46*	NA	NA	NA	NA
024.	Cincinnati, University of *Microbiology*	13 *47*	16 *50*	12 *46*	.62 *55*	6.3 *48*	.92 *60*	.58 *56*
025.	Colorado State University-Fort Collins *Microbiology*	35 *67*	19 *53*	25 *53*	.08 *36*	6.5 *45*	.67 *38*	.33 *42*
026.	Columbia University *Microbiology*	22 *55*	16 *50*	28 *54*	.39 *47*	6.1 *50*	.77 *47*	.46 *49*
027.	Connecticut, University of-Storrs *Biological Sciences*	11 *45*	6 *42*	6 *43*	NA	NA	NA	NA
028.	Cornell University-Ithaca *Microbiology*	27 *60*	15 *49*	24 *52*	.29 *44*	6.0 *51*	.82 *52*	.41 *46*
029.	Cornell University-Medical Center *Microbiology*	17 *51*	15 *49*	15 *48*	.46 *49*	5.8 *55*	1.00 *67*	.62 *57*
030.	Duke University *Microbiology and Immunology*	39 *70*	35 *67*	55 *67*	.88 *64*	5.9 *53*	.82 *52*	.61 *57*
031.	Emory University *Microbiology*	8 *42*	4 *40*	9 *45*	NA	NA	NA	NA
032.	Florida, University of-Gainesville *Immunol & Med Microbio/ Microbio & Cell Sci*	46 *77*	48 *78*	54 *66*	.36 *46*	5.4 *60*	.69 *40*	.43 *47*
033.	George Washington University *Microbiology*	7 *42*	30 *63*	14 *47*	.14 *38*	10.5 *1*	.57 *30*	.07 *27*
034.	Georgetown University *Microbiology*	8 *42*	16 *50*	15 *48*	.80 *61*	6.5 *45*	.73 *44*	.07 *26*
035.	Georgia, University of-Athens *Microbiology*	10 *44*	34 *66*	14 *47*	.30 *44*	6.7 *43*	.83 *53*	.53 *53*
036.	Hahnemann Medical College *Microbiology and Immunology*	14 *48*	13 *48*	15 *48*	.09 *37*	6.5 *45*	.82 *52*	.36 *43*
037.	Hawaii, University of *Microbiology*	10 *44*	8 *43*	12 *46*	NA	NA	NA	NA
038.	Health Sciences, Univ of/Chicago Med School *Medical Microbiology*	9 *43*	6 *42*	3 *42*	NA	NA	NA	NA
039.	Idaho, University of-Moscow *Bacteriology and Biochemistry*	10 *44*	6 *42*	3 *42*	NA	NA	NA	NA
040.	Illinois, University of-Medical Center *Microbiology and Immunology*	23 *56*	44 *75*	76 *77*	.41 *48*	6.1 *51*	.71 *42*	.50 *51*

* indicates program was initiated since 1970.

NOTE: On the first line of data for every program, raw values for each measure are reported; on the second line values are reported in standardized form, with mean = 50 and standard deviation = 10. "NA" indicates that the value for a measure is not available.

TABLE 6.1 Program Measures (Raw and Standardized Values) in Microbiology

Prog No.	Survey Results (08)	(09)	(10)	(11)	University Library (12)	Research Support (13)	(14)	Published Articles (15)	(16)	Survey Ratings Standard Error (08)	(09)	(10)	(11)
021.	3.4	2.1	1.4	0.6	0.9	.80	17589	88		.13	.08	.11	.08
	57	59	60	48	56	65	65	60	60				
022.	3.7	2.2	1.2	1.0	0.9	NA	17589	88		.11	.08	.09	.08
	61	60	50	61	56		65	60	60				
023.	4.2	2.3	1.5	1.1	0.9	.85	17589	88		.09	.07	.09	.09
	68	64	63	64	56	67	65	60	60				
024.	2.5	1.5	0.9	0.6	-0.2	.39	9365	43		.15	.09	.10	.07
	46	43	40	47	44	47	52	49	46				
025.	2.4	1.7	1.0	0.5	-1.1	.11	8863	17		.13	.08	.10	.07
	44	48	43	44	35	35	51	43	42				
026.	4.0	2.3	1.5	1.1	1.7	.73	11090	63		.08	.07	.09	.07
	64	63	61	62	65	62	54	54	52				
027.	2.9	1.8	1.1	0.7	-0.5	.64	15199	18		.13	.09	.11	.07
	51	50	47	53	42	58	61	43	44				
028.	3.5	2.1	1.3	0.8	1.6	.33	14597	71		.12	.08	.13	.09
	58	58	56	54	64	45	60	56	49				
029.	3.6	2.1	1.2	0.8	NA	.18	14597	45		.12	.08	.09	.09
	60	57	52	56		38	60	50	57				
030.	4.2	2.5	1.4	1.3	0.3	.54	11320	98		.09	.07	.08	.08
	67	67	59	70	50	54	55	63	63				
031.	2.7	1.6	1.8	0.6	-0.6	NA	2874	15		.14	.12	.09	.08
	49	46	73	49	41		41	42	44				
032.	3.3	2.0	1.6	0.7	0.8	.48	3486	62		.11	.07	.10	.08
	56	56	65	51	55	51	42	54	50				
033.	2.3	1.5	0.9	0.4	NA	NA	2641	17		.24	.15	.14	.07
	44	44	39	42			40	43	44				
034.	2.6	1.5	0.8	0.5	-0.6	NA	4200	26		.13	.10	.12	.06
	47	43	36	46	40		43	45	45				
035.	2.8	1.8	1.3	0.8	0.4	.50	10714	68		.13	.08	.12	.08
	50	51	53	55	52	52	54	55	49				
036.	2.2	1.5	1.2	0.5	NA	.43	NA	13		.13	.10	.09	.07
	42	42	51	46		49		42	43				
037.	2.5	1.4	1.1	0.4	-0.1	.20	4440	13		.13	.13	.11	.06
	46	41	45	43	46	39	43	42	43				
038.	1.7	NA	NA	0.2	NA	NA	NA	3		.27	NA	NA	.05
	35			37				39	41				
039.	1.6	1.2	1.1	0.3	NA	.20	1842	14		.24	.15	.17	.06
	34	35	48	38		39	39	42	43				
040.	3.0	2.0	1.1	0.7	NA	.35	4393	95		.11	.08	.13	.06
	52	54	45	52		46	43	62	58				

NOTE: On the first line of data for every program, raw values for each measure are reported; on the second line values are reported in standardized form, with mean = 50 and standard deviation = 10. "NA" indicates that the value for a measure is not available. Since the scale used to compute measure 16 is entirely arbitrary, only values in standardized form are reported for this measure.

TABLE 6.1 Program Measures (Raw and Standardized Values) in Microbiology

Prog No.	University - Department/Academic Unit	Program Size (01)	(02)	(03)	Characteristics of Program Graduates (04)	(05)	(06)	(07)
041.	Illinois, University-Urbana/Champaign *Microbiology*	20 *53*	26 *59*	58 *68*	.71 *58*	6.5 *45*	.83 *53*	.53 *53*
042.	Indiana State University-Terre Haute *Life Sciences*	13 *47*	8 *43*	7 *44*	NA	NA	NA	NA
043.	Indiana University-Bloomington *Biology*	11 *45*	12 *47*	18 *49*	.67 *56*	5.9 *52*	.87 *56*	.53 *53*
044.	Indiana University-Purdue University *Microbiology and Immunology*	14 *48*	16 *50*	10 *45*	.46 *49*	6.3 *47*	.92 *61*	.39 *44*
045.	Iowa State University-Ames *Microbiology*	7 *42*	14 *49*	26 *53*	.00 *33*	6.3 *48*	.75 *46*	.50 *51*
046.	Iowa, University of-Iowa City *Microbiology*	21 *54*	20 *54*	15 *48*	.11 *37*	5.4 *59*	.95 *63*	.67 *60*
047.	Johns Hopkins University *Microbiology*	11 *45*	14 *49*	9 *45*	.89 *64*	6.5 *45*	.81 *51*	.75 *65*
048.	Kansas State University-Manhattan *Biology*	13 *47*	11 *46*	15 *48*	NA	NA	NA	NA
049.	Kansas, University of *Microbiology (Graduate School)*	12 *46*	24 *57*	17 *49*	.67 *56*	4.9 *66*	.88 *56*	.75 *65*
050.	Kansas, University of *Microbiology (Schl of Medicine-Kansas City)*	12 *46*	11 *46*	14 *47*	.73 *58*	NA	.91 *59*	.55 *54*
051.	Kentucky, University of *Biological Sciences*	18 *51*	8 *43*	8 *44*	NA	NA	NA	NA
052.	Louisiana State University-Baton Rouge *Microbiology*	10 *44*	10 *45*	5 *43*	.09 *37*	5.8 *55*	.46 *20*	.27 *38*
053.	Louisiana State Univ-School of Medicine *Microbiology and Immunology*	26 *59*	7 *43*	11 *46*	NA	NA	NA	NA
054.	Louisville, University of *Microbiology and Immunology*	15 *49*	12 *47*	28 *54*	NA	NA	NA	NA
055.	Loyola University of Chicago *Microbiology*	12 *46*	11 *46*	17 *49*	NA	NA	NA	NA
056.	Maryland, University of-Baltimore Prof Schl *Dental Microbiology*	7 *42*	12 *47*	11 *46*	NA	NA	NA	NA
057.	Maryland, University of-Baltimore Prof Schl *Microbiology (School of Medicine)*	14 *48*	8 *43*	4 *42*	NA	NA	NA	NA
058.	Maryland, University of-College Park *Microbiology*	13 *47*	NA	24 *52*	.11 *37*	7.0 *39*	.67 *38*	.11 *29*
059.	Massachusetts Institute of Technology *Biology*	16 *50*	28 *61*	27 *54*	.88 *64*	5.8 *54*	.87 *56*	.57 *55*
060.	Massachusetts, University of-Amherst *Microbiology*	12 *46*	20 *54*	29 *54*	.42 *48*	5.7 *56*	.92 *60*	.83 *70*

* indicates program was initiated since 1970.

NOTE: On the first line of data for every program, raw values for each measure are reported; on the second line values are reported in standardized form, with mean = 50 and standard deviation = 10. "NA" indicates that the value for a measure is not available.

TABLE 6.1 Program Measures (Raw and Standardized Values) in Microbiology

Prog No.	Survey Results (08)	(09)	(10)	(11)	University Library (12)	Research Support (13)	(14)	Published Articles (15)	(16)	Survey Ratings Standard Error (08)	(09)	(10)	(11)
041.	4.0	2.5	1.2	1.2	2.0	.65	6074	38		.10	.06	.08	.08
	65	67	52	65	68	59	46	48	47				
042.	1.6	NA	NA	0.2	NA	.39	NA	0		.23	NA	NA	.06
	34			37		47		38	41				
043.	3.2	2.0	1.1	0.9	0.9	.55	NA	15		.11	.08	.11	.08
	54	55	45	58	57	54		42	44				
044.	2.5	1.7	1.1	0.5	NA	.43	2940	NA		.12	.08	.11	.07
	46	48	46	45		49	41		NA				
045.	2.6	1.8	0.7	0.6	-0.5	NA	5287	39		.13	.10	.10	.07
	47	50	33	48	42		45	48	47				
046.	3.0	2.1	1.3	0.8	0.3	.71	7088	59		.08	.06	.12	.07
	52	57	55	54	50	62	48	53	48				
047.	4.3	2.5	1.2	1.3	-0.4	.46	19837	122		.09	.07	.09	.07
	68	67	52	70	43	50	69	69	68				
048.	2.6	1.7	1.2	0.5	NA	.39	2496	25		.13	.09	.10	.07
	47	47	51	47		47	40	45	44				
049.	2.5	1.8	1.0	0.6	0.1	.25	3161	5		.13	.09	.10	.08
	46	49	45	48	48	41	41	40	41				
050.	2.1	1.4	1.0	0.3	0.1	.25	3161	42		.15	.14	.14	.06
	41	41	43	39	48	41	41	49	47				
051.	2.1	1.4	0.8	0.6	-0.1	.56	484	35		.12	.10	.11	.07
	41	40	36	48	46	55	37	47	46				
052.	2.3	1.4	1.2	0.5	-0.3	.10	5116	8		.18	.12	.11	.08
	43	41	49	44	43	35	44	40	41				
053.	2.5	1.4	1.3	0.4	NA	.23	5116	37		.15	.11	.12	.06
	45	41	55	44		41	44	48	45				
054.	2.6	1.6	1.1	0.4	NA	.40	NA	15		.14	.12	.10	.06
	47	44	45	43		48		42	43				
055.	2.4	1.7	1.5	0.4	NA	.00	NA	10		.13	.10	.11	.06
	45	47	61	43		31		41	42				
056.	1.7	1.2	0.9	0.3	NA	NA	6061	62		.17	.11	.08	.05
	35	35	38	38			46	54	49				
057.	2.1	1.4	0.8	0.4	NA	.21	6061	62		.16	.14	.11	.07
	41	40	36	44		40	46	54	49				
058.	3.0	1.9	1.0	0.7	0.2	.31	1623	10		.14	.09	.11	.09
	52	53	44	52	49	44	39	41	42				
059.	4.9	2.9	1.4	1.7	-0.3	.94	17348	85		.03	.04	.06	.06
	77	77	59	83	43	71	65	60	65				
060.	3.2	1.9	1.1	0.7	-0.7	.83	3022	41		.11	.07	.10	.08
	55	53	48	52	39	67	41	49	48				

NOTE: On the first line of data for every program, raw values for each measure are reported;
on the second line values are reported in standardized form, with mean = 50 and
standard deviation = 10. "NA" indicates that the value for a measure is not available.
Since the scale used to compute measure 16 is entirely arbitrary, only values in
standardized form are reported for this measure.

TABLE 6.1 Program Measures (Raw and Standardized Values) in Microbiology

Prog No.	University - Department/Academic Unit	Program Size			Characteristics of Program Graduates			
		(01)	(02)	(03)	(04)	(05)	(06)	(07)
061.	Medical College of Wisconsin	11	9	8	NA	NA	NA	NA
	Microbiology	45	44	44				
062.	Medical University of South Carolina	19	8	15	NA	NA	NA	NA
	*Basic & Clinical Immunology & Microbiology**	52	43	48				
063.	Miami University-Ohio	7	13	6	NA	NA	NA	NA
	*Microbiology**	42	48	43				
064.	Miami, University of-Florida	17	24	14	.21	5.2	.83	.72
	Microbiology	51	57	47	41	61	53	64
065.	Michigan State University-East Lansing	33	30	29	.59	6.2	.83	.48
	Microbiology and Public Health	65	63	54	54	49	52	50
066.	Michigan, University of-Ann Arbor	26	24	19	.60	5.9	.93	.67
	Microbiology	59	57	50	54	53	61	60
067.	Minnesota, University of	18	23	39	.65	6.3	.69	.50
	Microbiology	51	56	59	56	48	40	51
068.	Mississippi State University-Starkville	11	7	7	NA	NA	NA	NA
	Biological Sciences	45	43	44				
069.	Mississippi, University of-Oxford	4	6	4	NA	NA	NA	NA
	Biology	39	42	42				
070.	Missouri, University of-Columbia	23	23	10	.16	5.0	.84	.53
	Microbiology	56	56	45	39	64	54	52
071.	Montana State University-Bozeman	10	7	8	NA	NA	NA	NA
	Microbiology	44	43	44				
072.	Nebraska, University of-Lincoln	10	15	19	.07	6.1	.67	.53
	Life Sciences	44	49	50	36	50	38	53
073.	New Hampshire, University of	7	12	8	.18	6.0	.91	.55
	Microbiology	42	47	44	40	51	59	54
074.	New Jersey, College of Medicine & Dentistry	20	8	15	NA	NA	NA	NA
	*Microbiology**	53	43	48				
075.	New York University	31	22	27	.77	7.5	1.00	.54
	Basic Medical Sciences	63	56	54	60	32	67	53
076.	North Carolina State University-Raleigh	16	20	25	.21	5.4	.74	.47
	Microbiology	50	54	53	41	59	45	49
077.	North Carolina, University of-Chapel Hill	24	24	36	.93	5.0	.93	.79
	Bacteriology and Immunology	57	57	58	65	64	61	67
078.	Northwestern University	17	12	12	.94	5.3	.94	.78
	Microbiology/Immunology	51	47	46	66	61	62	67
079.	Notre Dame, University of	11	19	18	.43	6.2	.89	.50
	Microbiology/Biology	45	53	49	48	49	58	51
080.	Ohio State University-Columbus	18	11	15	.25	5.5	.67	.33
	*Medical Microbiology and Immunology**	51	46	48	42	58	38	42

* indicates program was initiated since 1970.

NOTE: On the first line of data for every program, raw values for each measure are reported; on the second line values are reported in standardized form, with mean = 50 and standard deviation = 10. "NA" indicates that the value for a measure is not available.

TABLE 6.1 Program Measures (Raw and Standardized Values) in Microbiology

Prog No.	Survey Results				University Library	Research Support		Published Articles		Survey Ratings Standard Error			
	(08)	(09)	(10)	(11)	(12)	(13)	(14)	(15)	(16)	(08)	(09)	(10)	(11)
061.	2.3	1.6	1.1	0.4	NA	.36	2085	20		.13	.10	.08	.06
	44	46	45	44		46	39	43	43				
062.	2.6	1.7	1.6	0.7	NA	.37	3178	55		.15	.10	.10	.07
	47	48	67	51		47	41	52	50				
063.	1.8	1.4	1.1	0.4	-0.8	NA	NA	5		.17	.16	.11	.06
	37	42	47	41	39			40	42				
064.	2.4	1.6	1.1	0.4	NA	.29	6101	17		.13	.09	.11	.06
	44	45	45	44		43	46	43	44				
065.	3.4	2.2	1.3	1.0	0.3	.70	10357	77		.09	.07	.09	.08
	57	60	56	62	50	61	53	58	52				
066.	3.8	2.4	1.6	1.2	1.8	.65	15431	54		.08	.06	.08	.07
	62	65	64	67	66	59	62	52	51				
067.	3.6	2.3	1.2	1.1	1.2	.61	13696	151		.08	.06	.09	.09
	60	62	51	63	59	57	59	76	63				
068.	1.5	0.9	1.0	0.2	NA	.00	2839	7		.20	.16	.10	.05
	33	28	43	37		31	41	40	42				
069.	0.8	0.7	NA	0.2	NA	NA	NA	4		.19	.15	NA	.05
	24	22		36				39	41				
070.	2.8	1.8	1.7	0.8	-0.2	.22	4628	NA		.11	.07	.09	.07
	49	50	69	55	45	40	44		NA				
071.	2.3	1.4	1.6	0.3	NA	.20	766	19		.21	.15	.15	.06
	44	41	66	40		39	37	43	42				
072.	2.1	1.6	1.1	0.4	-0.5	.50	2965	37		.18	.13	.14	.06
	41	45	45	42	42	52	41	48	45				
073.	2.1	1.4	1.2	0.5	NA	NA	NA	9		.17	.12	.15	.07
	41	41	50	44				41	42				
074.	2.5	1.4	1.4	0.4	NA	.30	4529	37		.14	.12	.13	.07
	46	41	59	43		44	43	48	48				
075.	4.0	2.2	1.2	1.0	0.5	.32	9934	98		.09	.07	.11	.08
	65	60	50	61	52	45	52	63	68				
076.	2.7	1.9	1.3	0.6	NA	.13	6741	38		.12	.07	.11	.09
	49	52	53	48		36	47	48	46				
077.	3.7	2.1	1.3	1.1	1.0	.75	9849	72		.09	.05	.09	.08
	60	57	56	65	57	63	52	56	51				
078.	2.8	1.8	1.1	0.5	0.3	.53	4760	48		.13	.10	.11	.07
	49	51	47	46	50	54	44	50	48				
079.	2.7	1.7	1.0	0.5	-1.3	.55	NA	8		.14	.10	.08	.07
	49	47	42	46	33	54		40	42				
080.	2.6	1.6	1.1	0.6	0.9	.17	8330	31		.11	.09	.10	.07
	47	45	45	49	56	38	50	46	46				

NOTE: On the first line of data for every program, raw values for each measure are reported; on the second line values are reported in standardized form, with mean = 50 and standard deviation = 10. "NA" indicates that the value for a measure is not available. Since the scale used to compute measure 16 is entirely arbitrary, only values in standardized form are reported for this measure.

TABLE 6.1 Program Measures (Raw and Standardized Values) in Microbiology

Prog No.	University - Department/Academic Unit	Program Size			Characteristics of Program Graduates			
		(01)	(02)	(03)	(04)	(05)	(06)	(07)
081.	Ohio State University-Columbus	13	41	47	.23	5.6	.79	.41
	Microbiology	47	72	63	41	57	49	46
082.	Ohio State University-Columbus	16	10	12	.60	NA	.90	.70
	Veterinary Pathobiology	50	45	46	54		59	62
083.	Oklahoma State University-Stillwater	5	4	8	NA	NA	NA	NA
	Microbiology	40	40	44				
084.	Oklahoma, University of-Norman	11	10	11	.30	7.0	.70	.20
	Botany/Microbiology (Graduate School)	45	45	46	44	39	41	34
085.	Oklahoma, University of-Norman	16	16	30	.20	5.5	.80	.60
	Microbiology and Immunology (Health Sci)	50	50	55	40	58	50	57
086.	Oregon State University-Corvallis	11	22	26	.24	6.1	.73	.27
	Microbiology	45	56	53	42	50	44	38
087.	Oregon, University of-Eugene	5	2	6	NA	NA	NA	NA
	Biology	40	38	43				
088.	Pennsylvania State University	12	21	21	.44	5.5	.92	.72
	Microbiology (Graduate School)	46	55	51	49	58	60	63
089.	Pennsylvania State University	13	5	14	NA	NA	NA	NA
	Microbiology Medical Center)*	47	41	47				
090.	Pennsylvania, University of	45	22	27	.81	6.2	.81	.48
	Immunology*	76	56	54	61	49	51	50
091.	Pennsylvania, University of	44	20	28	.85	6.2	.77	.39
	Microbiology	75	54	54	63	49	47	44
092.	Pennsylvania, University of	14	6	7	NA	NA	NA	NA
	Parasitology	48	42	44				
093.	Pittsburgh, University of	29	6	14	.15	6.6	.50	.30
	Biological Sciences (Arts and Sciences)*	61	42	47	39	43	24	40
094.	Pittsburgh, University of	6	8	5	NA	NA	NA	NA
	Microbiology (Grad School of Public Health)	41	43	43				
095.	Pittsburgh, University of	12	10	13	NA	NA	NA	NA
	Microbiology (School of Medicine)	46	45	47				
096.	Puerto Rico, University of	9	3	1	NA	NA	NA	NA
	Microbiology and Medical Zoology	43	39	41				
097.	Purdue University-West Lafayette	13	23	43	.25	6.0	.75	.50
	Biological Sciences	47	56	61	42	51	46	51
098.	Rensselaer Polytechnic Institute	7	10	6	NA	NA	NA	NA
	Biology	42	45	43				
099.	Rhode Island, University of	9	15	11	.19	6.0	.56	.25
	Microbiology	43	49	46	40	51	29	37
100.	Rochester, University of	22	28	34	.84	6.4	.89	.72
	Microbiology	55	61	57	62	47	58	64

* indicates program was initiated since 1970.

NOTE: On the first line of data for every program, raw values for each measure are reported; on the second line values are reported in standardized form, with mean = 50 and standard deviation = 10. "NA" indicates that the value for a measure is not available.

TABLE 6.1 Program Measures (Raw and Standardized Values) in Microbiology

Prog No.	Survey Results (08)	(09)	(10)	(11)	University Library (12)	Research Support (13)	(14)	Published Articles (15)	(16)	Survey Ratings Standard Error (08)	(09)	(10)	(11)
081.	2.5	1.7	0.8	0.6	0.9	.15	8330	49		.14	.09	.10	.07
	45	47	37	49	56	37	50	51	46				
082.	2.4	NA	NA	0.1	0.9	.31	8330	31		.25	NA	NA	.04
	45			35	56	44	50	46	46				
083.	1.8	1.0	0.7	0.5	-1.9	NA	3127	11		.20	.13	.12	.08
	37	30	30	45	26		41	41	42				
084.	1.9	1.4	0.9	0.4	-0.6	.27	NA	7		.17	.12	.14	.07
	38	40	41	42	41	42		40	41				
085.	2.2	1.7	1.2	0.3	-0.6	.25	NA	11		.14	.11	.10	.06
	42	47	51	39	41	41		41	42				
086.	2.8	1.9	1.1	0.6	NA	.64	7108	39		.13	.06	.10	.08
	50	52	49	48		58	48	48	45				
087.	3.4	1.9	1.2	0.5	-0.9	NA	NA	3		.20	.14	.10	.08
	57	54	51	47	37			39	42				
088.	2.3	1.5	0.4	0.6	0.7	.50	8024	40		.15	.12	.13	.07
	43	43	20	48	54	52	49	48	46				
089.	3.1	1.9	1.1	1.0	0.7	.85	8024	35		.10	.07	.09	.07
	53	53	49	61	54	67	49	47	48				
090.	4.2	2.4	1.5	1.0	0.7	.51	23550	130		.09	.08	.12	.09
	67	64	63	61	54	53	75	71	81				
091.	4.0	2.3	1.3	1.2	0.7	.48	23550	130		.08	.06	.09	.07
	64	62	56	66	54	51	75	71	81				
092.	NA	NA	NA	0.2	0.7	.57	23550	130		NA	NA	NA	.05
				35	54	55	75	71	81				
093.	3.1	1.9	1.3	0.6	0.1	.69	6462	25		.13	.07	.13	.07
	54	53	54	49	48	61	47	45	45				
094.	2.3	1.5	0.6	0.4	0.1	NA	6462	43		.19	.12	.11	.07
	43	43	28	43	48		47	49	48				
095.	2.8	1.7	1.0	0.6	0.1	.67	6462	43		.12	.09	.09	.07
	49	48	44	49	48	60	47	49	48				
096.	NA	NA	NA	0.1	NA	NA	NA	1		NA	NA	NA	.03
				34				39	41				
097.	3.6	2.2	1.2	1.1	-0.5	.54	10337	31		.09	.07	.08	.08
	60	59	52	63	41	54	53	46	48				
098.	2.4	NA	NA	0.2	NA	NA	NA	6		.18	NA	NA	.05
	44			37				40	42				
099.	2.2	1.3	NA	0.3	NA	NA	NA	7		.15	.13	NA	.06
	42	37		40				40	42				
100.	3.2	2.1	1.3	0.7	-0.6	.55	15969	57		.11	.08	.12	.08
	55	57	54	51	40	54	63	53	56				

NOTE: On the first line of data for every program, raw values for each measure are reported; on the second line values are reported in standardized form, with mean = 50 and standard deviation = 10. "NA" indicates that the value for a measure is not available. Since the scale used to compute measure 16 is entirely arbitrary, only values in standardized form are reported for this measure.

TABLE 6.1 Program Measures (Raw and Standardized Values) in Microbiology

Prog No.	University – Department/Academic Unit	Program Size			Characteristics of Program Graduates			
		(01)	(02)	(03)	(04)	(05)	(06)	(07)
101.	Rockefeller University	33	20	23	.42	6.1	.84	.76
	Microbiology	65	54	52	48	50	53	66
102.	Rutgers, The State University-New Brunswick	65	66	198	.56	5.8	.83	.44
	Microbiology	94	94	99	53	54	53	47
103.	SUNY Upstate Medical Center	8	9	10	NA	NA	NA	NA
	Microbiology	42	44	45				
104.	SUNY at Buffalo	18	12	5	NA	NA	NA	NA
	Microbiology (Roswell Park Graduate Div)	51	47	43				
105.	SUNY at Buffalo	28	28	49	.57	6.0	.78	.30
	Microbiology (School of Medicine)	61	61	64	53	51	48	40
106.	SUNY-Downstate Medical Center	13	7	10	NA	NA	NA	NA
	Microbiology and Immunology	47	43	45				
107.	Saint Louis University	9	5	7	NA	NA	NA	NA
	Microbiology	43	41	44				
108.	Southern California, University of	16	3	7	NA	NA	NA	NA
	Microbiology	50	39	44				
109.	Southern Illinois University-Carbondale	16	5	9	NA	NA	NA	NA
	Microbiology	50	41	45				
110.	Stanford University	9	22	10	.71	5.9	.83	.54
	Medical Microbiology	43	56	45	58	53	53	53
111.	Syracuse University	9	9	11	NA	NA	NA	NA
	*Biology**	43	44	46				
112.	Temple University	17	23	28	.82	5.9	.82	.25
	Microbiology and Immunology	51	56	54	62	53	52	37
113.	Tennessee, Univ of-Ctr for Health Sciences	16	4	5	NA	NA	NA	NA
	Microbiology and Immunology	50	40	43				
114.	Tennessee, University of-Knoxville	15	12	21	NA	NA	NA	NA
	Microbiology	49	47	51				
115.	Texas A & M University	6	7	12	NA	NA	.60	.20
	Biology	41	43	46			33	34
116.	Texas, U of-Health Science Center, Houston	26	14	24	.30	NA	.80	.40
	Virology/ Devl Therapeut/ Organ Transplant	59	49	52	44		50	45
117.	Texas, University of-Austin	19	32	58	.83	6.8	.86	.55
	Microbiology	52	64	68	62	42	55	54
118.	Texas, U of-Health Science Ctr, San Antonio	25	13	12	.09	7.5	.91	.46
	*Microbiology**	58	48	46	37	32	59	48
119.	Texas, University of-Med Branch, Galveston	17	7	18	NA	NA	NA	NA
	*Microbiology**	51	43	49				
120.	Thomas Jefferson University	12	9	13	.00	5.8	.70	.40
	Microbiology	46	44	47	33	54	41	45

* indicates program was initiated since 1970.

NOTE: On the first line of data for every program, raw values for each measure are reported; on the second line values are reported in standardized form, with mean = 50 and standard deviation = 10. "NA" indicates that the value for a measure is not available.

TABLE 6.1 Program Measures (Raw and Standardized Values) in Microbiology

Prog No.	Survey Results				University Library	Research Support		Published Articles		Survey Ratings Standard Error			
	(08)	(09)	(10)	(11)	(12)	(13)	(14)	(15)	(16)	(08)	(09)	(10)	(11)
101.	4.8	2.7	1.2	1.5	NA	.79	27299	120		.05	.05	.06	.06
	75	72	51	76		65	81	69	94				
102.	3.8	2.3	1.2	1.3	0.8	.26	7505	37		.09	.07	.09	.08
	62	63	52	70	55	42	48	48	45				
103.	2.0	1.6	NA	0.3	NA	NA	NA	17		.24	.14	NA	.06
	40	44		39				43	43				
104.	2.6	1.7	1.2	0.5	0.3	.00	6799	6		.16	.09	.12	.06
	47	47	52	46	50	31	47	40	42				
105.	3.1	1.9	1.2	0.7	0.3	.29	6799	82		.13	.08	.11	.07
	53	53	50	52	50	43	47	59	55				
106.	2.5	1.5	1.1	0.3	NA	.46	3077	39		.18	.10	.10	.05
	46	43	47	40		51	41	48	50				
107.	2.6	1.6	0.8	0.5	NA	NA	3674	25		.14	.10	.08	.07
	47	46	35	46			42	45	46				
108.	3.2	1.7	1.3	0.7	0.4	.56	2405	49		.14	.10	.10	.07
	55	48	55	52	51	55	40	51	50				
109.	1.8	1.2	1.2	0.5	-0.2	.19	NA	11		.14	.13	.14	.07
	37	36	49	46	45	39		41	43				
110.	4.0	2.2	1.4	1.0	2.0	NA	12514	112		.08	.08	.10	.07
	64	61	58	62	68		57	66	75				
111.	2.5	1.7	0.8	0.7	-0.3	NA	NA	6		.13	.09	.11	.08
	46	48	36	52	43			40	42				
112.	2.7	1.7	0.9	0.8	-0.4	.53	6914	27		.12	.10	.12	.08
	49	47	38	54	42	54	47	45	46				
113.	2.9	1.6	1.3	0.7	NA	.13	2127	30		.11	.09	.08	.08
	51	44	55	52		36	39	46	46				
114.	2.6	1.9	1.3	0.7	-0.4	.60	NA	8		.12	.07	.10	.08
	47	52	55	52	43	57		40	42				
115.	1.5	0.9	NA	0.3	-0.5	NA	3199	23		.23	.22	NA	.07
	33	27		40	42		41	44	45				
116.	3.1	1.8	1.3	0.8	NA	.50	4151	NA		.11	.08	.11	.07
	53	51	56	54		52	43		NA				
117.	3.3	2.1	1.2	0.9	1.6	.74	5757	53		.09	.08	.10	.08
	56	57	52	57	64	63	46	52	50				
118.	2.6	1.6	1.5	0.6	NA	.32	6064	NA		.12	.09	.12	.07
	47	45	62	49		44	46		NA				
119.	2.7	1.7	1.7	0.4	NA	.47	4581	NA		.18	.13	.10	.07
	48	47	70	44		51	44		NA				
120.	2.0	1.4	0.9	0.4	NA	.17	1851	25		.17	.11	.11	.06
	40	39	39	42		38	39	45	49				

NOTE: On the first line of data for every program, raw values for each measure are reported;
on the second line values are reported in standardized form, with mean = 50 and
standard deviation = 10. "NA" indicates that the value for a measure is not available.
Since the scale used to compute measure 16 is entirely arbitrary, only values in
standardized form are reported for this measure.

TABLE 6.1 Program Measures (Raw and Standardized Values) in Microbiology

Prog No.	University - Department/Academic Unit	Program Size			Characteristics of Program Graduates			
		(01)	(02)	(03)	(04)	(05)	(06)	(07)
121.	Tufts University	19	8	16	NA	NA	NA	NA
	*Immunology**	52	43	48				
122.	Tulane University	6	4	8	NA	NA	NA	NA
	Microbiology and Immunology	41	40	44				
123.	Tulane University	7	7	10	NA	NA	NA	NA
	Parasitology	42	43	45				
124.	Vanderbilt University	11	9	13	NA	NA	NA	NA
	Microbiology	45	44	47				
125.	Virginia Commonwealth University/Medical Col	25	25	32	.65	6.8	.80	.50
	Microbiology	58	58	56	56	42	50	51
126.	Virginia Polytechnic Institute & State Univ	17	15	16	.14	5.5	1.00	.57
	Biology & Anaerobic Microbiology	51	49	48	38	58	67	55
127.	Virginia, University of	13	21	24	.95	5.3	1.00	.61
	Microbiology	47	55	52	66	61	67	57
128.	Wake Forest University	14	8	21	NA	NA	NA	NA
	Microbiology and Immunology	48	43	51				
129.	Washington State University-Pullman	10	13	15	NA	NA	NA	NA
	Bacteriology and Public Health	44	48	48				
130.	Washington, University of-Seattle	25	28	20	.81	5.6	.87	.55
	Microbiology and Immunology	58	61	50	61	57	56	54
131.	Wayne State University	32	16	14	.27	5.3	.73	.27
	Immunology and Microbiology	64	50	47	43	60	44	38
132.	West Virginia University	17	22	8	.21	6.4	.85	.45
	Microbiology	51	56	44	41	47	54	48
133.	Wisconsin, University of-Madison	11	37	36	.58	5.3	.75	.39
	Bacteriology	45	69	58	53	60	46	45
134.	Yale University	25	22	35	.86	7.7	.62	.43
	Epidemiology and Public Health/ Biology	58	56	57	63	30	34	47

* indicates program was initiated since 1970.

NOTE: On the first line of data for every program, raw values for each measure are reported; on the second line values are reported in standardized form, with mean = 50 and standard deviation = 10. "NA" indicates that the value for a measure is not available.

TABLE 6.1 Program Measures (Raw and Standardized Values) in Microbiology

Prog No.	Survey Results (08)	(09)	(10)	(11)	University Library (12)	Research Support (13)	(14)	Published Articles (15)	(16)	Survey Ratings Standard Error (08)	(09)	(10)	(11)
121.	3.3	1.9	1.5	0.7	NA	.63	3518	48		.16	.08	.10	.08
	56	54	62	50		58	42	50	52				
122.	1.9	1.2	0.8	0.4	−1.0	NA	3690	25		.22	.15	.15	.06
	38	35	36	44	36		42	45	43				
123.	2.2	NA	NA	0.1	−1.0	NA	3690	25		.35	NA	NA	.04
	43			35	36		42	45	43				
124.	3.4	2.0	1.1	0.9	−0.7	.82	5204	26		.11	.06	.08	.08
	58	55	47	56	39	66	45	45	46				
125.	2.9	1.9	1.5	0.6	NA	.48	6556	52		.11	.06	.10	.08
	50	52	63	48		51	47	51	48				
126.	3.1	2.1	1.5	0.6	−0.0	.41	3108	46		.12	.10	.11	.08
	54	57	64	50	47	48	41	50	47				
127.	3.3	2.0	1.2	0.8	0.7	.77	6224	48		.11	.06	.11	.08
	56	56	52	55	55	64	46	50	49				
128.	2.5	1.6	1.2	0.6	NA	.50	3010	32		.13	.10	.10	.07
	45	46	52	47		52	41	46	45				
129.	2.4	1.6	NA	0.3	−0.3	.30	998	34		.20	.17	NA	.07
	44	46		40	44	44	38	47	46				
130.	4.3	2.4	1.5	1.3	1.5	.52	14164	112		.06	.07	.08	.08
	69	66	61	70	62	53	60	66	65				
131.	3.0	1.9	1.5	0.7	−0.4	.34	6372	37		.12	.07	.11	.07
	52	53	61	51	43	45	47	48	48				
132.	2.4	1.4	1.2	0.5	NA	.24	NA	15		.15	.12	.14	.07
	44	40	50	44		41		42	42				
133.	3.8	2.5	1.3	1.2	1.6	.73	19738	124		.11	.07	.09	.08
	62	66	53	65	63	62	69	70	62				
134.	3.9	2.2	0.9	1.0	2.1	.56	4337	100		.10	.06	.10	.08
	63	61	40	61	69	55	43	63	67				

NOTE: On the first line of data for every program, raw values for each measure are reported; on the second line values are reported in standardized form, with mean = 50 and standard deviation = 10. "NA" indicates that the value for a measure is not available. Since the scale used to compute measure 16 is entirely arbitrary, only values in standardized form are reported for this measure.

TABLE 6.2 Summary Statistics Describing Each Program Measure--Microbiology

Measure	Number of Programs Evaluated	Mean	Standard Deviation	DECILES								
				1	2	3	4	5	6	7	8	9
Program Size												
01 Raw Value	134	16	11	7	9	10	12	13	16	17	22	29
Std Value	134	50	10	42	43	44	46	47	50	51	55	61
02 Raw Value	132	16	11	4	7	8	10	12	15	20	23	28
Std Value	132	50	10	40	43	43	45	47	49	54	56	61
03 Raw Value	134	20	21	5	8	10	12	14	16	21	27	36
Std Value	134	50	10	43	44	45	46	47	48	51	54	58
Program Graduates												
04 Raw Value	75	.48	.29	.10	.19	.24	.30	.44	.59	.67	.81	.87
Std Value	75	50	10	37	40	42	44	49	54	57	61	63
05 Raw Value	71	6.1	.8	7.0	6.5	6.3	6.2	6.0	5.9	5.8	5.5	5.3
Std Value	71	50	10	39	45	48	49	51	53	54	58	60
06 Raw Value	76	.80	.12	.65	.70	.75	.80	.82	.83	.87	.91	.93
Std Value	76	50	10	38	42	46	50	52	53	56	59	61
07 Raw Value	76	.48	.18	.25	.33	.40	.45	.50	.53	.57	.62	.72
Std Value	76	50	10	37	42	46	48	51	53	55	58	63
Survey Results												
08 Raw Value	131	2.8	.8	1.8	2.2	2.4	2.6	2.7	3.0	3.2	3.6	4.0
Std Value	131	50	10	37	42	45	47	48	52	55	60	65
09 Raw Value	125	1.8	.4	1.3	1.4	1.6	1.7	1.7	1.9	2.0	2.2	2.3
Std Value	125	50	10	38	41	46	48	48	53	55	60	63
10 Raw Value	116	1.2	.3	.8	1.0	1.1	1.1	1.2	1.2	1.3	1.4	1.5
Std Value	116	50	10	35	43	47	47	51	51	55	58	62
11 Raw Value	134	.6	.3	.2	.4	.4	.5	.6	.7	.7	.9	1.1
Std Value	134	50	10	37	43	43	46	49	52	52	58	64
University Library												
12 Raw Value	85	.3	.9	-.8	-.5	-.4	-.1	.2	.4	.8	.9	1.8
Std Value	85	50	10	38	42	43	46	49	51	55	56	66
Research Support												
13 Raw Value	102	.45	.23	.16	.22	.30	.37	.46	.51	.56	.65	.77
Std Value	102	50	10	37	40	43	47	50	53	55	59	64
14 Raw Value	108	8449	6012	2612	3161	4359	5381	6462	7807	9900	14096	17682
Std Value	108	50	10	40	41	43	45	47	49	52	59	65
Publication Records												
15 Raw Value	129	46	40	7	10	17	26	37	43	54	83	100
Std Value	129	50	10	40	41	43	45	48	49	52	59	63
16 Std Value	129	50	10	42	42	43	45	46	48	50	58	63

NOTE: Standardized values reported in the preceding table have been computed from exact values of the mean and standard deviation and not the rounded values reported here. Since the scale used to compute measure 16 is entirely arbitrary, only data in standardized form are reported for this measure.

TABLE 6.3   Intercorrelations Among Program Measures on 134 Programs in Microbiology

								Measure								
	01	02	03	04	05	06	07	08	09	10	11	12	13	14	15	16
Program Size																
01		.61	.64	.12	.05	.00	.03	.50	.50	.42	.51	.23	.07	.24	.44	.38
02			.80	.18	.02	.07	.12	.48	.55	.19	.58	.27	.20	.18	.44	.29
03				.17	.06	.02	.04	.42	.46	.15	.50	.22	.14	.08	.29	.18
Program Graduates																
04					.09	.37	.37	.57	.54	.07	.48	.41	.42	.43	.52	.51
05						.33	.41	.08	.12	.19	.13	-.03	.00	.05	.02	-.03
06							.58	.23	.30	.16	.24	.08	.25	.12	.10	.13
07								.38	.37	.12	.31	.13	.35	.27	.26	.27
Survey Results																
08									.96	.46	.91	.54	.64	.68	.72	.75
09										.46	.90	.54	.65	.65	.69	.68
10											.39	.23	.26	.12	.27	.27
11												.39	.61	.50	.63	.62
University Library																
12													.16	.49	.63	.54
Research Support																
13														.29	.39	.40
14															.73	.78
Publication Records																
15																.90
16																

NOTE: Since in computing correlation coefficients program data must be available for both of the measures being correlated, the actual number of programs on which each coefficient is based varies.

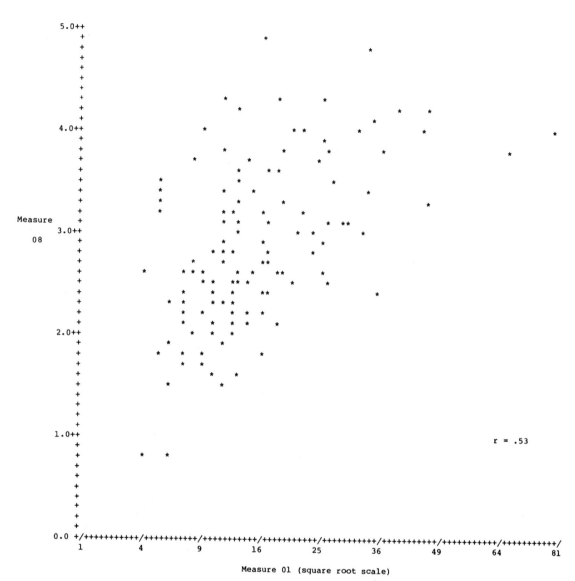

FIGURE 6.1 Mean rating of scholarly quality of faculty (measure 08) versus number of faculty members (measure 01)--131 programs in microbiology.

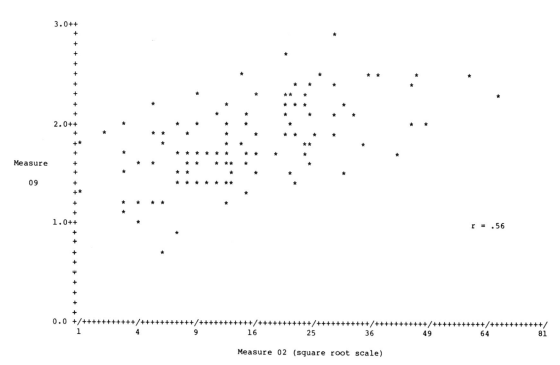

FIGURE 6.2 Mean rating of program effectiveness in educating research scholars/scientists (measure 09) versus number of graduates in last five years (measure 02)--123 programs in microbiology.

TABLE 6.4 Characteristics of Survey Participants in Microbiology

	Respondents	
	N	%
Field of Specialization		
Immunology	49	21
Microbiology/Bacteriology	108	47
Molecular Biology	32	14
Other/Unknown	42	18
Faculty Rank		
Professor	116	50
Associate Professor	65	28
Assistant Professor	50	22
Year of Highest Degree		
Pre-1950	11	5
1950-59	55	24
1960-69	89	39
Post-1969	76	33
Evaluator Selection		
Nominated by Institution	196	85
Other	35	15
Survey Form		
With Faculty Names	213	92
Without Names	18	8
Total Evaluators	231	100

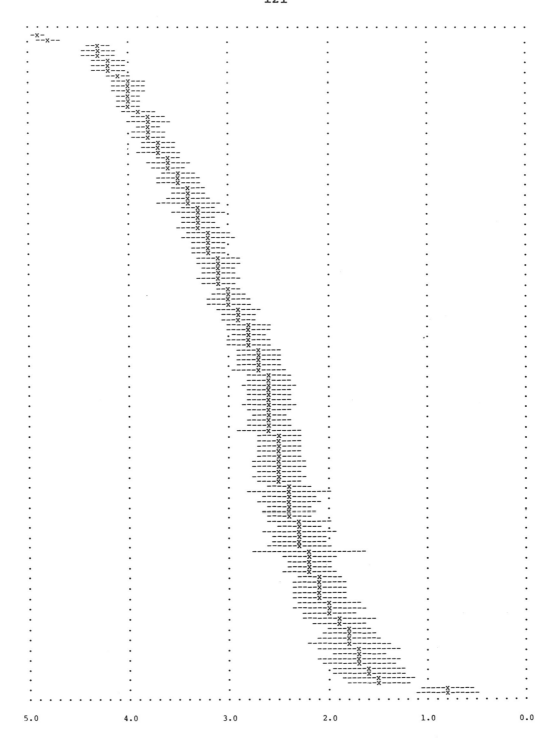

Mean Survey Rating (measure 08)

FIGURE 6.3 Mean rating of scholarly quality of faculty in 131 programs in microbiology.

NOTE: Programs are listed in sequence of mean rating, with the highest-rated program appearing at the top of the page. The broken lines (---) indicate a confidence interval of ±1.5 standard errors around the reported mean (x) of each program.

VII
Physiology Programs

In this chapter 101 research-doctorate programs in physiology are assessed. These programs, according to the information supplied by their universities, have accounted for 1,369 doctoral degrees awarded during the FY1976-80 period--approximately 87 percent of the aggregate number of physiology doctorates earned from U.S. universities in this five-year span.[1] Because physiology programs may be found in a variety of settings within universities, the committee encountered difficulty in identifying a comprehensive set of research-doctorate programs that have produced graduates in this discipline. On the average, 16 full-time and part-time students intending to earn doctorates were enrolled in a program in December 1980, with an average faculty size of 19 members.[2] Most of the 101 programs, listed in Table 7.1, are located in departments within schools of medicine. Six programs were initiated since 1970. Each of seven institutions--University of Arizona, University of California (San Diego), Iowa State University, University of Kansas, Ohio State University, Oklahoma State University, and SUNY at Buffalo--has two physiology programs included in the assessment. The University of Minnesota has three programs evaluated in this discipline. In addition to the 92 institutions represented in this discipline, another 11 were initially identified as meeting the criteria[3] for inclusion in the assessment:

> University of California--Riverside
> CUNY--Graduate School
> Florida State University--Tallahassee
> Massachusetts Institute of Technology

---

[1] Data from the NRC's Survey of Earned Doctorates indicate that 1,570 research doctorates in physiology were awarded by U.S. universities between FY1976 and FY1980.

[2] See the reported means for measures 03 and 01 in Table 7.2.

[3] As mentioned in Chapter I, the primary criterion for inclusion was that a university had awarded at least 11 doctorates in physiology during the FY1976-78 period.

University of Massachusetts--Amherst
University of Nebraska--Lincoln
University of New Mexico--Albuquerque
Oregon State University
Princeton University
University of Mississippi--Medical Center
University of Texas--Health Science Center, Dallas

The latter two institutions chose not to participate in the assessment in any discipline. Physiology programs at the other nine institutions have not been included in the evaluations in this discipline, since in each case the study coordinator either indicated that the institution did not at that time have a research-doctorate program in physiology or failed to provide the information requested by the committee.

Before examining individual program results presented in Table 7.1, the reader is urged to refer to Chapter II, in which each of the 16 measures used in the assessment is discussed. Summary statistics describing every measure are given in Table 7.2. For seven of the measures, data are reported for at least 94 of the 101 physiology programs. For measures 04-07, which pertain to characteristics of the program graduates, data are presented for slightly less than half of the programs; the other programs had too few graduates on which to base statistics.[4] For measure 12, a composite index of the size of a university library, data are available for 71 programs. With respect to measure 13, the fraction of faculty with research grants from the National Institutes of Health, the National Science Foundation, or the Alcohol, Drug Abuse, and Mental Health Administration, data are reported for 80 programs that had at least 10 faculty members. For measure 14, the total university expenditures for research in the biological sciences, data are available for 88 programs. The programs not evaluated on measures 12, 13, and 14 are typically smaller--in terms of faculty size and graduate student enrollment--than other physiology programs. Were data on these three measures available for all 101 programs, it is likely that their reported means would be appreciably lower (and that some of the correlations of these measures with others would be higher). With regard to reputational survey measures 09 and 10, results were not reported for any programs with fewer than 15 ratings.

Intercorrelations among the 16 measures (Pearson product-moment coefficients) are given in Table 7.3. Of particular note are the high positive correlations of reputational survey ratings (08, 09) with measures of publication records (15, 16) and number of program faculty (01). Figure 7.1 illustrates the relation between the mean rating of the scholarly quality of faculty (measure 08) and the number of faculty members (measure 01) for each of 94 programs in physiology. Figure 7.2

---

[4]As mentioned in Chapter II, data for measures 04-07 are not reported if they are based on the survey responses of fewer than 10 FY1975-79 program graduates.

plots the mean rating of program effectiveness (measure 09) against the total number of FY1976-80 program graduates (measure 02). Although in both figures there is a significant positive correlation between program size and reputational rating, it is quite apparent that some of the smaller programs received high mean ratings.

Table 7.4 describes the 146 faculty members who participated in the evaluation of physiology programs. These individuals constituted 48 percent of those asked to respond to the survey in this discipline and 7 percent of the faculty population in the 101 research-doctorate programs being evaluated.[5] More than two-thirds of the survey participants had earned their highest degree prior to 1970, and almost half held the rank of full professor.

One exception should be noted with regard to the survey evaluations in this discipline. It has been called to the attention of the committee that the University of Arizona's research-doctorate program in the physiology department in the College of Medicine was incorrectly identified as "Physiology (Human)." The committee has decided to report the survey results for this program but cautions that the reputational ratings may possibly have been influenced by the use of an inaccurate program title on the survey form.

To assist the reader in interpreting results of the survey evaluations, estimated standard errors have been computed for mean ratings of the scholarly quality of faculty in 94 physiology programs (and are given in Table 7.1). For each program the mean rating and an associated "confidence interval" of 1.5 standard errors are illustrated in Figure 7.3 (listed in order of highest to lowest mean rating). In comparing two programs, if their confidence intervals do not overlap, one may conclude that there is a significant difference in their mean ratings at a .05 level of significance.[6] From this figure it is also apparent that one should have somewhat more confidence in the accuracy of the mean ratings of higher-rated programs than lower-rated programs. This generalization results primarily from the fact that evaluators are not as likely to be familiar with the less prestigious programs, and consequently the mean ratings of these programs are usually based on fewer survey responses.

---

[5] See Table 2.3 in Chapter II.
[6] See pp. 31-33 for a discussion of the interpretation of mean ratings and associated confidence intervals.

TABLE 7.1 Program Measures (Raw and Standardized Values) in Physiology

Prog No.	University - Department/Academic Unit	Program Size			Characteristics of Program Graduates			
		(01)	(02)	(03)	(04)	(05)	(06)	(07)
001.	Alabama, University of-Birmingham	32	22	14	.31	8.0	.79	.71
	Physiology	59	58	49	41	29	48	60
002.	Albany Medical College	14	10	13	NA	NA	NA	NA
	Physiology	46	47	48				
003.	Albert Einstein College of Medicine	14	3	3	NA	NA	NA	NA
	Physiology	46	40	41				
004.	Arizona, University of-Tucson	11	11	15	NA	NA	NA	NA
	Animal Physiology	44	48	49				
005.	Arizona, University of-Tucson	13	12	13	NA	NA	NA	NA
	Physiology (College of Medicine)	45	49	48				
006.	Baylor College of Medicine-Houston	15	13	4	NA	NA	NA	NA
	Physiology	47	49	42				
007.	Brown University	17	7	10	NA	NA	NA	NA
	Biology and Medicine	48	44	46				
008.	California, University of-Irvine	17	7	8	NA	NA	NA	NA
	Physiol & Biophys/Developmental & Cell Biol	48	44	44				
009.	California, University of-Berkeley	14	29	48	.67	6.6	.78	.52
	Physiology	46	64	72	55	44	47	47
010.	California, University of-Davis	74	44	40	.33	6.3	.83	.66
	Physiology	90	78	67	42	49	52	56
011.	California, University of-Los Angeles	36	15	11	.90	5.1	.84	.79
	Physiology	62	51	47	64	62	54	65
012.	California, University of-San Diego	7	8	10	NA	NA	NA	NA
	Biology	41	45	46				
013.	California, University of-San Diego	12	8	41	NA	NA	NA	NA
	*Physiology/Pharmacology**	45	45	67				
014.	California, University of-San Francisco	50	23	9	.60	6.8	.95	.75
	Physiology	72	59	45	53	42	64	62
015.	Case Western Reserve University	9	5	5	NA	NA	NA	NA
	Physiology	42	42	42				
016.	Chicago, University of	23	20	25	NA	NA	NA	NA
	Pharmacological and Physiological Sciences	53	56	56				
017.	Cincinnati, University of	12	14	11	.20	5.0	.90	.70
	Physiology	45	50	47	37	63	59	59
018.	Colorado State University-Fort Collins	22	8	18	NA	NA	NA	NA
	Physiology and Biophysics	52	45	51				
019.	Colorado, University of	12	2	1	NA	NA	NA	NA
	Physiology	45	39	40				
020.	Columbia University	23	7	15	NA	NA	NA	NA
	Physiology	53	44	49				

* indicates program was initiated since 1970.

NOTE: On the first line of data for every program, raw values for each measure are reported; on the second line values are reported in standardized form, with mean = 50 and standard deviation = 10. "NA" indicates that the value for a measure is not available.

TABLE 7.1 Program Measures (Raw and Standardized Values) in Physiology

Prog No.	Survey Results (08)	(09)	(10)	(11)	University Library (12)	Research Support (13)	(14)	Published Articles (15)	(16)	Survey Ratings Standard Error (08)	(09)	(10)	(11)
001.	3.4	2.0	1.7	0.7	NA	.56	4467	40		.14	.10	.09	.08
	55	54	71	53		52	43	62	60				
002.	2.6	1.8	1.1	0.5	NA	.64	3066	10		.21	.10	.14	.08
	45	49	48	47		55	41	46	45				
003.	3.6	2.0	1.1	0.8	NA	.71	9184	17		.13	.11	.12	.08
	58	53	46	56		58	51	50	52				
004.	NA	NA	NA	0.2	0.9	.00	7828	4		NA	NA	NA	.06
				37	56	28	49	43	43				
005.	3.3	2.0	1.4	0.7	0.9	.62	7828	13		.13	.09	.11	.08
	53	53	61	54	56	54	49	48	47				
006.	2.9	1.6	0.9	0.5	NA	.27	14051	11		.18	.14	.15	.07
	49	43	39	48		39	59	47	48				
007.	3.3	1.9	1.1	0.6	-1.1	.59	NA	11		.12	.08	.10	.08
	54	51	48	52	37	53		47	47				
008.	3.1	2.1	1.5	0.6	NA	.77	6547	14		.15	.14	.15	.09
	52	56	65	50		60	47	48	48				
009.	3.4	2.1	0.9	0.9	2.2	.79	18977	23		.12	.12	.07	.09
	55	56	39	61	69	61	67	53	61				
010.	3.7	2.3	1.5	1.0	0.6	.42	18053	26		.13	.08	.10	.09
	60	62	66	62	54	46	65	55	51				
011.	4.3	2.3	1.1	1.3	2.0	.64	15581	75		.09	.07	.07	.08
	67	63	49	73	67	55	61	82	82				
012.	2.8	1.8	NA	0.3	-0.0	NA	8706	16		.29	.14	NA	.07
	47	49		42	47		50	49	49				
013.	3.7	2.0	1.5	0.8	-0.0	.83	8706	36		.15	.10	.11	.08
	59	53	64	56	47	63	50	60	55				
014.	4.5	2.5	1.4	1.4	NA	.78	13194	77		.09	.08	.08	.08
	70	67	59	77		61	57	83	83				
015.	2.7	1.3	0.6	0.4	-1.3	NA	7721	1		.15	.14	.14	.07
	46	35	27	45	35		48	41	42				
016.	3.6	2.1	1.2	1.0	0.9	.78	17589	29		.14	.11	.14	.07
	58	57	50	63	56	61	64	56	59				
017.	2.7	1.8	1.3	0.4	-0.2	.75	9365	9		.18	.13	.13	.07
	46	48	56	45	45	60	51	45	47				
018.	3.2	2.1	1.4	0.4	-1.1	.41	8863	3		.19	.13	.12	.08
	52	56	60	45	37	45	50	42	42				
019.	3.0	1.5	1.3	0.5	-0.9	.83	11967	39		.20	.16	.11	.08
	50	41	56	45	39	63	55	62	63				
020.	4.0	2.1	1.2	0.9	1.7	.70	11090	27		.09	.09	.09	.08
	63	58	53	61	65	57	54	55	54				

NOTE: On the first line of data for every program, raw values for each measure are reported; on the second line values are reported in standardized form, with mean = 50 and standard deviation = 10. "NA" indicates that the value for a measure is not available. Since the scale used to compute measure 16 is entirely arbitrary, only values in standardized form are reported for this measure.

TABLE 7.1 Program Measures (Raw and Standardized Values) in Physiology

Prog No.	University - Department/Academic Unit	Program Size (01)	(02)	(03)	Characteristics of Program Graduates (04)	(05)	(06)	(07)
021.	Connecticut, University of-Storrs	7	8	9	.39	6.8	.85	.69
	Biological Sciences	*41*	*45*	*45*	*44*	*43*	*54*	*58*
022.	Cornell University-Ithaca	34	12	13	.45	6.7	.75	.45
	Physiology	*61*	*49*	*48*	*47*	*44*	*45*	*42*
023.	Cornell University-Medical Center	8	6	6	NA	NA	NA	NA
	Physiology	*42*	*43*	*43*				
024.	Duke University	37	39	28	.84	5.4	.75	.57
	Physiology	*63*	*74*	*58*	*62*	*59*	*44*	*50*
025.	Emory University	10	8	10	.70	6.5	NA	NA
	Physiology	*43*	*45*	*46*	*57*	*46*		
026.	Florida, University of-Gainesville	15	7	9	NA	NA	NA	NA
	Physiology (Human)	*47*	*44*	*45*				
027.	Georgetown University	13	18	21	.43	5.2	.71	.21
	Physiology and Biophysics	*45*	*54*	*53*	*46*	*61*	*41*	*26*
028.	Georgia, University of-Athens	10	6	7	NA	NA	NA	NA
	Physiology and Pharmacology	*43*	*43*	*44*				
029.	Harvard University	46	54	76	.57	6.1	.77	.56
	Biology (Organismic & Evolutionary)	*69*	*88*	*92*	*51*	*51*	*46*	*49*
030.	Hawaii, University of	13	17	15	.09	5.3	.91	.55
	Physiology	*45*	*53*	*49*	*32*	*59*	*60*	*48*
031.	Houston, University of	7	11	6	.10	7.5	.80	.50
	Biology	*41*	*48*	*43*	*33*	*34*	*50*	*45*
032.	Howard University	18	10	12	NA	NA	NA	NA
	Physiology	*49*	*47*	*47*				
033.	Illinois, University of-Medical Center	25	25	32	.56	6.6	.87	.73
	Physiology and Biophysics	*54*	*61*	*61*	*51*	*44*	*56*	*61*
034.	Illinois, University-Urbana/Champaign	35	31	78	.77	6.5	.77	.59
	Physiology and Biophysics	*61*	*66*	*93*	*60*	*46*	*47*	*52*
035.	Indiana State University-Terre Haute	10	6	7	NA	NA	NA	NA
	Life Sciences	*43*	*43*	*44*				
036.	Indiana University-Bloomington	9	12	7	NA	NA	NA	NA
	Physiology	*42*	*49*	*44*				
037.	Indiana University-Purdue University	15	13	11	NA	NA	NA	NA
	Physiology	*47*	*49*	*47*				
038.	Iowa State University-Ames	8	8	25	NA	NA	NA	NA
	Animal Science	*42*	*45*	*56*				
039.	Iowa State University-Ames	18	1	16	NA	NA	NA	NA
	Veterinary Physiology and Pharmacology	*49*	*38*	*50*				
040.	Iowa, University of-Iowa City	23	13	10	.79	5.0	.90	.79
	Physiology and Biophysics	*53*	*49*	*46*	*60*	*63*	*59*	*65*

* indicates program was initiated since 1970.

NOTE: On the first line of data for every program, raw values for each measure are reported; on the second line values are reported in standardized form, with mean = 50 and standard deviation = 10. "NA" indicates that the value for a measure is not available.

TABLE 7.1 Program Measures (Raw and Standardized Values) in Physiology

Prog No.	Survey Results (08)	(09)	(10)	(11)	University Library (12)	Research Support (13)	(14)	Published Articles (15)	(16)	Survey Ratings Standard Error (08)	(09)	(10)	(11)
021.	2.5	1.3	1.1	0.3	-0.5	NA	15199	2		.17	.18	.17	.06
	43	36	46	42	43		61	42	43				
022.	3.5	2.2	1.2	0.7	1.6	.41	14597	15		.14	.09	.12	.08
	57	60	52	52	63	45	60	49	50				
023.	3.2	1.9	1.0	0.6	NA	NA	14597	5		.13	.08	.11	.08
	53	52	42	51			60	43	43				
024.	3.9	2.4	1.0	1.2	0.3	.65	11320	34		.10	.06	.10	.08
	63	64	44	69	51	55	54	59	62				
025.	2.7	1.7	0.8	0.6	-0.6	.90	2874	14		.13	.10	.14	.07
	46	45	33	51	42	66	41	48	48				
026.	2.9	1.8	1.2	0.8	0.8	.47	3486	20		.13	.10	.11	.08
	48	48	52	56	55	48	42	52	49				
027.	2.8	1.8	1.0	0.5	-0.6	.46	4200	10		.21	.12	.10	.08
	48	48	43	46	41	47	43	46	46				
028.	2.0	NA	NA	0.3	0.4	.00	10714	3		.27	NA	NA	.07
	36			40	52	28	53	42	42				
029.	4.1	2.5	1.1	0.8	3.0	.74	34979	6		.15	.08	.12	.09
	65	67	49	55	77	59	93	44	44				
030.	2.6	1.5	NA	0.3	-0.1	.39	4440	3		.22	.16	NA	.06
	44	41		41	46	44	43	42	42				
031.	1.6	NA	NA	0.2	-0.9	NA	NA	2		.26	NA	NA	.05
	31			36	39			42	43				
032.	2.1	1.3	1.3	0.4	-0.4	.06	NA	1		.19	.16	.18	.07
	38	34	55	42	44	30		41	42				
033.	3.0	1.8	1.1	0.6	NA	.44	4393	33		.14	.10	.14	.07
	49	49	45	50		47	43	59	58				
034.	3.8	2.2	1.4	1.0	2.0	.74	6074	5		.12	.09	.12	.09
	61	59	59	63	67	59	46	43	42				
035.	1.1	NA	NA	0.2	NA	.10	NA	0		.28	NA	NA	.05
	24			37		32		41	41				
036.	2.6	1.6	0.8	0.4	0.9	NA	NA	1		.15	.10	.14	.07
	44	44	33	45	57			41	42				
037.	3.4	1.9	1.0	0.9	NA	.60	2940	NA		.14	.09	.11	.09
	56	52	43	59		53	41		NA				
038.	2.5	1.5	NA	0.3	-0.5	NA	5287	8		.30	.24	NA	.07
	43	40		40	43		44	45	43				
039.	2.6	1.5	NA	0.3	-0.5	.06	5287	8		.26	.19	NA	.07
	44	41		42	43	30	44	45	43				
040.	3.4	2.1	1.3	1.1	0.3	.70	7088	48		.12	.09	.11	.08
	56	57	56	65	50	57	47	67	61				

NOTE: On the first line of data for every program, raw values for each measure are reported; on the second line values are reported in standardized form, with mean = 50 and standard deviation = 10. "NA" indicates that the value for a measure is not available. Since the scale used to compute measure 16 is entirely arbitrary, only values in standardized form are reported for this measure.

TABLE 7.1 Program Measures (Raw and Standardized Values) in Physiology

Prog No.	University - Department/Academic Unit	Program Size (01)	(02)	(03)	Characteristics of Program Graduates (04)	(05)	(06)	(07)
041.	Johns Hopkins University	10	8	8	.90	NA	.80	.60
	Physiology	*43*	*45*	*44*	*65*		*50*	*52*
042.	Kansas State University-Manhattan	9	7	12	NA	NA	NA	NA
	Anatomy and Physiology	*42*	*44*	*47*				
043.	Kansas, University of	17	5	9	NA	NA	NA	NA
	Physiology (Schl of Medicine-Kansas City)	*48*	*42*	*45*				
044.	Kansas, University of	11	12	4	.06	7.2	.67	.33
	Physiology and Cell Biology (Graduate Schl)	*44*	*49*	*42*	*31*	*38*	*36*	*34*
045.	Kent State University	16	9	30	NA	NA	NA	NA
	Biological Sciences	*48*	*46*	*60*				
046.	Kentucky, University of	19	9	10	NA	NA	NA	NA
	Physiology and Biophysics	*50*	*46*	*46*				
047.	Louisiana State University-Baton Rouge	5	3	6	NA	NA	NA	NA
	*Zoology and Physiology**	*40*	*40*	*43*				
048.	Louisiana State Univ-School of Medicine	37	12	17	NA	NA	NA	NA
	Physiology and Biophysics	*63*	*49*	*51*				
049.	Louisville, University of	9	8	6	NA	NA	NA	NA
	Physiology	*42*	*45*	*43*				
050.	Loyola University of Chicago	8	6	14	NA	NA	NA	NA
	Physiology	*42*	*43*	*49*				
051.	Maryland, University of-College Park	6	8	11	NA	NA	NA	NA
	*Animal Sciences**	*40*	*45*	*47*				
052.	Medical College of Wisconsin	9	19	7	.56	5.5	.78	.67
	Physiology	*42*	*55*	*44*	*51*	*57*	*47*	*57*
053.	Medical University of South Carolina	14	6	4	NA	NA	NA	NA
	Physiology	*46*	*43*	*42*				
054.	Miami, University of-Florida	15	8	8	.46	6.1	.54	.39
	Physiology and Biophysics	*47*	*45*	*44*	*47*	*50*	*24*	*38*
055.	Michigan State University-East Lansing	34	33	19	.19	6.3	.84	.61
	Physiology	*61*	*68*	*52*	*36*	*48*	*53*	*53*
056.	Michigan, University of-Ann Arbor	22	27	20	.78	6.1	.87	.61
	Physiology	*52*	*63*	*53*	*60*	*50*	*56*	*53*
057.	Minnesota, University of	6	5	8	NA	NA	NA	NA
	Animal Sci/Ecol & Behav Biol/Gen & Cell Bio	*40*	*42*	*44*				
058.	Minnesota, University of	13	2	5	NA	NA	NA	NA
	Physiol & Biophysics Mayo Grad Sch of Med)	*45*	*39*	*42*				
059.	Minnesota, University of	24	17	35	.67	9.0	.64	.36
	Physiology (Graduate School)	*53*	*53*	*63*	*55*	*17*	*34*	*36*
060.	Missouri, University of-Columbia	15	21	15	.52	6.5	.75	.46
	Physiology	*47*	*57*	*49*	*49*	*46*	*45*	*43*

* indicates program was initiated since 1970.

NOTE: On the first line of data for every program, raw values for each measure are reported;
on the second line values are reported in standardized form, with mean = 50 and
standard deviation = 10. "NA" indicates that the value for a measure is not available.

TABLE 7.1 Program Measures (Raw and Standardized Values) in Physiology

Prog No.	Survey Results (08)	(09)	(10)	(11)	University Library (12)	Research Support (13)	(14)	Published Articles (15)	(16)	Survey Ratings Standard Error (08)	(09)	(10)	(11)
041.	3.5	2.0	0.7	0.7	-0.4	.70	19837	45		.15	.09	.10	.08
	56	53	30	53	44	58	68	65	61				
042.	2.2	NA	NA	0.3	NA	NA	2496	2		.31	NA	NA	.06
	39			40			40	42	42				
043.	2.8	1.6	1.2	0.5	0.1	.53	3161	18		.16	.12	.10	.07
	47	44	53	48	49	50	41	50	49				
044.	2.1	1.5	1.0	0.3	0.1	.36	3161	1		.22	.14	.12	.06
	38	40	43	40	49	43	41	41	42				
045.	NA	NA	NA	0.2	-1.8	.06	NA	1		NA	NA	NA	.05
				36	30	31		41	42				
046.	2.6	1.6	1.0	0.5	-0.1	.42	484	6		.17	.12	.17	.07
	44	43	43	45	47	46	37	44	44				
047.	1.3	NA	NA	0.2	-0.3	NA	5116	3		.23	NA	NA	.05
	26			36	44		44	42	42				
048.	3.0	1.8	1.6	0.7	NA	.35	5116	5		.14	.10	.11	.09
	49	49	68	54		43	44	43	43				
049.	2.0	1.1	NA	0.3	NA	NA	NA	0		.17	.12	NA	.06
	36	30		42				41	41				
050.	2.6	1.6	1.0	0.5	NA	NA	NA	10		.17	.13	.13	.09
	45	43	41	48				46	47				
051.	NA	NA	NA	0.1	0.2	NA	1623	1		NA	NA	NA	.04
				34	49		39	41	42				
052.	2.2	1.4	1.3	0.4	NA	NA	2085	9		.18	.17	.17	.08
	40	37	54	45			39	45	45				
053.	2.3	1.4	NA	0.4	NA	.43	3178	3		.23	.17	NA	.07
	40	38		43		46	41	42	43				
054.	3.3	1.7	1.3	0.6	NA	.53	6101	10		.14	.13	.13	.08
	54	45	56	52		50	46	46	47				
055.	3.5	2.2	1.3	1.0	0.3	.38	10357	17		.11	.10	.12	.09
	57	59	56	62	51	44	53	50	50				
056.	4.1	2.3	1.2	1.2	1.8	.77	15431	35		.11	.08	.08	.08
	65	62	50	71	65	61	61	60	59				
057.	1.8	1.1	NA	0.3	1.2	NA	13696	NA		.24	.19	NA	.07
	34	30		40	59		58		NA				
058.	3.7	2.1	1.2	0.8	1.2	.00	13696	29		.14	.15	.12	.09
	60	56	50	56	59	28	58	56	56				
059.	3.5	1.9	1.1	0.8	1.2	.63	13696	12		.14	.10	.12	.09
	57	53	48	57	59	54	58	47	48				
060.	3.6	2.2	1.1	0.7	-0.2	.60	4628	NA		.12	.08	.10	.09
	58	60	48	54	46	53	43		NA				

NOTE: On the first line of data for every program, raw values for each measure are reported; on the second line values are reported in standardized form, with mean = 50 and standard deviation = 10. "NA" indicates that the value for a measure is not available. Since the scale used to compute measure 16 is entirely arbitrary, only values in standardized form are reported for this measure.

132

TABLE 7.1 Program Measures (Raw and Standardized Values) in Physiology

Prog No.	University - Department/Academic Unit	Program Size (01)	(02)	(03)	Characteristics of Program Graduates (04)	(05)	(06)	(07)
061.	New Jersey, College of Medicine & Dentistry *Physiology**	15 *47*	8 *45*	12 *47*	NA	NA	NA	NA
062.	New York University *Basic Medical Sciences*	25 *54*	5 *42*	6 *43*	NA	NA	NA	NA
063.	North Carolina State University-Raleigh *Physiology*	19 *50*	14 *50*	15 *49*	.42 *45*	6.0 *52*	.83 *53*	.25 *28*
064.	North Carolina, University of-Chapel Hill *Physiology*	77 *92*	9 *46*	21 *53*	NA	NA	NA	NA
065.	North Dakota, University of-Grand Forks *Physiology*	6 *40*	11 *48*	7 *44*	.92 *65*	4.5 *69*	.75 *45*	.67 *57*
066.	Northwestern University *Physiology/Pharmacology/Pathology/Biol Sci*	27 *55*	15 *51*	37 *65*	.53 *50*	5.8 *54*	.77 *46*	.53 *47*
067.	Ohio State University-Columbus *Physiology*	20 *50*	23 *59*	22 *54*	.56 *51*	5.3 *60*	.61 *31*	.33 *34*
068.	Ohio State University-Columbus *Veterinary Physiology and Pharmacology*	6 *40*	10 *47*	5 *42*	NA	NA	NA	NA
069.	Oklahoma State University-Stillwater *Animal Science*	16 *48*	71 *99*	12 *47*	.24 *38*	4.5 *70*	.95 *65*	.67 *57*
070.	Oklahoma State University-Stillwater *Physiological Sciences*	17 *48*	9 *46*	8 *44*	NA	NA	NA	NA
071.	Oklahoma, University of-Norman *Physiology and Biostatistics*	13 *45*	8 *45*	7 *44*	NA	NA	NA	NA
072.	Oregon, University of-Eugene *Biology*	12 *45*	3 *40*	7 *44*	NA	NA	NA	NA
073.	Pennsylvania State University *Physiology (Grad School and Medical Center)*	37 *63*	34 *69*	35 *63*	.33 *42*	5.5 *57*	.68 *38*	.42 *40*
074.	Pennsylvania, University of *Physiology*	46 *69*	14 *50*	30 *60*	.75 *59*	7.0 *40*	.88 *57*	.56 *50*
075.	Purdue University-West Lafayette *Biological Sciences*	13 *45*	26 *62*	28 *58*	.46 *47*	5.7 *55*	.91 *60*	.76 *63*
076.	Rochester, University of *Physiology*	13 *45*	10 *47*	16 *50*	.83 *62*	7.2 *38*	.92 *61*	.58 *51*
077.	Rockefeller University *Physiology*	40 *65*	20 *56*	26 *57*	.56 *51*	5.5 *58*	.81 *51*	.75 *62*
078.	Rutgers, The State University-New Brunswick *Physiology*	26 *55*	21 *57*	72 *89*	.09 *32*	6.5 *46*	.82 *51*	.55 *48*
079.	SUNY Upstate Medical Center *Physiology*	13 *45*	9 *46*	7 *44*	NA	NA	NA	NA
080.	SUNY at Buffalo *Physiology (Roswell Park Graduate Division)*	15 *47*	10 *47*	16 *50*	NA	NA	NA	NA

* indicates program was initiated since 1970.

NOTE: On the first line of data for every program, raw values for each measure are reported; on the second line values are reported in standardized form, with mean = 50 and standard deviation = 10. "NA" indicates that the value for a measure is not available.

TABLE 7.1 Program Measures (Raw and Standardized Values) in Physiology

Prog No.	Survey Results (08)	(09)	(10)	(11)	University Library (12)	Research Support (13)	(14)	Published Articles (15)	(16)	Survey Ratings Standard Error (08)	(09)	(10)	(11)
061.	2.6	1.6	1.1	0.3	NA	.47	4529	15		.21	.16	.13	.06
	44	42	49	41		48	43	49	47				
062.	3.3	1.8	1.4	0.6	0.5	.60	9934	11		.17	.15	.15	.09
	54	48	61	51	52	53	52	47	49				
063.	2.7	1.7	NA	0.3	NA	.26	6741	4		.24	.16	NA	.07
	45	45		41		39	47	43	42				
064.	3.8	2.1	1.4	1.0	1.0	.61	9849	29		.10	.09	.10	.08
	61	57	61	62	57	54	52	56	56				
065.	1.4	1.0	NA	0.3	NA	NA	NA	2		.23	.19	NA	.06
	28	27		39				42	42				
066.	3.4	2.0	1.7	0.8	0.3	.78	4760	19		.12	.10	.13	.09
	55	54	73	55	50	61	44	51	52				
067.	2.6	1.5	NA	0.4	0.9	.35	8330	8		.22	.14	NA	.08
	44	41		44	56	43	49	45	44				
068.	1.9	NA	NA	0.3	0.9	NA	8330	8		.30	NA	NA	.07
	35			39	56		49	45	44				
069.	NA	NA	NA	0.2	-1.9	.00	3127	4		NA	NA	NA	.05
				37	29	28	41	43	43				
070.	NA	NA	NA	0.2	-1.9	.35	3127	4		NA	NA	NA	.07
				38	29	43	41	43	43				
071.	2.3	1.4	1.1	0.5	-0.6	.46	NA	7		.15	.15	.19	.07
	40	39	46	46	42	47		44	44				
072.	3.0	1.9	1.2	0.4	-0.9	.58	NA	6		.25	.14	.10	.07
	50	51	51	43	39	53		44	43				
073.	3.5	2.1	1.3	0.7	0.7	.49	8024	32		.14	.08	.14	.09
	57	58	57	54	54	48	49	58	54				
074.	4.3	2.5	1.3	1.4	0.7	.70	23550	104		.10	.07	.08	.07
	67	66	54	77	54	57	74	98	91				
075.	3.1	1.9	1.0	0.5	-0.5	.85	10337	17		.17	.09	.15	.07
	51	52	45	46	42	64	53	50	52				
076.	3.4	2.2	0.9	0.8	-0.6	.85	15969	39		.13	.07	.08	.09
	55	58	41	56	42	64	62	62	60				
077.	4.3	2.6	1.2	1.0	NA	.73	27299	29		.09	.07	.09	.09
	68	70	52	62		59	80	56	67				
078.	3.1	2.0	1.1	0.7	0.8	.15	7505	5		.13	.06	.10	.08
	51	53	48	52	55	34	48	43	44				
079.	2.8	1.8	NA	0.4	NA	.54	NA	8		.15	.14	NA	.07
	47	48		45		51		45	44				
080.	NA	NA	NA	0.2	0.3	.00	6799	6		NA	NA	NA	.06
				38	50	28	47	44	42				

NOTE: On the first line of data for every program, raw values for each measure are reported; on the second line values are reported in standardized form, with mean = 50 and standard deviation = 10. "NA" indicates that the value for a measure is not available. Since the scale used to compute measure 16 is entirely arbitrary, only values in standardized form are reported for this measure.

134

TABLE 7.1 Program Measures (Raw and Standardized Values) in Physiology

Prog No.	University - Department/Academic Unit	Program Size			Characteristics of Program Graduates			
		(01)	(02)	(03)	(04)	(05)	(06)	(07)
081.	SUNY at Buffalo	29	15	9	.67	6.0	.83	.75
	Physiology (School of Medicine)	57	51	45	55	52	53	62
082.	SUNY-Downstate Medical Center	17	3	3	NA	NA	NA	NA
	Physiology	48	40	41				
083.	Southern California, University of	14	12	9	.67	6.5	.92	.50
	Physiology and Biophysics	46	49	45	55	46	61	45
084.	Stanford University	8	13	14	.75	6.0	.92	.75
	Physiology	42	49	49	59	52	61	62
085.	Temple University	8	7	9	.23	6.5	.58	.33
	Physiology	42	44	45	38	46	28	34
086.	Tennessee, Univ of-Ctr for Health Sciences	21	4	3	NA	NA	NA	NA
	Physiology & Biophysics	51	41	41				
087.	Texas, U of-Health Science Center, Houston	65	12	40	NA	6.5	.70	.40
	Physiol & Cell Biol/Pharm/Neuro & Anatomy	83	49	67		46	40	39
088.	Thomas Jefferson University	10	13	10	.13	5.2	.87	.67
	Physiology	43	49	46	34	61	56	57
089.	Tufts University	4	4	2	NA	NA	NA	NA
	Physiology*	39	41	40				
090.	Tulane University	10	3	4	NA	NA	NA	NA
	Physiology	43	40	42				
091.	Vanderbilt University	18	11	2	NA	NA	NA	NA
	Physiology	49	48	40				
092.	Vermont, University of	8	13	5	.50	5.5	.83	.58
	Physiology and Biophysics	42	49	42	49	57	53	51
093.	Virginia Commonwealth University/Medical Col	22	11	24	.42	5.8	.83	.50
	Physiology	52	48	56	45	55	53	45
094.	Virginia, University of	17	17	19	.93	5.8	.87	.73
	Physiology	48	53	52	66	54	56	61
095.	Washington State University-Pullman	8	8	7	NA	NA	NA	NA
	Zoophysiology	42	45	44				
096.	Washington University-Saint Louis	44	9	33	NA	NA	NA	NA
	Biology and Biomedical Sciences*	68	46	62				
097.	Washington, University of-Seattle	34	25	8	.96	7.5	.85	.62
	Physiology and Biophysics	61	61	44	67	34	54	53
098.	Wayne State University	19	17	12	.47	6.5	.60	.40
	Physiology	50	53	47	47	46	30	39
099.	West Virginia University	18	10	12	NA	NA	NA	NA
	Physiology	49	47	47				
100.	Wisconsin, University of-Madison	14	17	20	.63	6.0	1.00	.69
	Physiology	46	53	53	54	52	69	58

* indicates program was initiated since 1970.

NOTE: On the first line of data for every program, raw values for each measure are reported; on the second line values are reported in standardized form, with mean = 50 and standard deviation = 10. "NA" indicates that the value for a measure is not available.

TABLE 7.1 Program Measures (Raw and Standardized Values) in Physiology

Prog No.	Survey Results (08)	(09)	(10)	(11)	University Library (12)	Research Support (13)	(14)	Published Articles (15)	(16)	Survey Ratings Standard Error (08)	(09)	(10)	(11)
081.	3.7	2.3	1.0	1.0	0.3	.48	6799	25		.13	.10	.11	.10
	60	61	43	62	50	48	47	54	50				
082.	2.8	1.7	0.7	0.5	NA	.41	3077	12		.15	.13	.11	.08
	48	45	31	48		45	41	47	48				
083.	3.1	1.8	1.3	0.5	0.4	.64	2405	19		.14	.08	.14	.07
	52	50	56	48	51	55	40	51	47				
084.	3.3	2.1	0.8	0.8	2.0	NA	12514	24		.18	.10	.11	.09
	54	56	34	57	67		56	54	56				
085.	2.1	1.3	NA	0.3	-0.4	NA	6914	15		.17	.11	NA	.07
	38	34		42	43		47	49	48				
086.	2.8	1.6	1.1	0.6	NA	.48	2127	9		.15	.11	.07	.08
	47	42	48	50		48	39	45	47				
087.	3.5	2.0	1.6	0.6	NA	.57	4151	NA		.15	.12	.15	.08
	57	55	67	50		52	43		NA				
088.	NA	NA	NA	0.3	NA	.60	1851	9		NA	NA	NA	.08
				41		53	39	45	46				
089.	1.4	0.8	0.5	0.2	NA	NA	3518	5		.28	.17	.13	.05
	28	23	21	38			42	43	44				
090.	2.5	1.4	1.1	0.3	-1.0	.40	3690	13		.21	.16	.18	.06
	43	39	46	41	38	45	42	48	45				
091.	3.5	2.0	1.0	0.5	-0.7	.78	5204	13		.21	.13	.14	.09
	56	54	43	48	41	61	44	48	47				
092.	2.9	1.9	1.2	0.5	NA	NA	4628	11		.15	.09	.08	.08
	49	50	51	48			43	47	49				
093.	3.1	1.8	1.4	0.8	NA	.68	6556	21		.16	.10	.12	.08
	51	49	61	57		57	47	52	51				
094.	3.8	2.3	1.2	0.9	0.7	.65	6224	17		.12	.07	.09	.08
	60	61	51	60	55	55	46	50	49				
095.	2.3	1.7	1.0	0.4	-0.3	NA	998	5		.21	.18	.00	.07
	40	46	43	44	45		38	43	43				
096.	4.0	2.3	1.4	0.9	-0.4	.86	16825	48		.12	.08	.09	.08
	63	63	59	61	44	64	63	67	75				
097.	4.3	2.6	1.3	1.3	1.5	.68	14164	54		.09	.07	.11	.08
	68	69	54	74	62	57	59	70	68				
098.	2.6	1.5	1.0	0.4	-0.4	.53	6372	19		.19	.15	.18	.06
	44	41	43	43	44	50	46	51	51				
099.	2.5	NA	NA	0.3	NA	.33	NA	2		.14	NA	NA	.06
	43			41		42		42	42				
100.	3.0	2.0	1.2	0.5	1.6	.64	19738	24		.16	.04	.17	.08
	50	53	52	47	63	55	68	54	52				

NOTE: On the first line of data for every program, raw values for each measure are reported; on the second line values are reported in standardized form, with mean = 50 and standard deviation = 10. "NA" indicates that the value for a measure is not available. Since the scale used to compute measure 16 is entirely arbitrary, only values in standardized form are reported for this measure.

TABLE 7.1 Program Measures (Raw and Standardized Values) in Physiology

Prog No.	University - Department/Academic Unit	Program Size			Characteristics of Program Graduates			
		(01)	(02)	(03)	(04)	(05)	(06)	(07)
101.	Yale University	33	17	20	.82	5.9	.88	.50
	Physiology/ Biology/ Neuroanatomy	*60*	*53*	*53*	*62*	*53*	*57*	*45*

* indicates program was initiated since 1970.

NOTE: On the first line of data for every program, raw values for each measure are reported; on the second line values are reported in standardized form, with mean = 50 and standard deviation = 10. "NA" indicates that the value for a measure is not available.

TABLE 7.1 Program Measures (Raw and Standardized Values) in Physiology

Prog No.	Survey Results				University Library	Research Support		Published Articles		Survey Ratings Standard Error			
	(08)	(09)	(10)	(11)	(12)	(13)	(14)	(15)	(16)	(08)	(09)	(10)	(11)
101.	4.3	2.5	1.4	1.3	2.1	.73	4337	64		.10	.07	.10	.08
	68	67	59	74	68	59	43	76	82				

NOTE: On the first line of data for every program, raw values for each measure are reported;
on the second line values are reported in standardized form, with mean = 50 and
standard deviation = 10. "NA" indicates that the value for a measure is not available.
Since the scale used to compute measure 16 is entirely arbitrary, only values in
standardized form are reported for this measure.

TABLE 7.2 Summary Statistics Describing Each Program Measure--Physiology

Measure	Number of Programs Evaluated	Mean	Standard Deviation	DECILES								
				1	2	3	4	5	6	7	8	9
Program Size												
01 Raw Value	101	19	14	8	9	12	13	15	17	21	26	37
Std Value	101	50	10	42	42	45	45	47	48	51	55	63
02 Raw Value	101	14	11	4	7	8	9	11	12	14	18	25
Std Value	101	50	10	41	44	45	46	48	49	50	54	61
03 Raw Value	101	16	14	4	7	8	9	11	14	16	22	33
Std Value	101	50	10	42	44	44	45	47	49	50	54	62
Program Graduates												
04 Raw Value	48	.53	.25	.13	.28	.42	.46	.56	.59	.67	.78	.85
Std Value	48	50	10	34	40	46	47	51	52	56	60	63
05 Raw Value	48	6.2	.9	7.2	6.7	6.5	6.5	6.1	6.0	5.7	5.5	5.2
Std Value	48	50	10	38	44	46	46	51	52	55	57	61
06 Raw Value	48	.80	.10	.64	.73	.77	.79	.83	.84	.87	.88	.92
Std Value	48	50	10	34	43	47	49	53	54	57	58	62
07 Raw Value	48	.57	.15	.33	.41	.50	.55	.58	.61	.67	.71	.75
Std Value	48	50	10	34	39	45	49	51	53	57	59	62
Survey Results												
08 Raw Value	94	3.0	.7	2.0	2.5	2.6	2.8	3.0	3.3	3.4	3.6	4.0
Std Value	94	50	10	36	43	44	47	50	54	55	58	63
09 Raw Value	87	1.9	.4	1.3	1.5	1.6	1.8	1.9	2.0	2.1	2.2	2.3
Std Value	87	50	10	35	41	43	49	51	54	57	59	62
10 Raw Value	75	1.2	.2	.8	1.0	1.1	1.1	1.2	1.2	1.3	1.4	1.4
Std Value	75	50	10	35	43	48	48	52	52	56	60	60
11 Raw Value	101	.6	.3	.2	.3	.4	.4	.5	.6	.7	.8	1.0
Std Value	101	50	10	37	41	44	44	47	50	54	57	63
University Library												
12 Raw Value	71	.3	1.0	-1.0	-.6	-.4	-.2	.2	.4	.8	1.0	1.7
Std Value	71	50	10	38	42	44	46	50	51	55	57	64
Research Support												
13 Raw Value	80	.52	.24	.06	.35	.42	.48	.57	.62	.68	.73	.78
Std Value	80	50	10	31	43	46	48	52	54	57	59	61
14 Raw Value	88	8687	6173	2798	3363	4492	5444	6799	8330	10349	13696	16140
Std Value	88	50	10	40	41	43	45	47	49	53	58	62
Publication Records												
15 Raw Value	97	17	18	2	4	6	9	11	15	19	28	39
Std Value	97	50	10	42	43	44	45	47	49	51	56	62
16 Std Value	97	50	10	42	43	43	45	47	48	51	56	61

NOTE: Standardized values reported in the preceding table have been computed from exact values of the mean and standard deviation and not the rounded values reported here. Since the scale used to compute measure 16 is entirely arbitrary, only data in standardized form are reported for this measure.

TABLE 7.3 Intercorrelations Among Program Measures on 101 Programs in Physiology

Measure

	01	02	03	04	05	06	07	08	09	10	11	12	13	14	15	16
Program Size																
01		.43	.49	.12	-.15	-.01	.08	.64	.62	.53	.63	.36	.18	.36	.52	.52
02			.54	-.09	.19	.14	.15	.46	.51	.19	.32	.25	.04	.30	.16	.17
03				.01	-.11	-.09	-.08	.42	.43	.29	.34	.41	.16	.37	.12	.14
Program Graduates																
04					.01	.15	.28	.47	.38	-.25	.60	.43	.60	.31	.51	.50
05						.19	.22	-.11	-.16	.00	-.17	-.13	-.17	-.16	-.15	-.12
06							.68	.27	.37	-.03	.22	.01	.17	.14	.30	.29
07								.30	.33	-.01	.32	.10	.32	.23	.32	.33
Survey Results																
08									.95	.38	.89	.49	.57	.51	.69	.71
09										.40	.84	.53	.47	.51	.63	.65
10											.29	.18	.06	-.01	.23	.20
11												.58	.57	.46	.80	.81
University Library																
12													.23	.50	.34	.37
Research Support																
13														.28	.48	.51
14															.43	.48
Publication Records																
15																.97
16																

NOTE: Since in computing correlation coefficients program data must be available for both of the measures being correlated, the actual number of programs on which each coefficient is based varies.

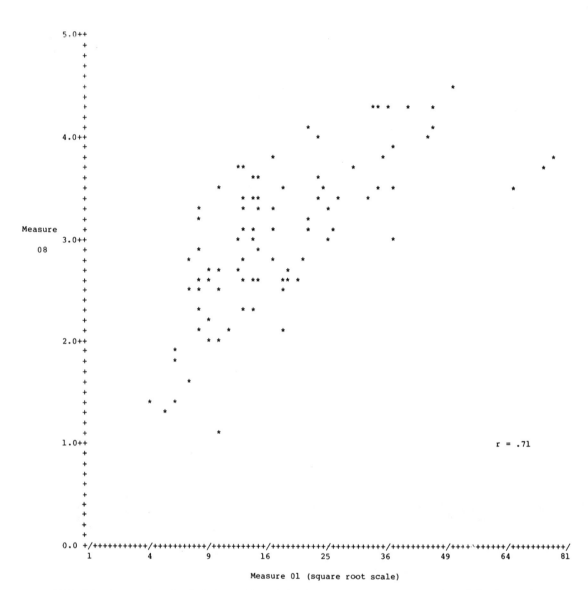

FIGURE 7.1 Mean rating of scholarly quality of faculty (measure 08) versus number of faculty members (measure 01)--94 programs in physiology.

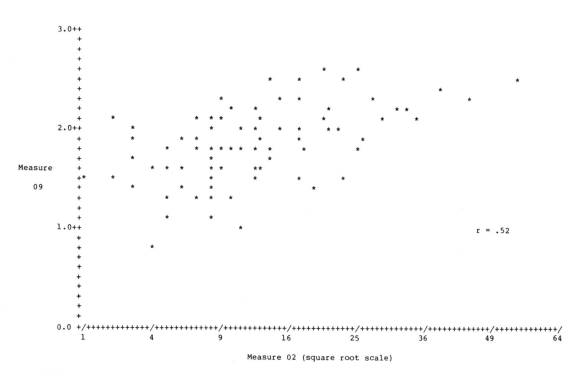

FIGURE 7.2 Mean rating of program effectiveness in educating research scholars/scientists (measure 09) versus number of graduates in last five years (measure 02)--87 programs in physiology.

TABLE 7.4 Characteristics of Survey Participants in Physiology

	Respondents	
	N	%
Field of Specialization		
Biophysics	11	8
Physiology, Animal/Human	113	77
Other/Unknown	22	15
Faculty Rank		
Professor	73	50
Associate Professor	45	31
Assistant Professor	28	19
Year of Highest Degree		
Pre-1950	8	6
1950-59	38	26
1960-69	57	39
Post-1969	42	29
Unknown	1	1
Evaluator Selection		
Nominated by Institution	120	82
Other	26	18
Survey Form		
With Faculty Names	136	93
Without Names	10	7
Total Evaluators	146	100

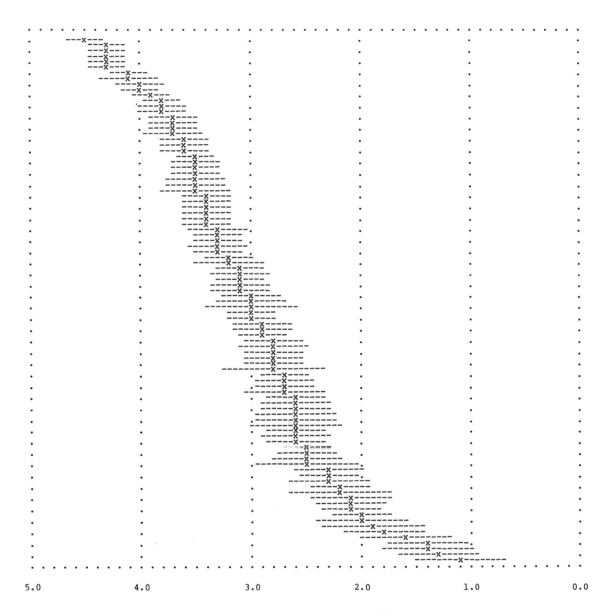

Mean Survey Rating (measure 08)

FIGURE 7.3 Mean rating of scholarly quality of faculty in 94 programs in physiology.

NOTE: Programs are listed in sequence of mean rating, with the highest-rated program appearing at the top of the page. The broken lines (---) indicate a confidence interval of ±1.5 standard errors around the reported mean (x) of each program.

VIII
Zoology Programs

In this chapter 70 research-doctorate programs in zoology are assessed. These programs, according to the information supplied by their
universities, have accounted for 1,753 doctoral degrees awarded during
the FY1976-80 period.[1] On the average, 33 full-time and part-time
students intending to earn doctorates were enrolled in a program in
December 1980, with an average faculty size of 21 members.[2] Most of
the 70 programs, listed in Table 8.1, are located in departments of
zoology. Approximately one-third are found in departments of biology
or biological sciences. Four programs were initiated since 1970, and
only one institution--Utah State University--had two zoology programs
included in the assessment. In addition to the 69 institutions represented in this discipline, another 8 were initially identified as meeting the criteria[3] for inclusion in the assessment:

> CUNY--Graduate School
> University of California--Santa Barbara
> Florida State University--Tallahassee
> Illinois Institute of Technology
> University of Illinois--Urbana-Champaign
> University of Kansas
> University of Michigan--Ann Arbor
> Tulane University

Zoology programs at these eight institutions have not been included in

---

[1]Data from the NRC's Survey of Earned Doctorates indicate that 1,219
research doctorates in zoology were awarded by U.S. universities between FY1976 and FY1980. Since the NRC figure is based on field of
degree and not department, it may exclude some doctorates included in
the numbers reported by the institutional coordinators.
[2]See the reported means for measures 03 and 01 in Table 8.2.
[3]As mentioned in Chapter I, the primary criterion for inclusion was
that a university had awarded 8 or more doctorates in zoology during
the FY1976-78 period.

the evaluations in this discipline, since in each case the study coordinator either indicated that the institution did not at that time have a research-doctorate program in zoology or failed to provide the information requested by the committee.

Before examining individual program results presented in Table 8.1, the reader is urged to refer to Chapter II, in which each of the 16 measures used in the assessment is discussed. Summary statistics describing every measure are given in Table 8.2. For 10 of the measures, data are reported for at least 66 of the 70 zoology programs. For measures 04-07, which pertain to characteristics of the program graduates, data are presented for approximately four-fifths of the programs; the other fifth had too few graduates on which to base statistics.[4] For measure 12, a composite index of the size of a university library, data are available for 49 programs; for measure 14, the total university expenditures for research in the biological sciences, data are available for 44 programs. The programs not evaluated on measures 12 and 14 are typically smaller--in terms of faculty size and graduate student enrollment--than other zoology programs. Were data on these two measures available for all 70 programs, it is likely that their reported means would be appreciably lower (and that some of the correlations of these measures with others would be higher).

Intercorrelations among the 16 measures (Pearson product-moment coefficients) are given in Table 8.3. Of particular note are the high positive correlations of reputational survey ratings (08, 09) with measures of research support (13, 14), publication records (15, 16), and number of program faculty members (02). Figure 8.1 illustrates the relation between the mean rating of the scholarly quality of faculty (measure 08) and the number of faculty members (measure 01) for each of 69 programs in zoology. Figure 8.2 plots the mean rating of program effectiveness (measure 09) against the total number of FY1976-80 program graduates (measure 02). Although in both figures there is a significant positive correlation between program size and reputational rating, it is quite apparent that some of the smaller programs received high mean ratings and that some of the larger programs received low mean ratings.

Table 8.4 describes the 123 faculty members who participated in the evaluation of zoology programs. These individuals constituted 59 percent of those asked to respond to the survey in this discipline and 8 percent of the faculty population in the 70 research-doctorate programs being evaluated.[5] A majority of the survey participants had earned their highest degree prior to 1970, and almost half held the rank of full professor.

To assist the reader in interpreting results of the survey evaluations, estimated standard errors have been computed for mean ratings

---

[4] As mentioned in Chapter II, data for measures 04-07 are not reported if they are based on the survey responses of fewer than 10 FY1975-79 program graduates.
[5] See Table 2.3 in Chapter II.

of the scholarly quality of faculty in 69 zoology programs (and are given in Table 8.1). For each program the mean rating and an associated "confidence interval" of 1.5 standard errors are illustrated in Figure 8.3 (listed in order of highest to lowest mean rating). In comparing two programs, if their confidence intervals do not overlap, one may conclude that there is a significant difference in their mean ratings at a .05 level of significance.[6] From this figure it is also apparent that one should have somewhat more confidence in the accuracy of the mean ratings of higher-rated programs than lower-rated programs. This generalization results primarily from the fact that evaluators are not as likely to be familiar with the less prestigious programs, and consequently the mean ratings of these programs are usually based on fewer survey responses.

---

[6] See pp. 31-33 for a discussion of the interpretation of mean ratings and associated confidence intervals.

TABLE 8.1 Program Measures (Raw and Standardized Values) in Zoology

Prog No.	University - Department/Academic Unit	Program Size			Characteristics of Program Graduates			
		(01)	(02)	(03)	(04)	(05)	(06)	(07)
001.	Arizona State University-Tempe	24	28	43	.29	7.7	.54	.32
	Zoology	53	51	54	48	44	42	51
002.	Arizona, University of-Tucson	19	21	NA	.24	7.3	.45	.20
	General Biology	48	47		46	48	35	43
003.	Auburn University	33	30	51	.17	6.9	.77	.24
	Zoology/Entomology	61	52	57	42	52	59	46
004.	Boston University	10	13	18	.83	7.2	.50	.25
	Biology	39	43	44	75	49	39	47
005.	California, University of-Irvine	15	15	18	.67	5.5	.92	.62
	Ecol & Evolut Biol/Devel & Cell Biology	44	44	44	67	66	71	70
006.	California, University of-Berkeley	29	105	78	.51	6.2	.72	.50
	Zoology	58	92	68	59	59	55	63
007.	California, University of-Davis	20	30	31	.19	6.8	.61	.39
	Zoology	49	52	49	43	54	47	56
008.	California, University of-Los Angeles	42	77	115	.38	6.7	.63	.40
	Biology	70	77	83	53	54	49	56
009.	Chicago, University of	11	14	15	NA	NA	NA	NA
	Biology	40	44	43				
010.	Clemson University	14	7	23	NA	NA	NA	NA
	Zoology	43	40	46				
011.	Colorado State University-Fort Collins	33	22	38	.11	8.0	.47	.16
	Zoology and Entomology	61	48	52	39	41	37	41
012.	Colorado, University of	16	43	27	.16	7.3	.50	.38
	Environmental, Population, & Organismic Bio	45	59	48	42	48	39	55
013.	Connecticut, University of-Storrs	16	15	25	.36	7.8	.50	.14
	Biological Sciences	45	44	47	52	43	39	40
014.	Cornell University-Ithaca	10	6	5	NA	NA	NA	NA
	Zoology	39	39	39				
015.	Duke University	24	47	63	.43	6.0	.71	.36
	Zoology	53	61	62	55	61	55	54
016.	Florida, University of-Gainesville	33	20	78	.18	6.0	.44	.31
	Zoology	61	47	68	43	61	34	51
017.	Georgia, University of-Athens	27	34	50	.29	7.7	.84	.61
	Zoology	56	54	57	48	44	65	70
018.	Harvard University	46	54	76	.50	6.1	.60	.40
	Biology (Organismic & Evolutionary)	74	65	67	59	60	46	56
019.	Hawaii, University of	24	21	39	.39	8.0	.72	.39
	Zoology	53	47	52	53	41	56	56
020.	Howard University	14	25	45	.31	10.1	.47	.07
	*Zoology**	43	50	55	49	20	36	35

* indicates program was initiated since 1970.

NOTE: On the first line of data for every program, raw values for each measure are reported; on the second line values are reported in standardized form, with mean = 50 and standard deviation = 10. "NA" indicates that the value for a measure is not available.

TABLE 8.1 Program Measures (Raw and Standardized Values) in Zoology

Prog No.	Survey Results (08)	(09)	(10)	(11)	University Library (12)	Research Support (13)	(14)	Published Articles (15)	(16)	Survey Ratings Standard Error (08)	(09)	(10)	(11)
001.	3.0	1.7	1.6	0.9	−0.3	.46	NA	17		.11	.08	.08	.08
	53	51	73	55	44	55		50	59				
002.	3.1	2.0	1.3	0.9	0.9	.26	7828	26		.09	.05	.11	.07
	55	57	58	57	56	45	48	57	55				
003.	1.9	1.4	1.1	0.2	NA	.00	NA	6		.16	.14	.14	.04
	39	44	45	35		32		42	40				
004.	2.6	1.5	0.9	0.7	−0.4	.50	NA	5		.14	.10	.11	.06
	48	47	35	49	44	57		41	41				
005.	3.3	2.0	1.3	1.0	NA	.60	6547	12		.13	.08	.10	.08
	57	57	56	58		62	47	47	55				
006.	4.4	2.5	1.0	1.4	2.2	.69	18977	73		.08	.06	.06	.07
	70	69	42	71	69	67	66	93	87				
007.	3.4	2.0	1.2	1.1	0.6	.50	18053	54		.09	.05	.09	.07
	58	58	54	62	53	57	64	79	84				
008.	4.1	2.4	1.2	1.3	2.0	.64	15581	30		.08	.07	.08	.07
	67	67	51	69	66	64	60	60	68				
009.	3.7	2.2	0.9	1.0	0.9	.55	17589	9		.13	.08	.09	.08
	62	62	35	59	56	59	64	44	45				
010.	1.9	1.2	1.4	0.5	NA	.21	1275	6		.16	.11	.12	.07
	40	39	60	45		43	38	42	40				
011.	2.8	1.8	1.5	0.8	−1.1	.27	8863	21		.14	.06	.11	.08
	50	52	66	53	37	46	50	53	59				
012.	3.0	1.9	1.5	0.9	−0.9	.75	11967	20		.13	.07	.09	.08
	54	55	68	55	39	70	55	53	58				
013.	2.8	1.6	1.2	0.7	−0.5	.38	15199	9		.12	.09	.11	.07
	50	48	51	49	43	51	60	44	46				
014.	3.6	2.1	1.0	0.9	1.6	.00	14597	39		.14	.09	.11	.08
	61	59	42	56	63	32	59	67	65				
015.	4.1	2.4	1.3	1.3	0.3	.67	11320	29		.09	.06	.08	.07
	67	67	56	67	51	65	54	60	55				
016.	3.2	1.8	1.4	1.0	0.8	.46	3486	27		.10	.07	.08	.07
	56	53	64	60	55	55	42	58	51				
017.	3.5	2.0	1.3	1.1	0.4	.44	10714	24		.10	.06	.09	.07
	59	58	56	63	52	54	53	56	56				
018.	4.7	2.7	1.1	1.5	3.0	.74	34979	18		.06	.05	.07	.07
	74	72	44	73	76	69	90	51	51				
019.	2.6	1.6	1.1	0.6	−0.1	.29	4440	10		.12	.09	.12	.08
	48	49	47	47	46	47	43	45	52				
020.	1.6	1.0	NA	0.2	−0.4	.14	NA	0		.16	.17	NA	.04
	36	35		35	44	40		37	38				

NOTE: On the first line of data for every program, raw values for each measure are reported; on the second line values are reported in standardized form, with mean = 50 and standard deviation = 10. "NA" indicates that the value for a measure is not available. Since the scale used to compute measure 16 is entirely arbitrary, only values in standardized form are reported for this measure.

TABLE 8.1 Program Measures (Raw and Standardized Values) in Zoology

Prog No.	University - Department/Academic Unit	Program Size			Characteristics of Program Graduates			
		(01)	(02)	(03)	(04)	(05)	(06)	(07)
021.	Idaho State University-Pocatello	12	10	12	.08	7.8	.58	.00
	Biology	*41*	*42*	*42*	*38*	*43*	*45*	*30*
022.	Indiana University-Bloomington	12	48	35	.35	7.0	.74	.54
	Biology	*41*	*62*	*51*	*51*	*51*	*57*	*66*
023.	Iowa State University-Ames	20	25	19	.15	6.3	.73	.39
	Zoology	*49*	*50*	*45*	*41*	*58*	*56*	*55*
024.	Iowa, University of-Iowa City	24	15	50	.83	6.3	.46	.27
	Zoology	*53*	*44*	*57*	*75*	*58*	*35*	*48*
025.	Kentucky, University of	21	7	11	NA	NA	NA	NA
	Biological Sciences	*50*	*40*	*41*				
026.	Louisiana State University-Baton Rouge	12	22	17	.13	6.9	.59	.27
	Zoology and Physiology	*41*	*48*	*44*	*40*	*52*	*46*	*48*
027.	Louisville, University of	17	15	36	.18	7.0	.46	.09
	Biology	*46*	*44*	*51*	*43*	*51*	*35*	*36*
028.	Maine, University of-Orono	20	17	16	.47	6.6	.36	.14
	Zoology	*49*	*45*	*43*	*57*	*55*	*28*	*40*
029.	Maryland, University of-College Park	35	43	41	.24	6.7	.62	.19
	Zoology	*63*	*59*	*53*	*46*	*54*	*48*	*43*
030.	Massachusetts, University of-Amherst	18	39	32	.28	7.4	.97	.66
	Zoology	*47*	*57*	*50*	*48*	*47*	*75*	*73*
031.	Miami University-Ohio	24	13	12	NA	NA	NA	NA
	*Zoology**	*53*	*43*	*42*				
032.	Michigan State University-East Lansing	28	43	58	.38	6.2	.55	.27
	Zoology	*57*	*59*	*60*	*52*	*59*	*43*	*48*
033.	Minnesota, University of	14	23	15	.32	8.2	.63	.08
	Ecol & Behavioral Biol/Genetics & Cell Biol	*43*	*49*	*43*	*50*	*39*	*48*	*36*
034.	Mississippi State University-Starkville	15	12	8	.23	6.9	.54	.23
	Biological Sciences	*44*	*43*	*40*	*45*	*52*	*42*	*45*
035.	Nebraska, University of-Lincoln	15	20	21	.18	7.3	.68	.29
	Life Sciences	*44*	*47*	*45*	*43*	*49*	*53*	*49*
036.	New Hampshire, University of	17	29	13	.12	7.2	.62	.12
	Zoology	*46*	*52*	*42*	*40*	*49*	*48*	*38*
037.	North Carolina State University-Raleigh	15	27	29	.30	8.3	.70	.15
	Zoology	*44*	*51*	*49*	*49*	*38*	*54*	*40*
038.	North Carolina, University of-Chapel Hill	23	29	38	.31	6.3	.85	.46
	Zoology	*52*	*52*	*52*	*49*	*59*	*65*	*60*
039.	North Dakota, University of-Grand Forks	12	5	10	NA	NA	NA	NA
	Biology	*41*	*39*	*41*				
040.	Notre Dame, University of	17	18	21	.42	7.2	.78	.39
	Biology	*46*	*46*	*45*	*55*	*49*	*60*	*56*

* indicates program was initiated since 1970.

NOTE: On the first line of data for every program, raw values for each measure are reported; on the second line values are reported in standardized form, with mean = 50 and standard deviation = 10. "NA" indicates that the value for a measure is not available.

TABLE 8.1 Program Measures (Raw and Standardized Values) in Zoology

Prog No.	Survey Results (08)	(09)	(10)	(11)	University Library (12)	Research Support (13)	(14)	Published Articles (15)	(16)	Survey Ratings Standard Error (08)	(09)	(10)	(11)
021.	1.7	1.0	1.2	0.4	NA	.17	NA	5		.16	.12	.13	.06
	37	35	49	41		41		41	39				
022.	3.2	2.0	0.7	0.8	0.9	.50	NA	10		.11	.07	.10	.07
	56	57	26	53	56	57		45	46				
023.	2.7	1.8	1.4	0.6	-0.5	.35	5287	14		.12	.08	.11	.07
	50	53	61	48	43	50	45	48	50				
024.	3.3	1.9	1.4	0.9	0.3	.71	7088	4		.09	.07	.08	.07
	57	55	63	57	50	67	47	40	44				
025.	2.2	1.3	1.1	0.4	-0.1	.48	484	9		.17	.11	.15	.06
	44	41	45	40	47	56	37	44	43				
026.	1.6	1.2	1.1	0.4	-0.3	.25	5116	24		.16	.14	.14	.06
	36	39	47	41	44	45	44	56	53				
027.	1.6	1.0	0.8	0.2	NA	.12	NA	0		.18	.15	.13	.05
	36	35	33	37		38		37	38				
028.	2.3	1.4	1.4	0.5	NA	.40	NA	14		.13	.13	.12	.07
	45	43	60	44		52		48	48				
029.	3.2	1.9	1.3	1.0	0.2	.26	1623	22		.09	.07	.10	.07
	56	54	56	58	49	45	39	54	55				
030.	2.8	1.8	1.0	0.8	-0.7	.44	3022	20		.11	.08	.11	.07
	51	52	43	53	41	54	41	53	55				
031.	2.2	1.4	1.0	0.5	-0.8	.33	NA	10		.13	.11	.08	.06
	43	44	44	45	40	49		45	42				
032.	3.0	1.9	1.2	0.8	0.3	.43	10357	30		.13	.08	.11	.08
	53	54	50	52	51	54	52	60	57				
033.	2.9	1.9	1.0	0.7	1.2	.29	13696	28		.14	.09	.13	.08
	51	55	42	49	59	47	58	59	57				
034.	1.6	0.9	0.9	0.2	NA	.13	2839	16		.18	.16	.11	.05
	35	32	39	37		39	41	50	46				
035.	2.4	1.4	1.2	0.5	-0.5	.40	2965	6		.14	.11	.10	.07
	45	44	50	45	43	52	41	42	40				
036.	2.2	1.5	1.3	0.4	NA	.24	NA	6		.13	.12	.09	.07
	43	45	58	42		44		42	43				
037.	2.5	1.6	1.2	0.5	NA	.20	6741	16		.14	.11	.10	.07
	47	48	49	44		42	47	50	47				
038.	3.4	2.0	1.3	1.0	1.0	.57	9849	15		.09	.05	.10	.07
	58	57	58	59	57	60	52	49	44				
039.	1.4	0.9	1.1	0.3	NA	.17	NA	5		.18	.14	.09	.06
	33	32	48	38		41		41	40				
040.	2.7	1.7	1.0	0.6	-1.3	.47	NA	7		.14	.09	.09	.07
	49	50	42	48	34	56		43	48				

NOTE: On the first line of data for every program, raw values for each measure are reported; on the second line values are reported in standardized form, with mean = 50 and standard deviation = 10. "NA" indicates that the value for a measure is not available. Since the scale used to compute measure 16 is entirely arbitrary, only values in standardized form are reported for this measure.

TABLE 8.1 Program Measures (Raw and Standardized Values) in Zoology

Prog No.	University - Department/Academic Unit	Program Size			Characteristics of Program Graduates			
		(01)	(02)	(03)	(04)	(05)	(06)	(07)
041.	Ohio State University-Columbus *Zoology*	41 *69*	42 *59*	63 *62*	.16 *42*	6.0 *61*	.65 *50*	.16 *41*
042.	Ohio University-Athens *Zoology/Microbiology*	19 *48*	10 *42*	30 *49*	NA	NA	NA	NA
043.	Oklahoma State University-Stillwater *Zoology*	15 *44*	6 *39*	17 *44*	NA	NA	NA	NA
044.	Oklahoma, University of-Norman *Zoology*	25 *54*	22 *48*	7 *40*	.23 *45*	8.0 *41*	.64 *49*	.18 *42*
045.	Oregon State University-Corvallis *Zoology*	16 *45*	24 *49*	13 *42*	.22 *45*	8.9 *32*	.48 *37*	.17 *42*
046.	Oregon, University of-Eugene *Biology*	17 *46*	3 *38*	5 *39*	NA	NA	NA	NA
047.	Pennsylvania State University *Zoology*	16 *45*	4 *38*	6 *39*	NA	NA	NA	NA
048.	Rhode Island, University of *Zoology*	20 *49*	15 *44*	32 *50*	.40 *54*	7.5 *46*	.70 *54*	.20 *43*
049.	Rutgers, The State University-New Brunswick *Zoology*	34 *62*	36 *55*	90 *73*	.35 *51*	7.4 *47*	.56 *44*	.33 *52*
050.	Rutgers, The State University-Newark *Zoology and Physiology**	19 *48*	27 *51*	46 *55*	.12 *40*	6.4 *58*	.68 *53*	.24 *46*
051.	SUNY-College of Environ Science & Forestry *Environmental and Forest Biology*	19 *48*	25 *50*	22 *46*	.29 *48*	6.9 *52*	.67 *52*	.25 *47*
052.	South Florida, University of-Tampa *Biology*	11 *40*	16 *45*	21 *45*	.23 *45*	7.8 *44*	.77 *59*	.39 *55*
053.	Southern Illinois University-Carbondale *Zoology*	24 *53*	16 *45*	19 *45*	.19 *43*	9.7 *24*	.63 *48*	.19 *43*
054.	Stanford University *Biological Sciences*	9 *38*	16 *45*	15 *43*	.90 *79*	6.5 *56*	.70 *54*	.60 *69*
055.	Syracuse University *Biology**	5 *34*	8 *40*	11 *41*	NA	NA	NA	NA
056.	Tennessee, University of-Knoxville *Zoology*	30 *58*	27 *51*	28 *48*	.35 *51*	6.7 *54*	.73 *56*	.46 *60*
057.	Texas A & M University *Biology*	12 *41*	10 *42*	26 *47*	.00 *34*	6.3 *58*	.73 *56*	.18 *42*
058.	Texas Tech University-Lubbock *Biological Sciences*	16 *45*	14 *44*	12 *42*	.08 *38*	5.9 *62*	.85 *65*	.31 *50*
059.	Texas, University of-Austin *Zoology*	45 *73*	70 *74*	80 *69*	.74 *71*	6.2 *59*	.63 *49*	.47 *61*
060.	Utah State University-Logan *Biology*	41 *69*	30 *52*	51 *57*	.33 *50*	6.8 *54*	.56 *43*	.22 *45*

* indicates program was initiated since 1970.

NOTE: On the first line of data for every program, raw values for each measure are reported; on the second line values are reported in standardized form, with mean = 50 and standard deviation = 10. "NA" indicates that the value for a measure is not available.

TABLE 8.1 Program Measures (Raw and Standardized Values) in Zoology

Prog No.	Survey Results (08)	(09)	(10)	(11)	University Library (12)	Research Support (13)	(14)	Published Articles (15)	(16)	Survey Ratings Standard Error (08)	(09)	(10)	(11)
041.	3.1	1.9	1.3	1.0	0.9	.27	8330	17		.11	.06	.07	.07
	55	54	58	57	56	46	49	50	51				
042.	1.7	1.1	0.9	0.4	NA	.26	NA	9		.16	.12	.17	.06
	37	37	39	42		45		44	42				
043.	1.9	1.3	1.1	0.4	-1.9	.20	3127	6		.18	.12	.10	.07
	39	40	44	42	29	42	41	42	40				
044.	2.6	1.7	1.2	0.6	-0.6	.32	NA	24		.13	.07	.11	.07
	48	52	53	48	42	48		56	54				
045.	3.0	1.8	1.4	0.9	NA	.63	7108	24		.09	.07	.11	.08
	54	52	61	56		63	47	56	56				
046.	3.1	1.8	1.0	0.9	-0.9	.53	NA	11		.10	.08	.09	.07
	55	54	42	55	38	59		46	47				
047.	2.5	1.5	1.0	0.6	0.7	.38	8024	13		.13	.11	.07	.07
	46	47	42	46	54	51	49	47	52				
048.	2.2	1.4	1.0	0.5	NA	.15	NA	14		.13	.08	.08	.06
	43	44	44	45		40		48	49				
049.	2.7	1.8	1.2	0.6	0.8	.15	7505	30		.11	.08	.11	.07
	50	54	50	46	55	40	48	60	55				
050.	2.2	1.6	NA	0.2	NA	.11	7505	3		.12	.12	NA	.05
	43	47		37		38	48	40	44				
051.	2.7	1.8	1.1	0.2	NA	.21	NA	5		.19	.11	.12	.05
	50	52	48	37		43		41	40				
052.	2.0	1.3	1.2	0.5	NA	.09	NA	8		.16	.12	.13	.07
	41	42	52	44		37		43	42				
053.	2.1	1.3	1.1	0.5	-0.2	.13	NA	3		.15	.15	.14	.07
	42	42	49	43	46	39		40	39				
054.	4.0	2.2	1.0	1.2	2.0	NA	12514	11		.09	.07	.08	.07
	66	63	41	65	67		56	46	46				
055.	2.7	1.6	0.9	0.7	-0.3	NA	NA	8		.17	.10	.07	.08
	50	47	35	50	44			43	44				
056.	2.7	1.7	1.3	0.6	-0.4	.23	NA	15		.12	.10	.10	.07
	49	50	58	49	43	44		49	49				
057.	1.8	1.2	1.0	0.4	-0.5	.17	3199	22		.18	.13	.17	.06
	38	40	39	40	43	41	41	54	49				
058.	2.4	1.4	1.4	0.4	NA	.19	NA	20		.15	.14	.11	.08
	46	44	63	43		42		53	50				
059.	4.0	2.3	1.2	1.2	1.6	.64	5757	19		.09	.06	.07	.07
	65	64	53	65	63	64	45	52	57				
060.	2.6	1.7	1.4	0.4	NA	.10	NA	16		.15	.13	.12	.06
	48	50	60	42		37		50	47				

NOTE: On the first line of data for every program, raw values for each measure are reported; on the second line values are reported in standardized form, with mean = 50 and standard deviation = 10. "NA" indicates that the value for a measure is not available. Since the scale used to compute measure 16 is entirely arbitrary, only values in standardized form are reported for this measure.

TABLE 8.1 Program Measures (Raw and Standardized Values) in Zoology

Prog No.	University - Department/Academic Unit	Program Size			Characteristics of Program Graduates			
		(01)	(02)	(03)	(04)	(05)	(06)	(07)
061.	Utah State University-Logan	11	17	24	.15	8.3	.77	.31
	Range Science	40	45	47	41	39	59	50
062.	Vanderbilt University	6	4	5	NA	NA	NA	NA
	General Biology	35	38	39				
063.	Virginia Polytechnic Institute & State Univ	26	27	22	.27	7.5	.73	.18
	Biology	55	51	46	47	46	56	42
064.	Washington State University-Pullman	23	15	15	.40	6.5	NA	NA
	Zoology	52	44	43	54	56		
065.	Washington, University of-Seattle	32	36	12	.61	7.1	.75	.47
	Zoology	60	55	42	64	50	58	61
066.	Wayne State University	10	NA	NA	.19	9.8	.50	.19
	Zoology	39			43	23	39	43
067.	Wisconsin, University of-Madison	27	60	70	.36	7.2	.79	.45
	Zoology	56	68	65	52	49	61	59
068.	Wisconsin, University of-Milwaukee	14	NA	NA	NA	NA	NA	NA
	Zoology	43						
069.	Wyoming, University of	18	21	13	.23	5.0	.62	.15
	Zoology	47	47	42	45	71	48	40
070.	Yale University	58	65	107	.80	5.9	.84	.56
	Biology/Human Genetics/Geology-Paleontology	86	71	80	74	62	64	67

* indicates program was initiated since 1970.

NOTE: On the first line of data for every program, raw values for each measure are reported; on the second line values are reported in standardized form, with mean = 50 and standard deviation = 10. "NA" indicates that the value for a measure is not available.

TABLE 8.1 Program Measures (Raw and Standardized Values) in Zoology

Prog No.	Survey Results				University Library	Research Support		Published Articles		Survey Ratings Standard Error			
	(08)	(09)	(10)	(11)	(12)	(13)	(14)	(15)	(16)	(08)	(09)	(10)	(11)
061.	NA	NA	NA	0.1	NA	.09	NA	16		NA	NA	NA	.04
				34		*37*		*50*	*47*				
062.	1.4	0.9	NA	0.2	−0.7	NA	5204	0		.24	.19	NA	.05
	33	*32*		*37*	*40*		*44*	*37*	*38*				
063.	2.8	1.8	1.5	0.7	−0.0	.31	3108	13		.14	.10	.09	.07
	51	*53*	*65*	*51*	*47*	*48*	*41*	*47*	*44*				
064.	2.8	1.8	1.3	0.7	−0.3	.48	998	14		.12	.10	.10	.07
	51	*52*	*55*	*49*	*45*	*56*	*38*	*48*	*46*				
065.	4.3	2.6	1.5	1.5	1.5	.72	14164	60		.08	.06	.07	.07
	69	*70*	*69*	*73*	*61*	*68*	*58*	*83*	*83*				
066.	1.5	0.9	0.8	0.3	−0.4	.50	6372	8		.18	.16	.18	.06
	35	*32*	*29*	*40*	*44*	*57*	*46*	*43*	*46*				
067.	4.0	2.3	1.0	1.2	1.6	.44	19738	26		.09	.07	.06	.07
	66	*65*	*44*	*65*	*62*	*54*	*67*	*57*	*55*				
068.	2.0	1.1	1.1	0.4	NA	.14	NA	NA		.20	.14	.12	.07
	40	*38*	*44*	*43*		*40*			*NA*				
069.	1.9	1.3	1.4	0.4	NA	.17	NA	8		.13	.11	.12	.06
	40	*42*	*60*	*40*		*41*		*43*	*43*				
070.	4.2	2.5	1.2	1.3	2.1	.78	4337	19		.09	.06	.08	.07
	69	*69*	*49*	*66*	*68*	*71*	*43*	*52*	*56*				

NOTE: On the first line of data for every program, raw values for each measure are reported; on the second line values are reported in standardized form, with mean = 50 and standard deviation = 10. "NA" indicates that the value for a measure is not available. Since the scale used to compute measure 16 is entirely arbitrary, only values in standardized form are reported for this measure.

TABLE 8.2 Summary Statistics Describing Each Program Measure--Zoology

Measure	Number of Programs Evaluated	Mean	Standard Deviation	DECILES								
				1	2	3	4	5	6	7	8	9
Program Size												
01 Raw Value	70	21	10	11	12	15	16	19	20	24	28	34
Std Value	70	50	10	40	41	44	45	48	49	53	57	62
02 Raw Value	68	26	19	7	13	15	17	21	25	29	36	47
Std Value	68	50	10	40	43	44	45	47	50	52	55	61
03 Raw Value	67	33	25	9	12	15	19	24	30	38	50	72
Std Value	67	50	10	41	42	43	45	47	49	52	57	66
Program Graduates												
04 Raw Value	57	.33	.20	.12	.16	.19	.23	.29	.32	.36	.41	.63
Std Value	57	50	10	40	42	43	45	48	50	52	54	65
05 Raw Value	57	7.1	1.0	8.3	7.8	7.5	7.2	7.0	6.8	6.5	6.3	6.0
Std Value	57	50	10	38	43	46	49	51	53	56	58	61
06 Raw Value	56	.65	.13	.46	.50	.56	.62	.63	.69	.72	.75	.81
Std Value	56	50	10	35	38	43	48	48	53	55	58	62
07 Raw Value	56	.30	.15	.13	.17	.19	.23	.27	.32	.39	.44	.52
Std Value	56	50	10	39	41	43	45	48	51	56	59	65
Survey Results												
08 Raw Value	69	2.7	.8	1.6	1.9	2.2	2.5	2.7	2.8	3.1	3.3	4.0
Std Value	69	50	10	36	40	43	47	50	51	55	57	66
09 Raw Value	69	1.7	.4	1.0	1.3	1.4	1.6	1.7	1.8	1.9	2.0	2.3
Std Value	69	50	10	35	42	44	48	51	53	55	58	64
10 Raw Value	66	1.2	.2	.9	1.0	1.0	1.1	1.2	1.2	1.3	1.4	1.4
Std Value	66	50	10	37	42	42	47	52	52	57	62	62
11 Raw Value	70	.7	.4	.2	.4	.4	.5	.6	.7	.9	1.0	1.2
Std Value	70	50	10	36	42	42	45	47	50	56	59	65
University Library												
12 Raw Value	49	.3	1.0	-.9	-.6	-.4	-.3	-.1	.4	.8	1.0	1.7
Std Value	49	50	10	39	41	43	44	46	51	55	57	64
Research Support												
13 Raw Value	67	.36	.20	.11	.16	.20	.26	.31	.41	.47	.52	.65
Std Value	67	50	10	38	40	42	45	48	53	56	58	65
14 Raw Value	44	8806	6503	2109	3123	4575	6126	7108	8146	10643	13790	16786
Std Value	44	50	10	40	41	44	46	47	49	53	58	62
Publication Records												
15 Raw Value	69	16	13	5	6	9	11	14	16	20	24	29
Std Value	69	50	10	41	42	44	46	48	50	53	56	60
16 Std Value	69	50	10	40	42	44	46	48	50	54	56	58

NOTE: Standardized values reported in the preceding table have been computed from exact values of the mean and standard deviation and not the rounded values reported here. Since the scale used to compute measure 16 is entirely arbitrary, only data in standardized form are reported for this measure.

TABLE 8.3   Intercorrelations Among Program Measures on 70 Programs in Zoology

Measure

	01	02	03	04	05	06	07	08	09	10	11	12	13	14	15	16
Program Size																
01		.66	.78	.26	.34	.05	.23	.53	.56	.35	.50	.48	.34	.20	.32	.36
02			.78	.27	.25	.19	.44	.66	.68	.09	.62	.60	.50	.42	.56	.59
03				.27	.26	.00	.31	.52	.53	.10	.50	.56	.34	.28	.32	.34
Program Graduates																
04					.26	.07	.48	.58	.53	-.11	.53	.49	.61	.21	.08	.16
05						.24	.36	.39	.40	.19	.34	.43	.26	.08	.20	.18
06							.64	.25	.30	-.12	.17	.16	.05	-.04	.10	.11
07								.63	.63	-.05	.60	.40	.56	.19	.32	.41
Survey Results																
08									.98	.19	.95	.78	.72	.65	.59	.64
09										.21	.91	.75	.66	.63	.61	.66
10											.22	-.08	.14	-.16	.20	.24
11												.74	.77	.62	.62	.68
University Library																
12													.39	.63	.50	.47
Research Support																
13														.37	.35	.46
14															.43	.46
Publication Records																
15																.94
16																

NOTE: Since in computing correlation coefficients program data must be available for both of the measures being correlated, the actual number of programs on which each coefficient is based varies.

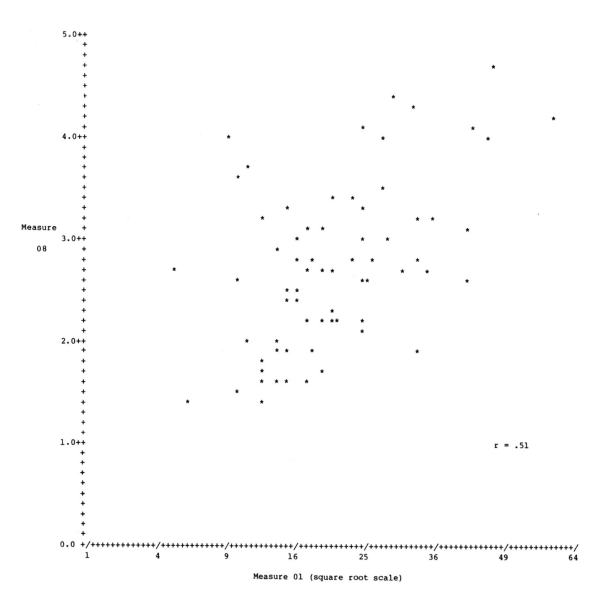

Measure 01 (square root scale)

FIGURE 8.1 Mean rating of scholarly quality of faculty (measure 08) versus number of faculty members
(measure 01)--69 programs in zoology.

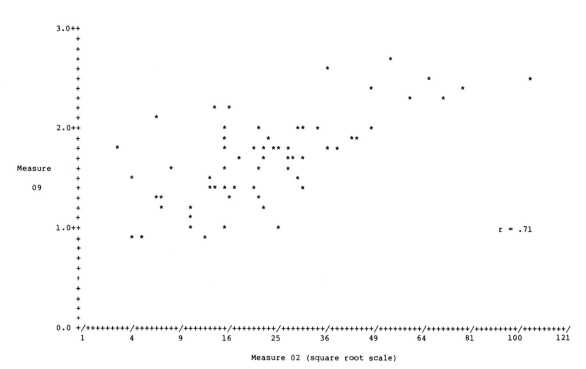

FIGURE 8.2 Mean rating of program effectiveness in educating research scholars/scientists (measure 09) versus number of graduates in last five years (measure 02)--67 programs in zoology.

TABLE 8.4   Characteristics of Survey Participants in Zoology

	Respondents	
	N	%
Field of Specialization		
Cell Biology	17	14
Ecology	35	29
Physiology, Animal/Human	14	11
Zoology	33	27
Other/Unknown	24	20
Faculty Rank		
Professor	55	45
Associate Professor	45	37
Assistant Professor	23	19
Year of Highest Degree		
Pre-1950	7	6
1950-59	16	13
1960-69	50	41
Post-1969	49	40
Unknown	1	1
Evaluator Selection		
Nominated by Institution	105	85
Other	18	15
Survey Form		
With Faculty Names	110	89
Without Names	13	11
Total Evaluators	123	100

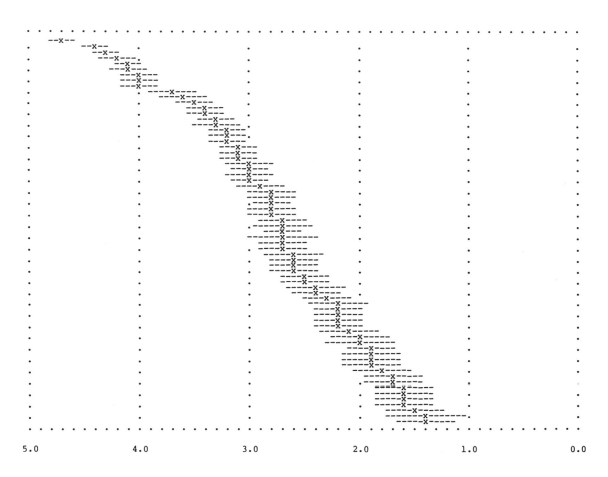

5.0   4.0   3.0   2.0   1.0   0.0

Mean Survey Rating (measure 08)

FIGURE 8.3 Mean rating of scholarly quality of faculty in 69 programs in zoology.

NOTE: Programs are listed in sequence of mean rating, with the highest-rated program appearing at the
       top of the page. The broken lines (---) indicate a confidence interval of +1.5 standard errors
       around the reported mean (x) of each program.

IX
Summary and Discussion

In the six preceding chapters results are presented of the assessment of 616 research-doctorate programs in biochemistry, botany, cellular/molecular biology, microbiology, physiology, and zoology. Included in each chapter are summary data describing the means and intercorrelations of the program measures in a particular discipline. In this chapter a comparison is made of the summary data reported in the six disciplines. Also presented here are an analysis of the reliability (consistency) of the reputational survey ratings and an examination of some factors that might possibly have influenced the survey results. This chapter concludes with suggestions for improving studies of this kind--with particular attention given to the types of measures one would like to have available for an assessment of research-doctorate programs.

This chapter necessarily involves a detailed discussion of various statistics (means, standard deviations, correlation coefficients) describing the measures. Throughout, the reader should bear in mind that all these statistics and measures are necessarily imperfect attempts to describe the real quality of research-doctorate programs. Quality and some differences in quality are real, but these differences cannot be subsumed completely under any one quantitative measure. For example, no single numerical ranking--by measure 08 or by any weighted average of measures--can rank the quality of different programs with precision.

However, the evidence for reliability indicates considerable stability in the assessment of quality. For instance, a program that comes out in the first decile of a ranking is quite unlikely to "really" belong in the third decile, or vice versa. If numerical ranks of programs were replaced by groupings (distinguished, strong, etc.), these groupings again would not fully capture actual differences in quality since there would likely be substantial ambiguity about the borderline between adjacent groups. Furthermore, any attempt at linear ordering (best, next best, . . .) may also be inaccurate. Programs of roughly comparable quality may be better in different ways, so that there simply is no one best program--as will also be indicated in some of the numerical analyses. However, these difficulties of formulating ranks should not hide the underlying reality of differences in quality or the importance of high quality for effective doctoral education.

SUMMARY OF THE RESULTS

Displayed in Table 9.1 are the numbers of programs evaluated (bottom line) and the mean values for each measure in the six biological science disciplines.[1] As can be seen, the mean values reported for individual measures vary considerably among disciplines. The pattern of means on each measure is summarized below, but the reader interested in a detailed comparison of the distribution of a measure should refer to the second table in each of the preceding chapters.[2]

<u>Program Size (Measures 01-03)</u>. Based on the information provided to the committee by the study coordinator at each university, cellular/ molecular biology programs had, on the average, the largest number of faculty members (26 in December 1980), followed by zoology (21). Zoology programs graduated the most students (26 Ph.D. recipients in the FY1975-79 period), and cellular/molecular programs had the largest enrollment (34 doctoral students in December 1980). In contrast, physiology programs were reported to have an average of 19 faculty members, 14 graduates, and 16 doctoral students.

<u>Program Graduates (Measures 04-07)</u>. The mean fraction of FY1975-79 doctoral recipients who as graduate students had received some national fellowship or training grant support (measure 04) ranges from .21 for graduates of botany programs to .59 for graduates in cellular/molecular biology. The relatively high fraction of support in cellular/molecular biology, biochemistry, microbiology, and physiology may be explained by the availability of National Institutes of Health (NIH) training grant support for graduate students in these disciplines. With respect to the median number of years from first enrollment in a graduate program to receipt of the doctorate (measure 05), graduates in biochemistry, cellular/molecular biology, microbiology, and physiology typically earned their degrees approximately a year sooner than graduates in zoology. In terms of employment status at graduation (measure 06), an average of 80 percent or more of the Ph.D. recipients in these same four disciplines reported that they had made firm job commitments by the time they had completed requirements for their degrees, contrasted with 65 percent of the program graduates in zoology and 67 percent in botany. A mean of 56 percent (or higher) of the program graduates in biochemistry, cellular/molecular biology, and physiology reported that they had made firm commitments to take positions in Ph.D.-granting institutions (measure 07), while only 30 percent of those in zoology and 32 percent in botany had made such plans.

---

[1]Means for measure 16, publication "influence," are omitted since arbitrary scaling of this measure prevents meaningful comparisons across disciplines.
[2]The second table in each of the six earlier chapters presents the standard deviation and decile values for each measure.

TABLE 9.1 Mean Values for Each Program Measure, by Discipline

	Bio-chemistry	Botany	Cell./Molec. Biology	Micro-biology	Physi-ology	Zoology
Program Size						
01	19	19	26	16	19	21
02	20	19	23	16	14	26
03	25	20	34	20	16	33
Program Graduates						
04	.47	.21	.59	.48	.53	.33
05	6.0	6.5	6.1	6.1	6.2	7.1
06	.81	.67	.80	.80	.80	.65
07	.56	.32	.56	.48	.57	.30
Survey Results						
08	2.6	3.0	2.9	2.8	3.0	2.7
09	1.7	1.8	1.9	1.8	1.9	1.7
10	1.2	1.2	1.2	1.2	1.2	1.2
11	.7	.7	.7	.6	.6	.7
University Library						
12	.2	.3	.3	.3	.3	.3
Research Support						
13	.63	.28	.64	.45	.52	.36
14	8419	8406	10243	8449	8687	8806
Publication Records						
15	92	60	133	46	17	16
Total Programs	139	83	89	134	101	70

Survey Results (Measures 08-11). Differences in the mean ratings derived from the reputational survey are small. In all six disciplines
the mean rating of scholarly quality of program faculty (measure 08)
is at or slightly below 3.0 ("good"), and programs were judged to be,
on the average, "reasonably" (2.0) to "moderately" (1.0) effective in
educating research scholars/scientists (measure 09). In the opinions
of the survey respondents, there has been "slight improvement" (an average of 1.2 in each discipline on measure 10) in the last five years
in the overall average quality of programs. The mean rating of an
evaluator's familiarity with the work of program faculty (measure 11)
falls below 1.0 ("some familiarity") in every discipline--about which
more will be said later in this chapter.

The reader should be reminded that the distribution of ratings may
vary from one discipline to another. If one examines, for example,
the top program ratings recorded for measure 08 in each discipline,
one finds noticeably higher top ratings in biochemistry (two programs
with ratings above 4.8) and cellular/molecular biology (three programs
with ratings above 4.7) than in either botany or physiology (no programs with ratings above 4.5). The study committee does not have an
explanation of this observation but wishes to emphasize that many
differences may be found in the distributions of survey ratings in the
various disciplines and that the determinants of these differences are
not known. As discussed in Chapter II, the survey ratings reflect each
program's standing relative to other programs in the same discipline
and provide no basis for making comparisons across disciplines.

University Library (Measure 12). Measure 12, based on a composite index of the size[3] of the library in the university in which a program
resides, is calculated on a scale from -2.0 to 3.0, with means ranging
from .2 in biochemistry to .3 in the other five disciplines. As mentioned earlier in this report, these data are not available for many
of the smaller universities. Were the program coverage complete for
this measure, it is likely that the reported means would be significantly lower.

Research Support (Measures 13-14). Measure 13, the proportion of program faculty who had received NIH, NSF, or ADAMHA[4] research grant
awards during the FY1978-80 period, has mean values ranging from as
high as .64 and .63 in cellular/molecular biology and biochemistry,
respectively, to .28 in botany. It should be emphasized that this
measure does not take into account research support that faculty mem-

---

[3] The index, derived by the Association of Research Libraries, reflects a number of different measures, including number of volumes,
fiscal expenditures, and other factors relevant to the size of a university library. See the description of this measure presented in Appendix D.
[4] National Institutes of Health; National Science Foundation; and Alcohol, Drug Abuse, and Mental Health Administration.

bers have received from sources other than these three federal agencies. In terms of total university expenditures for R&D in the biological sciences (measure 14), the mean values are reported to range from $8,406,000 in botany to $10,243,000 in cellular/molecular biology. In considering this measure it must be remembered that it reflects the overall university expenditures in the biological sciences and not expenditures in individual disciplines within the biological sciences.

Publication Records (Measures 15 and 16). Considerable diversity is also found in the mean number of articles associated with a research-doctorate program (measure 15). An average of 133 articles published in the 1978-79 period is reported for programs in cellular/molecular biology and 92 articles for programs in biochemistry; in physiology and zoology the mean number of articles is fewer than 20. These large differences reflect several factors, including the program size in a particular discipline (i.e., the total number of faculty and other staff members involved in research), the frequency with which scientists in that discipline publish, and the length of a typical paper in a discipline. Another important factor is the fact that journals in biochemistry and cellular/molecular biology far outnumber those in the other four biological disciplines. (As decribed in Chapter II, data on published articles were identified by field of journal—not by matching the names of program faculty with authors' names.) Mean scores are not reported on measure 16, the estimated "overall influence" of the articles attributed to a program. Since this measure is calculated from an average of journal influence weights,[5] normalized for the journals covered in a particular discipline, mean differences between disciplines are uninterpretable.

CORRELATIONS AMONG MEASURES

Relations among the program measures are of intrinsic interest and are relevant to the issue of validity of the measures as indices of the quality of a research-doctorate program. Measures that are logically related to program quality are expected to be related to each other. To the extent that they are, a stronger case might be made for the validity of each as a quality measure.

A reasonable index of the relationship between any two measures is the Pearson product-moment correlation coefficient. A table of correlation coefficients of all possible pairs of measures is presented in each of the six preceding chapters. This chapter presents selected correlations to determine the extent to which coefficients are comparable in the six disciplines. Special attention is given to the correlations involving the number of FY1975-79 program graduates (measure 02), survey rating of the scholarly quality of program faculty (measure

---

[5] See Appendix F for a description of the derivation of this measure.

08), university R&D expenditures in a particular discipline (measure 14), and the influence-weighted number of publications (measure 16). These four measures have been selected because of their relatively high correlations with several other measures. Readers interested in correlations other than those presented in Tables 9.2-9.5 may refer to the third table in each of the preceding six chapters.

Correlations with Measure 02. Table 9.2 presents the correlations of measure 02 with each of the other measures used in the assessment. As might be expected, correlations of this measure with the other two measures of program size--the number of faculty (01) and doctoral student enrollment (03)--are moderately high in all six disciplines. Of greater interest are the strong positive correlations between measure 02 and measures derived from the reputational survey ratings (08, 09, and 11). In biochemistry and zoology these coefficients are all above .60; in cellular/molecular biology, microbiology, and physiology most of the coefficients are above .40. In botany the correlations are somewhat lower. It is quite apparent that the programs that received high survey ratings and with which evaluators were more likely to be familiar were also ones that had larger numbers of graduates. Although the committee gave serious consideration to presenting an alternative set of survey measures that were adjusted for program size, a satisfactory algorithm for making such an adjustment was not found. In attempting such an adjustment on the basis of the regression of survey ratings on measures of program size, it was found that some exceptionally large programs appeared to be unfairly penalized and that some very small programs received unjustifiably high adjusted scores.

Measure 02 also has positive correlations in most disciplines with measure 12, an index of university library size, with measures 13 and 14, which pertain to the level of support for research in a program, and with measures 15 and 16, which reflect publication productivity. Of particular note are the moderately large coefficients--in disciplines other than botany and physiology--for the latter two measures. The relation of the number of program graduates and the publication records of that program is especially strong in biochemistry and zoology. The correlations of measure 02 with measures 04, 05, 06, and 07 are below .20 in all disciplines except biochemistry and zoology. From this analysis it is apparent that the number of program graduates tends to be positively correlated with all other variables except those pertaining to recent program graduates (04-07). It is also apparent that the relationship of measure 02 with the other variables tends to be strongest for programs in biochemistry and zoology.

Correlations with Measure 08. Table 9.3 shows the correlation coefficients for measure 08, the mean rating of the scholarly quality of program faculty, with each of the other variables. The correlations of measure 08 with measures of program size (01, 02, and 03) are typically greater than .40. Not surprisingly, the larger the program, the more likely its faculty is to be rated high in quality.

Correlations of measure 08 with measure 04, the fraction of students with national fellowship or traineeship awards, are .47 or

TABLE 9.2 Correlations of the Number of Program Graduates (Measure 02) with Other Measures, by Discipline

	Bio-chemistry	Botany	Cell./Molec. Biology	Micro-biology	Physi-ology	Zoology
Program Size						
01	.48	.42	.54	.61	.43	.66
03	.72	.55	.83	.80	.54	.78
Program Graduates						
04	.47	-.14	.16	.18	-.09	.27
05	.16	.04	-.11	.02	.19	.25
06	.23	-.06	.12	.07	.14	.19
07	.27	-.07	-.02	.12	.15	.44
Survey Results						
08	.63	.29	.42	.48	.46	.66
09	.67	.34	.47	.55	.51	.68
10	.14	.11	.09	.19	.19	.09
11	.63	.27	.40	.58	.32	.62
University Library						
12	.46	-.01	.19	.27	.25	.60
Research Support						
13	.35	.03	.18	.20	.04	.50
14	.46	.09	.02	.18	.30	.42
Publication Records						
15	.66	.23	.32	.44	.16	.56
16	.65	.24	.34	.29	.17	.59

TABLE 9.3   Correlations of the Survey Ratings of Scholarly Quality of Program Faculty
(Measure 08) with Other Measures, by Discipline

	Bio-chemistry	Botany	Cell./Molec. Biology	Micro-biology	Physi-ology	Zoology
Program Size						
01	.58	.56	.39	.50	.64	.53
02	.63	.29	.42	.48	.46	.66
03	.60	.51	.43	.42	.42	.52
Program Graduates						
04	.70	.31	.58	.57	.47	.58
05	.15	.26	.38	.08	-.11	.39
06	.24	.36	.33	.23	.27	.25
07	.35	.59	.41	.38	.30	.63
Survey Results						
09	.96	.97	.96	.96	.95	.98
10	.21	.29	.33	.46	.38	.19
11	.96	.83	.94	.91	.89	.95
University Library						
12	.63	.66	.47	.54	.49	.78
Research Support						
13	.62	.49	.58	.64	.57	.72
14	.69	.62	.57	.68	.51	.65
Publication Records						
15	.83	.60	.69	.72	.69	.59
16	.83	.62	.71	.75	.71	.64

greater in all disciplines except botany. For programs in the mathematical and physical sciences and in engineering, the corresponding coefficients (reported in earlier volumes) are found to be considerably lower, typically in the range of .10 to .30. In the biological sciences (especially in the biomedical fields), there is a far greater reliance on training grant and fellowship support, and fewer graduate students are supported by research assistantships or teaching assistantships. Correlations of rated faculty quality with measure 05, the shortness of time from matriculation in graduate school to award of the doctorate, are small but positive for programs in botany, cellular/ molecular biology, and zoology and close to zero for programs in the other three disciplines.

Correlations of ratings of faculty quality with measure 06, the fraction of program graduates with definite employment plans, range between .23 and .36 in the six biological disciplines. In every discipline the correlation of measure 08 is higher with measure 07, the fraction of graduates having agreed to employment at a Ph.D.-granting institution. These coefficients are approximately .60 in botany and zoology and .30 or above in the other four disciplines. Thus, those programs with the larger fractions of graduates intending to take academic positions tended to receive higher survey ratings.

The correlations of measure 08 with measure 09, the rated effectiveness of doctoral education, are uniformly very high, at or above .95 in every discipline. This finding is consistent with results from the Cartter and Roose-Andersen studies.[6] The coefficients describing the relationship between measure 08 and measure 11, the familiarity with the work of program faculty, are also very high, ranging from .83 to .96. In general, evaluators were more likely to have high regard for the quality of faculty in those programs with which they were most familiar. That the correlation coeffients are as large as observed may simply reflect the fact that "known" programs tend to be those that have earned strong reputations.

Correlations of ratings of faculty quality with measure 10, the ratings of perceived improvement in program quality, are much smaller-- ranging from .19 in zoology to .46 in microbiology. One might have expected that a program judged to have improved in quality would have been somewhat more likely to receive high ratings on measure 08 than would a program judged to have declined--thereby imposing a small positive correlation between these two variables.

Moderately high correlations are observed in most disciplines between measure 08 and university library size (measure 12), support for research (measures 13 and 14), and publication records (measures 15 and 16). With few exceptions these coefficients are .50 or greater in all disciplines. Of particular note are the strong correlations with the two publication measures--as high as .83 in biochemistry. In all disciplines the correlations with measure 16 are as high as or slightly higher than those with measure 15; the "weighted influence" of journals

---

[6] Roose and Andersen, p. 19.

in which articles are published yields an index that tends to relate more closely to faculty reputation than does an unadjusted count of the number of articles published. Although the observed differences between the coefficients for measures 15 and 16 are not large, this result is consistent with earlier findings of Anderson et al.[7]

Correlations with Measure 14. Correlations of measure 14, the reported dollars of support for R&D, with other measures are shown in Table 9.4. The reader is reminded that this measure reflects total university expenditures in the biological sciences and not expenditures in the six separate biological science disciplines. The pattern of relations is quite similar for programs in all six disciplines: moderately high correlations with reputational survey results (except measure 10), university library size, and publication measures. Measure 14 is also positively correlated with measures of program size (01-03), the fraction of recent graduates with fellowship/traineeship support (04), the fraction with definite commitments for employment in Ph.D.-granting universities (07), and the fraction of program faculty with federal research grants (13). In interpreting these relationships one must keep in mind the fact that the research expenditure data have not been adjusted for the number of faculty and other staff members involved in research in a program.

Correlations with Measure 16. Measure 16 is the number of published articles attributed to a program and adjusted for the "average influence" of the journals in which the articles appear. The correlations of this measure with all others appear in Table 9.5. Of particular interest are the high correlations with the reputational survey results (excluding measure 10). All of those coefficients exceed .60, and for biochemistry programs the coefficients are approximately .80. Moderately high correlations are also observed between measure 16 and measures 12, 13, and 14; with few exceptions these correlations are .40 or higher. It should be pointed out that the exceptionally large coefficients reported for measure 15 result from the fact that the two publication measures are logically as well as empirically interdependent.

Despite the appreciable correlations between reputational ratings of quality and program size measures, the functional relations between the two probably are complex. If there is a minimum size for a high-quality program, this size is likely to vary from discipline to discipline. Increases in size beyond the minimum may represent more high-quality faculty, or a greater proportion of inactive faculty, or a faculty with heavy teaching responsibilities. In attempting to select among these alternative interpretations, a single correlation coefficient provides insufficient guidance. Nonetheless, certain similarities across disciplines may be seen in the correlations among the measures. High correlations consistently appear among measures 08, 09, and 11 from the reputational survey, and these measures also are prom-

---

[7]Anderson, Narin, and McAllister, p. 95.

TABLE 9.4 Correlations of the University Research Expenditures in a Discipline
(Measure 14) with Other Measures, by Discipline

	Bio-chemistry	Botany	Cell./Molec. Biology	Micro-biology	Physi-ology	Zoology
Program Size						
01	.33	.31	.16	.24	.36	.20
02	.46	.09	.02	.18	.30	.42
03	.27	.17	.02	.08	.37	.28
Program Graduates						
04	.50	.20	.30	.43	.31	.21
05	.03	.12	.25	.05	-.16	.08
06	.12	.04	.18	.12	.14	-.04
07	.29	.28	.20	.27	.23	.19
Survey Results						
08	.69	.62	.57	.68	.51	.65
09	.64	.61	.47	.65	.51	.63
10	.03	-.07	-.16	.12	-.01	-.16
11	.69	.48	.58	.50	.46	.62
University Library						
12	.56	.55	.42	.48	.50	.63
Research Support						
13	.30	.36	.24	.29	.28	.37
Publication Records						
15	.71	.47	.58	.73	.43	.43
16	.71	.52	.59	.78	.48	.46

TABLE 9.5 Correlations of the Influence-Weighted Number of Publications
(Measure 16) with Other Measures, by Discipline

	Bio-chemistry	Botany	Cell./Molec. Biology	Micro-biology	Physi-ology	Zoology
Program Size						
01	.58	.55	.37	.38	.52	.36
02	.65	.24	.34	.29	.17	.59
03	.55	.32	.35	.18	.14	.34
Program Graduates						
04	.62	-.11	.42	.51	.50	.16
05	.12	.16	.29	-.03	-.12	.18
06	.22	.18	.26	.13	.29	.11
07	.34	.26	.32	.27	.33	.41
Survey Results						
08	.83	.62	.71	.75	.71	.64
09	.79	.63	.61	.68	.65	.66
10	.28	.24	.17	.27	.20	.24
11	.85	.56	.74	.62	.81	.68
University Library						
12	.66	.37	.59	.54	.37	.47
Research Support						
13	.47	.04	.40	.40	.51	.46
14	.71	.52	.59	.78	.48	.46
Publication Records						
15	.98	.96	.99	.90	.97	.94

inently related to program size (measures 01, 02, and 03), to publication productivity (measures 15 and 16), to R&D expenditures (measure 14), and to library size (measure 12). These results show that for all disciplines the reputational rating measures (08, 09, and 11) tend to be associated with program size and with other correlates of size: publication volume, R&D expenditures, and library size. Also, for most disciplines the reputational measures 08, 09, and 11 tend to be positively related to fellowship/traineeship support (measure 04), to employment prospects of program graduates (especially measure 07), and to the fraction of faculty holding research grants (measure 13).

ANALYSIS OF THE SURVEY RESPONSE

Measures 08-11, derived from the reputational survey, may be of particular interest to many readers since measures of this type have been the most widely used (and frequently criticized) indices of quality of graduate education. In designing the survey instrument for this assessment the committee made several changes in the form that had been used in the Roose-Andersen study. The modifications served two purposes: to provide the evaluators with a clearer understanding of the programs that they were asked to judge and to provide the committee with supplemental information for the analysis of the survey response. One change was to restrict to 50 the number of programs that any individual was asked to evaluate. Probably the most important change was the inclusion of lists of names and ranks of individual faculty members involved in the research-doctorate programs to be evaluated on the survey form, together with the number of doctoral degrees awarded in the previous five years. Ninety percent of the evaluators were sent forms with faculty names and numbers of degrees awarded; the remaining 10 percent were given forms without this information, so that an analysis could be made of the effect of this modification on survey results. Another change was the addition of a question concerning an evaluator's familiarity with each of the programs. In addition to providing an index of program recognition (measure 11), the inclusion of this question permits a comparison between the ratings furnished by individuals who had considerable familiarity with a particular program and the ratings by those not as familiar with the program. Each evaluator was also asked to identify his or her own institution of highest degree and current field of specialization. This information enables us to compare, for each program, the ratings furnished by alumni of that institution with the ratings by other evaluators, as well as to examine differences in the ratings supplied by evaluators in certain specialty fields.

Before examining factors that may have influenced the survey results, some mention should be made of the distributions of responses to the four survey items and the reliability (consistency) of the ratings. For example, in judging the scholarly quality of faculty (measure 08), survey respondents in each discipline rated between 5 and 8 percent of the programs as being "distinguished" and approximately 1 percent as "not sufficient for doctoral education" (see Table 9.6). In evaluating the effectiveness in educating research scholars/scientists,

TABLE 9.6 Distribution of Responses to Each Survey Item, by Discipline

Survey Measure	Total	Bio-chem.	Botany	Cell./ Molec.	Micro-biology	Physi-ology	Zoology
08 SCHOLARLY QUALITY OF PROGRAM FACULTY							
Distinguished	6.3	7.0	5.9	8.1	5.3	6.0	5.4
Strong	14.5	12.7	16.1	16.9	14.1	14.4	14.5
Good	16.9	17.0	16.7	17.8	17.0	14.7	18.5
Adequate	10.3	12.0	8.8	8.6	10.5	8.1	12.8
Marginal	3.9	5.5	2.8	3.1	3.5	2.9	4.9
Not Sufficient for Doctoral Education	1.1	1.4	1.1	1.0	1.0	.8	1.3
Don't Know Well Enough to Evaluate	47.0	44.5	48.5	44.4	48.5	53.3	42.6
TOTAL	100.0	100.0	100.0	100.0	100.0	100.0	100.0
09 EFFECTIVENESS OF PROGRAM IN EDUCATING SCIENTISTS							
Extremely Effective	7.2	7.2	7.6	8.1	6.8	6.7	6.9
Reasonably Effective	24.6	22.3	27.7	22.4	25.4	22.0	28.8
Minimally Effective	8.4	8.6	8.1	6.7	8.4	7.4	11.0
Not Effective	1.4	1.6	1.1	1.3	1.2	1.1	2.4
Don't Know Well Enough to Evaluate	58.5	60.3	55.5	61.5	58.2	62.7	51.0
TOTAL	100.0	100.0	100.0	100.0	100.0	100.0	100.0
10 CHANGE IN PROGRAM QUALITY IN LAST FIVE YEARS							
Better	9.8	8.5	10.2	11.1	9.9	8.4	11.5
Little or No Change	19.6	19.3	22.6	18.3	18.4	17.6	22.1
Poorer	3.8	3.6	3.8	3.8	3.6	3.7	4.5
Don't Know Well Enough to Evaluate	66.9	68.6	63.4	66.7	68.1	70.3	61.9
TOTAL	100.0	100.0	100.0	100.0	100.0	100.0	100.0
11 FAMILIARITY WITH WORK OF PROGRAM FACULTY							
Considerable	15.2	13.8	17.4	18.4	15.1	12.1	15.0
Some	34.3	36.3	31.5	34.0	33.5	32.6	37.5
Little or None	47.8	46.2	48.3	44.3	50.3	50.9	45.7
No Response	2.8	3.6	2.8	3.3	1.1	4.4	1.8
TOTAL	100.0	100.0	100.0	100.0	100.0	100.0	100.0

NOTE: For survey measures 08, 09, 10 the "don't know" category includes a small number of cases for which the respondents provided no response to the survey item.

they rated 7 to 8 percent of the programs as being "extremely effective" and approximately 1 to 2 percent as "not effective." Of particular interest in this table are the frequencies with which evaluators failed to provide responses to measures 08, 09, and 10. Approximately 47 percent of the total number of evaluations requested for measure 08 were not furnished because survey respondents in the biological sciences felt that they were not familiar enough with a particular program to evaluate it. The corresponding percentages of "don't know" responses for measures 09 and 10 are considerably larger--58 and 67 percent, respectively--suggesting that survey respondents found it more difficult (or were less willing) to judge program effectiveness and change than to judge the scholarly quality of program faculty. The percentages of "don't know" responses are greater in the biological disciplines than in most other science, engineering, or humanities disciplines. This finding may be attributed, in part, to the fact that many different academic units or departmental fields are represented in the assessment in each biological discipline and that survey evaluators were less likely to be familiar with programs outside their own fields of specialty.

The large fractions of "don't know" responses are a matter of some concern. However, given the broad coverage of research-doctorate programs, it is not surprising that faculty members would be unfamiliar with many of the less distinguished programs. As shown in Table 9.7, survey respondents in each discipline were much more likely to furnish evaluations for programs with high reputational standing than they were for programs of lesser distinction. For example, for biological science programs that received mean ratings of 4.0 or higher on measure 08, almost 85 percent of the evaluations requested on measure 08 were provided; 72 and 57 percent, respectively, were provided on measures 09 and 10. In contrast, the corresponding response rates for programs with mean ratings below 2.0 are much lower--30, 22, and 16 percent response on measures 08, 09, and 10, respectively.

Of great importance to the interpretation of the survey results is the reliability of the responses. How much confidence can one have in the reliability of a mean rating reported for a particular program? In the second table in each of the preceding six chapters, estimated standard errors associated with the mean ratings of every program are presented for all four survey items (measures 08-11). While there is some variation in the magnitude of the standard errors reported in every discipline, they rarely exceed .20 for any of the four measures and typically range from .10 to .15. For programs with higher mean ratings the estimated errors associated with these means are generally smaller--a finding consistent with the fact that survey respondents were more likely to furnish evaluations for programs with high reputational standing. The "split-half" correlations[8] presented in Table 9.8

---

[8]For a discussion of the interpretation of "split-half" coefficients, see Robert L. Thorndike and Elizabeth Hagan, Measurement and Evaluation in Psychology and Education, John Wiley & Sons, New York, 1969, pp. 182-185.

TABLE 9.7 Survey Item Response Rates, by Discipline and Mean Rating on Measure 08

Survey Measure	Total	Bio-chem.	Botany	Cell./ Molec.	Micro-biology	Physi-ology	Zoology
08 SCHOLARLY QUALITY OF PROGRAM FACULTY							
Mean Rating on Measure 08							
4.0 or Higher	84.7	95.9	67.7	89.9	82.0	81.6	91.1
3.0 - 3.9	65.9	76.0	57.9	72.6	64.2	57.0	75.4
2.0 - 2.9	44.8	48.8	43.9	43.8	44.1	36.3	50.1
Less than 2.0	29.9	32.2	34.2	23.4	27.6	21.8	35.3
09 EFFECTIVENESS OF PROGRAM IN EDUCATING SCIENTISTS							
Mean Rating on Measure 08							
4.0 or Higher	72.2	78.3	61.5	72.3	69.9	70.9	83.4
3.0 - 3.9	52.3	56.1	51.3	49.7	52.5	45.1	65.2
2.0 - 2.9	33.8	33.5	36.5	27.7	35.1	28.1	41.6
Less than 2.0	21.6	19.8	26.7	15.6	21.9	18.1	29.1
10 CHANGE IN PROGRAM QUALITY IN LAST FIVE YEARS							
Mean Rating on Measure 08							
4.0 or Higher	57.3	62.0	51.4	60.5	51.3	56.0	64.4
3.0 - 3.9	42.5	45.3	43.2	44.1	39.9	36.1	51.7
2.0 - 2.9	27.1	26.8	29.2	24.6	27.3	22.6	32.2
Less than 2.0	15.9	14.0	20.0	11.7·	16.5	13.4	21.6

give an indication of the overall reliability of the survey results in each discipline and for each measure. In the derivation of these correlations individual ratings of each program were randomly divided into two groups (A and B), and a separate mean rating was computed for each group. The last column in Table 9.8 reports the correlations between the mean program ratings of the two groups and is not corrected for the fact that the mean ratings of each group are based on only half rather than a full set of responses.[9] As the reader will note, the coefficients reported for measure 08, the scholarly quality of program faculty, are in the range of .91 to .96--indicating a high degree of consistency in evaluators' judgments. The correlations reported for measures 09 and 11, the rated effectiveness of a program and the evaluators' familiarity with a program, are somewhat lower but still at a level of .87 or higher in every discipline, except physiology. Not surprisingly, the reliability coefficients for ratings of change in program quality in the last five years (measure 10) are considerably lower, ranging from .48 to .68 in the six biological science disci-

---

[9]To compensate for the smaller sample size the "split-half" coefficient may be adjusted using the Spearman-Brown formula: $r' = 2r/(1 + r)$. This adjustment would have the effect of increasing a correlation of .70, for example, to .82, a correlation of .80 to .89, a correlation of .90 to .95, and a correlation of .95 to .97.

TABLE 9.8 Correlations Between Two Sets of Average Ratings from Two Randomly
Selected Groups of Evaluators in the Biological Sciences

MEASURE 08: SCHOLARLY QUALITY OF PROGRAM FACULTY

Discipline	Mean Rating		Std. Deviation		Correlation	
	Group A	Group B	Group A	Group B	N	r
Biochemistry	2.65	2.62	.94	.98	138	.96
Botany	3.02	3.03	.84	.82	83	.95
Cell/Molec. Biol.	2.86	2.90	1.02	.97	88	.96
Microbiology	2.83	2.81	.79	.82	134	.93
Physiology	2.93	2.94	.83	.77	101	.91
Zoology	2.71	2.74	.84	.78	70	.95

MEASURE 09: EFFECTIVENESS OF PROGRAM IN EDUCATING SCHOLARS

Discipline	Mean Rating		Std. Deviation		Correlation	
	Group A	Group B	Group A	Group B	N	r
Biochemistry	1.67	1.63	.52	.54	138	.88
Botany	1.82	1.84	.45	.45	83	.90
Cell/Molec. Biol.	1.73	1.75	.52	.53	88	.89
Microbiology	1.75	1.76	.45	.42	134	.87
Physiology	1.76	1.76	.43	.46	101	.81
Zoology	1.66	1.69	.45	.45	70	.89

MEASURE 10: IMPROVEMENT IN PROGRAM IN LAST FIVE YEARS

Discipline	Mean Rating		Std. Deviation		Correlation	
	Group A	Group B	Group A	Group B	N	r
Biochemistry	1.11	1.12	.27	.24	138	.55
Botany	1.15	1.17	.20	.22	83	.64
Cell/Molec. Biol.	1.17	1.17	.29	.27	88	.48
Microbiology	1.14	1.15	.28	.28	134	.68
Physiology	1.13	1.12	.27	.28	101	.55
Zoology	1.17	1.15	.21	.24	70	.64

MEASURE 11: FAMILIARITY WITH WORK OF PROGRAM FACULTY

Discipline	Mean Rating		Std. Deviation		Correlation	
	Group A	Group B	Group A	Group B	N	r
Biochemistry	.67	.65	.42	.42	138	.95
Botany	.68	.68	.30	.29	83	.87
Cell/Molec. Biol.	.72	.73	.43	.44	88	.95
Microbiology	.64	.64	.34	.33	134	.90
Physiology	.58	.61	.32	.32	101	.87
Zoology	.68	.69	.36	.36	70	.92

plines. While these coefficients represent tolerable reliability, it is quite evident that the responses to measure 10 are not as reliable as the responses to the other three items. In interpreting program ratings for this measure the reader is urged to refer to the standard error estimates reported with the ratings.

Further evidence of the reliability of the survey responses is presented in Table 9.9. As mentioned in Chapter VI, 11 mathematics programs[10] selected at random were included on a second form sent to 178 survey respondents in this discipline, and 116 individuals (65 percent) furnished responses to the second survey. A comparison of the overall results of the two survey administrations (columns 2 and 4 in Table 9.9) demonstrates the consistency of the ratings provided for each of the 11 programs. The average, absolute observed difference in the two sets of mean ratings is less than 0.1 for each measure. Columns 6 and 8 of Table 9.9 report the results based on the responses of only those evaluators who had been asked to consider a particular program in both administrations of the survey. (For a given program approximately 40-45 percent of the 116 respondents to the second survey had been asked to evaluate that program in the prior survey.) It is not surprising to find comparable small differences in the mean ratings provided by this subgroup of evaluators.

Critics of past reputational studies have expressed concern about the credibility of reputational assessments when evaluators provide judgments of programs about which they may know very little. As already mentioned, survey participants in this study were offered the explicit alternative, "Don't know well enough to evaluate." This response option was quite liberally used for measures 08, 09, and 10, as is shown in Table 9.6. In addition, evaluators were asked to indicate their degree of familiarity with each program. Respondents reported "considerable" familiarity with an average of only one program in every six or seven. While this finding supports the conjecture that many program ratings are based on limited information, the availability of reported familiarity permits us to analyze how ratings vary as a function of familiarity.

This issue can be addressed in more than one way. It is evident from the data reported in Table 9.10 that mean ratings of the scholarly quality of program faculty tend to be higher if the evaluator has considerable familiarity with the program. There is nothing surprising or, for that matter, disconcerting about such an association. When a particular program fails to provoke more than vague images in the evaluator's mind, he or she is likely to take this as some indication that the program is not an extremely lustrous one on the national scene. While visibility and quality are scarcely the same, the world of research in higher education is structured to encourage high quality to achieve high visibility, so that any association of the two is far from spurious.

_____

[10]Mathematics is the only discipline in which results were obtained from two separate administrations of the survey.

TABLE 9.9 Comparison of Mean Ratings for 11 Mathematics Programs
Included in Two Separate Survey Administrations

| | Survey Measure | All Evaluators | | | | Evaluators Rating the Same Program in Both Surveys | | | |
| | | First | | Second | | First | | Second | |
		N	$\bar{X}$	N	$\bar{X}$	N	$\bar{X}$	N	$\bar{X}$
Program A	08	100	4.9	114	4.9	50	4.9	50	4.9
	09	90	2.7	100	2.8	42	2.7	43	2.7
	10	74	1.2	83	1.2	38	1.1	34	1.2
	11	100	1.6	115	1.6	50	1.5	50	1.6
Program B	08	94	4.6	115	4.6	48	4.6	50	4.5
	09	81	2.6	91	2.5	40	2.6	39	2.5
	10	69	1.0	82	1.0	37	1.0	36	0.9
	11	98	1.4	116	1.4	50	1.5	50	1.5
Program C	08	86	3.4	103	3.6	42	3.4	44	3.5
	09	56	2.0	66	2.1	28	2.1	29	2.0
	10	55	1.1	62	1.3	30	1.2	27	1.4
	11	99	1.0	116	1.1	50	1.1	50	1.0
Program D	08	74	3.0	93	3.0	37	2.8	38	2.9
	09	50	1.8	48	1.6	27	1.7	16	1.6
	10	46	1.4	52	1.5	24	1.4	23	1.5
	11	90	1.0	113	0.9	46	1.0	46	0.9
Program E	08	69	3.0	95	3.1	39	3.0	46	3.1
	09	40	1.8	60	1.9	25	1.8	30	1.8
	10	36	0.8	58	0.9	24	0.8	29	0.9
	11	96	0.8	115	0.9	52	0.9	52	1.0
Program F	08	63	2.9	90	3.0	26	3.0	32	3.1
	09	35	1.8	46	1.7	10	1.6	13	1.8
	10	32	1.1	43	1.1	11	1.3	12	1.2
	11	95	0.7	115	0.8	43	0.7	44	0.7
Program G	08	69	2.7	92	2.8	39	2.7	39	3.0
	09	35	1.7	45	1.6	17	1.7	19	1.7
	10	36	1.1	43	1.2	17	1.1	19	1.2
	11	85	0.9	116	0.8	46	0.9	46	0.9
Program H	08	58	2.2	73	2.5	36	2.2	37	2.4
	09	32	1.3	43	1.3	22	1.2	19	1.3
	10	30	1.5	39	1.5	20	1.7	17	1.4
	11	90	0.7	116	0.6	51	0.7	52	0.6
Program I	08	55	2.0	74	1.9	30	1.9	30	2.0
	09	33	1.0	41	0.9	19	1.0	18	0.8
	10	27	1.2	31	1.1	15	1.1	13	1.2
	11	99	0.5	115	0.5	50	0.5	50	0.5
Program J	08	51	1.5	67	1.5	26	1.4	28	1.4
	09	31	0.8	36	0.7	14	0.6	14	0.7
	10	26	1.2	23	1.1	14	1.2	12	1.3
	11	96	0.5	113	0.3	49	0.4	48	0.4
Program K	08	33	1.2	48	1.2	17	1.1	21	1.4
	09	19	0.8	21	0.5	11	0.6	8	0.4
	10	12	0.8	15	0.9	5	1.0	5	0.8
	11	99	0.2	114	0.2	48	0.2	47	0.2

TABLE 9.10 Mean Ratings of Scholarly Quality of Program Faculty,
by Evaluator's Familiarity with Work of Faculty

| | MEAN RATINGS | | CORRELATION | |
	Consid-erable	Some/ Little	r	N
Biochemistry	2.99	2.59	.86	133
Botany	3.30	2.90	.85	82
Cellular/Molecular Biology	3.33	2.88	.90	83
Microbiology	3.17	2.73	.89	130
Physiology	3.54	2.83	.77	97
Zoology	3.09	2.62	.88	69

NOTE: N reported in last column represents the number of programs
with a rating from at least one evaluator in each of the two groups.

From the data presented in Table 9.10 it is evident that if mean
ratings were computed on the basis of the responses of only those most
familiar with programs, the values reported for individual programs
would be increased. A largely independent question is whether a restriction of this kind would substantially change our sense of the
relative standings of programs on this measure. Quite naturally, the
answer depends in some degree on the nature of the restriction imposed.
For example, if we exclude evaluations provided by those who confessed
"little or no" familiarity with particular programs, then the revised
mean ratings would be correlated at a level of at least .99 with the
mean ratings computed using all of the data. (This similarity arises,
in part, because only a small fraction of evaluations are given on the
basis of no more than "little" familiarity with the program.)

The third column in Table 9.10 presents the correlation in each
discipline between the array of mean ratings supplied by respondents
claiming "considerable" familiarity and the mean ratings of those in-
dicating "some" or "little or no" familiarity with particular programs.
This coefficient is a rather conservative estimate of agreement since
there is not a sufficient number of ratings from those with "considerable" familiarity to provide highly stable means. Were more such ratings available, one might expect the correlations to be higher. However, even in the form presented, the correlations, which are at least
.85 in all disciplines but physiology, are high enough to suggest that
the relative standing of programs on measure 08 is not greatly affected
by the admixtures of ratings from evaluators who recognize that their
knowledge of a given program is limited.

As mentioned previously, 90 percent of the survey sample members
were supplied the names of faculty members associated with each program
to be evaluated, along with the reported number of program graduates
(Ph.D. or equivalent degrees) in the previous five years. Since earlier reputational surveys had not provided such information, 10 percent

TABLE 9.11 Item Response Rate on Measure 08, by Selected Characteristics of Survey Evaluators in the Biological Sciences

	Total	Bio-chem.	Botany	Cell./ Molec.	Micro-biology	Physi-ology	Zoology
EVALUATOR'S FAMILIARITY WITH PROGRAM							
Considerable	99.9	99.9	99.5	100.0	100.0	100.0	100.0
Some	95.3	95.3	94.8	94.4	95.5	95.1	96.7
Little or None	10.3	14.3	8.5	10.7	8.6	6.5	12.8
TYPE OF SURVEY FORM							
Names	53.1	56.0	51.4	56.1	51.8	47.0	56.1
No Names	52.2	52.0	52.0	48.0	48.1	43.2	68.2
INSTITUTION OF HIGHEST DEGREE							
Alumni	91.6	96.0	84.0	94.1	91.4	95.1	96.4
Nonalumni	52.6	55.3	50.9	55.2	51.2	46.5	57.0
EVALUATOR'S PROXIMITY TO PROGRAM							
Same Region	64.4	66.1	63.3	64.1	64.0	56.7	75.3
Outside Region	51.4	54.1	50.0	54.3	49.6	45.3	55.3

NOTE: The item response rate is the percentage of the total ratings requested from survey participants that included a response other than "don't know."

of the sample members, randomly selected, were given forms without faculty names or doctoral data, as a "control group." Although one might expect that those given faculty names would have been more likely than other survey respondents to provide evaluations of the scholarly quality of program faculty, no appreciable differences were found (see Table 9.11) between the two groups in their frequency of response to this survey item. (The reader may recall that the provision of faculty names apparently had a positive effect on survey sample members' willingness to complete and return their questionnaires.[11])

The mean ratings provided by the group furnished faculty names are generally lower than the mean ratings supplied by other respondents (Table 9.12). Although the differences are small, they attract attention because they are reasonably consistent from discipline to discipline (except in physiology and zoology) and because the direction of the differences was not anticipated. After all, those programs more familiar to evaluators tended to receive higher ratings, yet when steps were taken to enhance the evaluator's familiarity, the resulting ratings are somewhat lower. One post hoc interpretation of this finding

[11]As shown in Table 2.3, the survey response rate for those furnished faculty names is approximately 7 percentage points higher than that for those not given this information.

TABLE 9.12 Mean Ratings of Scholarly Quality of Program Faculty, by Type of Survey Form Provided to Evaluator

	MEAN RATINGS		CORRELATION	
	Names	No Names	r	N
Biochemistry	2.63	2.83	.76	137
Botany	3.01	3.19	.75	83
Cellular/Molecular Biology	2.94	3.33	.80	79
Microbiology	2.84	3.14	.57	126
Physiology	3.06	2.86	.52	84
Zoology	2.72	2.71	.88	70

NOTE: N reported in last column represents the number of programs with a rating from at least one evaluator in each of the two groups.

is that a program may be considered to have distinguished faculty if even only a few of its members are considered by the evaluator to be outstanding in their field. However, when a full list of program faculty is provided, the evaluator may be influenced by the number of individuals whom he or she could not consider to be distinguished. Thus, the presentation of these additional, unfamiliar names may occasionally result in a lower rating of program faculty.

However interesting these effects may be, one should not lose sight of the fact that they are small at best and that their existence does not necessarily imply that a program's relative standing on measure 08 would differ much whichever type of survey form was used. Since only about 1 in 10 ratings was supplied without the benefit of faculty names, it is hard to establish any very stable picture of relative mean ratings of individual programs. However, the correlations between the mean ratings supplied by the two groups are reasonably high—.75 or greater in four disciplines and .57 and .52 in microbiology and physiology, respectively (see Table 9.12). Were these coefficients adjusted for the fact that the group furnished forms without names constituted only about 10 percent of the survey respondents they would be substantially larger. From this result it seems reasonable to conclude that differences in the alternative survey forms used are not likely to be responsible for any large-scale reshuffling in the reputational ranking of programs on measure 08. It also suggests that the inclusion of faculty names in the committee's assessment need not prevent comparisons of the results with those obtained from the Roose-Andersen survey.

Another factor that might be thought to influence an evaluator's judgment about a particular program is the geographic proximity of that program to the evaluator. There is enough regional traffic in academic life that one might expect proximate programs to be better known than

TABLE 9.13 Mean Ratings of Scholarly Quality of Program Faculty, by Evaluator's Proximity to Region of Program

	MEAN RATINGS		CORRELATION	
	Nearby	Outside	r	N
Biochemistry	2.71	2.63	.92	134
Botany	2.99	3.03	.88	80
Cellular/Molecular Biology	2.91	2.91	.84	83
Microbiology	2.89	2.84	.87	131
Physiology	2.99	2.97	.76	97
Zoology	2.80	2.73	.86	68

NOTE: N reported in last column represents the number of programs with a rating from at least one evaluator in each of the two groups.

those in distant regions of the country. This hypothesis may apply especially to the smaller and less visible programs and is confirmed by the survey results. For purposes of analysis, programs were assigned to one of nine geographic regions[12] in the United States, and ratings of programs within an evaluator's own region are categorized in Table 9.13 as "nearby." Ratings of programs in any of the other eight regions were put in the "outside" group. Findings reported elsewhere in this chapter confirm that evaluators were more likely to provide ratings if a program was within their own region of the country,[13] and it is reasonable to imagine that the smaller and the less visible programs received a disproportionate share of their ratings either from evaluators within their own region or from others who for one reason or another were particularly familiar with programs in that region.

Although the data in Table 9.13 show that "nearby" programs were given higher ratings than those outside the evaluator's region in four of the disciplines, the differences in reported means are quite small and probably represent no more than a secondary effect that might be expected, because, as we have already seen, evaluators tended to rate higher those programs with which they were more familiar. Furthermore, the reasonably high correlations found between the mean ratings of the two groups indicate that the relative standings of programs are not dramatically influenced by the geographic proximity of those evaluating them.

Another consideration that troubles some critics is that large programs may be unfairly favored in a faculty survey because they are

---

[12]See Appendix I for a list of the states included in each region.
[13]See Table 9.11.

TABLE 9.14 Mean Ratings of Scholarly Quality of Program Faculty,
by Evaluator's Institution of Highest Degree

| | MEAN RATINGS | | NUMBER OF PROGRAMS WITH ALUMNI RATINGS |
	Alumni	Nonalumni	N
Biochemistry	3.80	3.60	31
Botany	3.76	3.43	46
Cellular/Molecular Biology	3.69	3.46	35
Microbiology	3.36	3.11	51
Physiology	3.82	3.30	29
Zoology	3.56	3.32	30

NOTE: The pairs of means reported in each discipline are computed
for a subset of programs with a rating from at least one alumnus and
are substantially greater than the mean ratings for the full set of
programs in each discipline.

likely to have more alumni contributing to their ratings who, it would
stand to reason, would be generous in the evaluations of their alma
maters. Information collected in the survey on each evaluator's institution of highest degree enables us to investigate this concern. The
findings presented in Table 9.14 support the hypothesis that alumni
provided generous ratings--with differences in the mean ratings (for
measure 08) of alumni and nonalumni ranging from .20 to .52 in the six
disciplines. Given the appreciable differences between the ratings
furnished by program alumni and other evaluators, one might ask how
much effect this has had on the overall results of the survey. The
answer is "very little." As shown in the table, in biochemistry only
one program in every four received ratings from any alumnus; in botany
slightly more than half of the programs were evaluated by one or more
alumni.[14] Even in the latter discipline, however, the fraction of
alumni providing ratings of a program is always quite small and should
have had minimal impact on the overall mean rating of any program. To
be certain that this was the case, mean ratings of the scholarly quality of faculty were recalculated for every biological science program--
with the evaluations provided by alumni excluded. The results were
compared with the mean scores based on a full set of evaluations. Out
of the 616 biological science programs evaluated in the survey, only 1
program (in physiology) had an observed difference as large as 0.2, and
for 574 programs (93 percent) their mean ratings remain unchanged (to

---

[14]Because of the small number of alumni ratings in every discipline,
the mean ratings for this group are unstable and therefore the correlations between alumni and nonalumni mean ratings are not reported.

the nearest tenth of a unit). On the basis of these findings the committee saw no reason to exclude alumni ratings in the calculation of
program means.

Another concern that some critics have is that a survey evaluation
may be affected by the interaction of the research interests of the
evaluator and the area(s) of focus of the research-doctorate program
to be rated. It is said, for example, that some narrowly focused programs may be strong in a particular area of research but that this
strength may not be recognized by a large fraction of evaluators who
happen to be unknowledgeable in this area. This is a concern more difficult to address than those discussed in the preceding pages since
little or no information is available about the areas of focus of the
programs being evaluated (although in certain disciplines the title of
a department or academic unit may provide a clue). To obtain a better
understanding of the extent to which an evaluator's field of specialty
may have influenced the ratings he or she has provided, an analysis was
made of ratings provided by evaluators in physics and statistics/
biostatistics. In each discipline the survey participants were divided
into two groups according to specialty field (as reported on the survey
questionnaire). The results of the analysis, which are presented in
the mathematical and physical sciences volume of the committee's report, indicate that there is a high degree of correlation in the mean
ratings provided by those in differing specialty fields within these
two disciplines. Although one cannot conclude from these findings that
an evaluator's specialty field has no bearing on how he or she rates a
program, these findings do suggest that the relative standings of programs in physics and statistics/biostatistics would not be greatly al-
tered if the ratings by either group were discarded.

In the biological science disciplines there is a corollary concern
that a survey evaluator may be influenced by the interaction of the
university setting in which the evaluator works and the setting in
which the program to be evaluated resides. For example, one might sus-
pect that medical school faculty members would tend to rate research-
doctorate programs in schools of medicine higher than would evaluators
from other university settings. To test this hypothesis evaluators in
each of the four biomedical disciplines--biochemistry, cellular/molec-
ular biology, microbiology, and physiology--were separated into two
groups: (1) those included on the faculties of programs located in
medical schools and (2) those in other programs. For purposes of
analysis, if a program spans both the medical and nonmedical school
settings, the survey evaluators selected from that program have been
included in the first group. The percentage of evaluators from medical
school programs varies considerably by disciplines: biochemistry (60
percent), cellular/molecular biology (32 percent), microbiology (46
percent), and physiology (68 percent). As shown in Table 9.15, there
is a high degree of correlation between the mean ratings provided by
medical school and other faculty members. For the four biomedical
disciplines the coefficients range from .83 to .96, suggesting that the
relative standings of programs in each discipline would not be greatly
affected if the survey responses of one of these two groups were ignored.

TABLE 9.15   Mean Ratings of Scholarly Quality of Program Faculty, by School in Which Evaluator's Own Program Is Located

| | MEAN RATINGS | | CORRELATION | |
	Medical School	Other	r	N
Biochemistry	2.61	2.67	.96	138
Cellular/Molecular Biology	2.80	2.91	.94	88
Microbiology	2.89	2.77	.93	134
Physiology	2.87	3.01	.83	101

NOTE: N reported in last column represents the number of programs with a rating from at least one evaluator in each of the two groups.

INTERPRETATION OF REPUTATIONAL SURVEY RATINGS

It is not hard to foresee that results from this survey will receive considerable attention through enthusiastic and uncritical reporting in some quarters and sharp castigation in others. The study committee understands the grounds for both sides of this polarized response but finds that both tend to be excessive. It is important to make clear how we view these ratings as fitting into the larger study of which they are a part.

The reputational results are likely to receive a disproportionate degree of attention for several reasons, including the fact that they reflect the opinions of a large group of faculty colleagues and that they form a bridge with earlier studies of graduate programs. But the results will also receive emphasis because they alone, among all of the measures, seem to address quality in an overall or global fashion. While most recognize that "objective" program characteristics (i.e., publication productivity, research funding, or library size) have some bearing on program quality, probably no one would contend that a single one of these measures encompasses all that need be known about the quality of research-doctorate programs. Each is obviously no more than an indicator of some aspect of program quality. In contrast, the reputational ratings are global from the start because the respondents are asked to take into account many objective characteristics and to arrive at a general assessment of the quality of the faculty and the effectiveness of the program. This generality has self-evident appeal.

On the other hand, it is wise to keep in mind that these reputational ratings are measures of _perceived_ program quality rather than of "quality" in some ideal or absolute sense. What this means is that, just as for all of the more objective measures, the reputational ratings represent only a partial view of what most of us would consider quality to be; hence, they must be kept in careful perspective.

Some critics may argue that such ratings are positively misleading because of a variety of methodological artifacts or because they are supplied by "judges" who often know very little about the programs they are rating. The committee has conducted the survey in a way that permits the empirical examination of a number of the alleged artifacts and, although our analysis is by no means exhaustive, the general conclusion is that their effects are slight.

Among the criticisms of reputational ratings from prior studies are some that represent a perspective that may be misguided. This perspective assumes that one asks for ratings in order to find out what "quality" really is and that to the degree that the ratings miss the mark of "quintessential quality," they are unreal, although the quality that they attempt to measure is real. What this perspective misses is the reality of quality and the fact that impressions of quality, if widely shared, have an imposing reality of their own and therefore are worth knowing about in their own right. After all, these perceptions govern a large-scale system of traffic around the nation's graduate institutions--for example, when undergraduate students seek the advice of professors concerning graduate programs that they might attend. It is possible that some professors put in this position disqualify themselves on grounds that they are not well informed about the relative merits of the programs being considered. Most faculty members, however, surely attempt to be helpful on the basis of impressions gleaned from their professional experience, and these assessments are likely to have major impact on student decision-making. In short, the impressions are real and have very real effects not only on students shopping for graduate schools but also on other flows, such as job-seeking young faculty and the distribution of research resources. At the very least, the survey results provide a snapshot of these impressions from discipline to discipline. Although these impressions may be far from ideally informed, they certainly show a strong degree of consensus within each discipline, and it seems safe to assume that they are more than passingly related to what a majority of keen observers might agree program quality is all about.

COMPARISON WITH RESULTS OF THE ROOSE-ANDERSEN STUDY

An analysis of the response to the committee's survey would not be complete without comparing the results with those obtained in the survey by Roose and Andersen 12 years earlier. Although there are obvious similarities in the two surveys, there are also some important differences that should be kept in mind in examining individual program ratings of the scholarly quality of faculty. Already mentioned in this chapter is the inclusion, on the form sent to 90 percent of the sample members in the committee's survey, of the names and academic ranks of faculty and the numbers of doctoral graduates in the previous five years. Other significant changes in the committee's form are the identification of the university department or academic unit in which each program may be found, the restriction of requesting evaluators to make judgments about no more than 50 research-doctorate programs in their discipline, and the presentation of these programs in random sequence on each survey form. The sampling frames used in the two surveys also differ. The sample selected in the earlier study included only individuals who had been nominated by the participating universities, while more than one-fourth of the sample in the committee's survey were chosen at random from full faculty lists. (Except for this difference the samples were quite similar--i.e., in terms of the number of evaluators in each discipline and the fraction of senior scholars.[15])

Several dissimilarities in the coverage of the Roose-Andersen study and this committee's reputational assessments should be mentioned. The former included a total of 130 institutions that had awarded at least 100 doctoral degrees in two or more disciplines during the FY1958-67 period. The institutional coverage in the committee's assessment was based on the number of doctorates awarded in each discipline (as described in Chapter I) and covered a total population of 228 universities. Most of the universities represented in the present study but not the earlier one are institutions that offered research-doctorate programs in a limited set of disciplines. In the Roose-Andersen study, programs in 10 biological science disciplines were rated: biochemistry, botany, developmental biology, entomology, microbiology, molecular biology, pharmacology, physiology, population biology, and zoology. For reasons explained in Chapter I, the committee in its assessment was able to include programs in the six disiplines with the largest numbers of doctoral awards in recent years.[16] Programs in the other four disciplines--developmental biology, entomology, pharmacology, and population biology--were not evaluated in the present assessment. Finally, in the Roose-Andersen study only <u>one</u> set of ratings was compiled from each institution represented in a discipline, whereas in the committee's survey separate ratings were requested if a university offered more than one research-doctorate program in a given discipline. In the committee's survey, evaluations were requested for a total of 616 research-doctorate programs in the six biological science disciplines, compared with 618 programs in these same disciplines in the Roose-Andersen study. Although the total numbers of programs included in the studies are nearly equal, there are many differences in the program coverage in each discipline.

Figures 9.1-9.6 plot the mean ratings of scholarly quality of faculty in programs included in both surveys; sets of ratings are graphed for 90 programs in biochemistry, 52 programs in botany, 53 programs in cellular/molecular biology, 82 programs in microbiology, 63 programs in physiology, and 48 programs in zoology. Since in the Roose-Andersen

---

[15]For a description of the sample group used in the earlier study, see Roose and Andersen, pp. 28-31.

[16]It should be noted that the "molecular biology" category used in the Roose-Andersen study was expanded in the committee's assessment to include cellular and molecular biology programs.

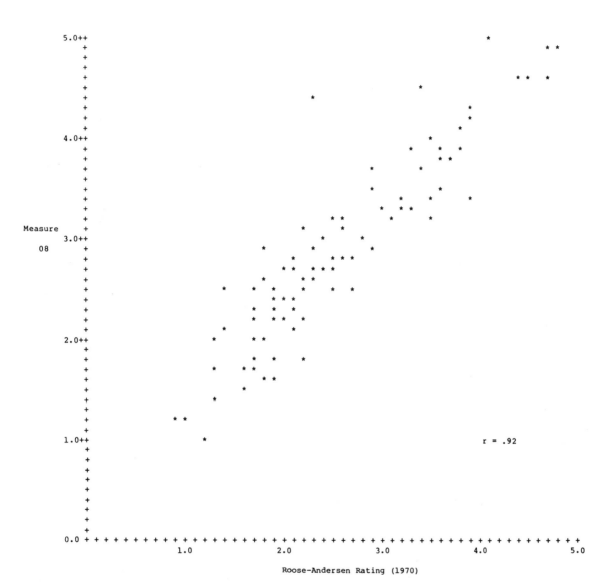

FIGURE 9.1 Mean rating of scholarly quality of faculty (measure 08) versus mean rating of faculty in the Roose-Andersen study--90 programs in biochemistry.

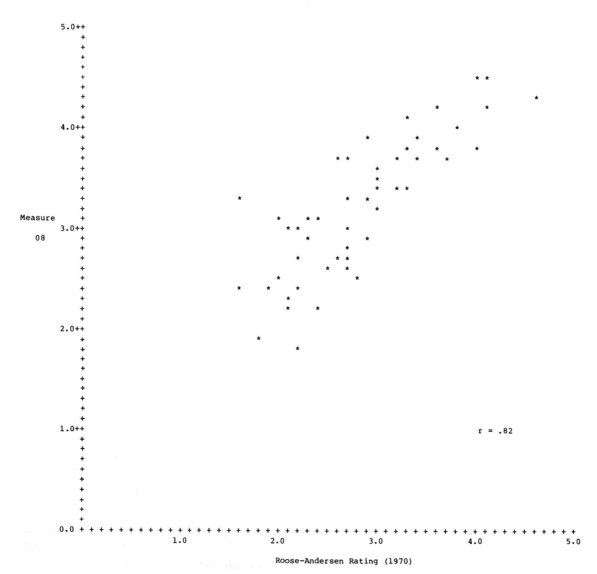

FIGURE 9.2 Mean rating of scholarly quality of faculty (measure 08) versus mean rating of faculty in the
Roose-Andersen study--52 programs in botany.

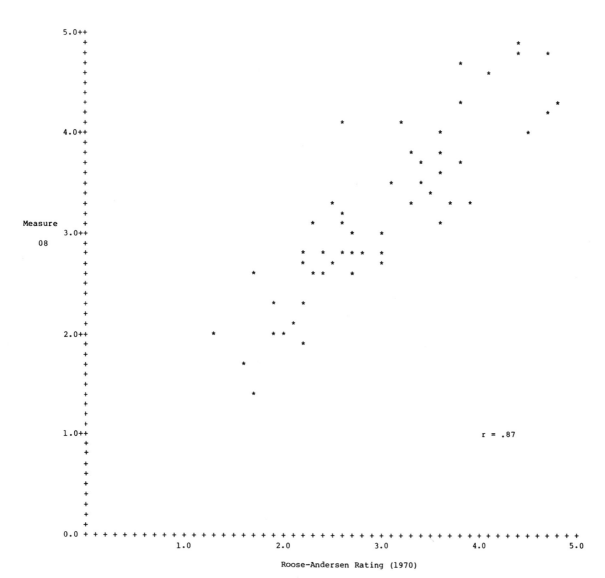

FIGURE 9.3 Mean rating of scholarly quality of faculty (measure 08) versus mean rating of faculty in the Roose-Andersen study--53 programs in cellular/molecular biology.

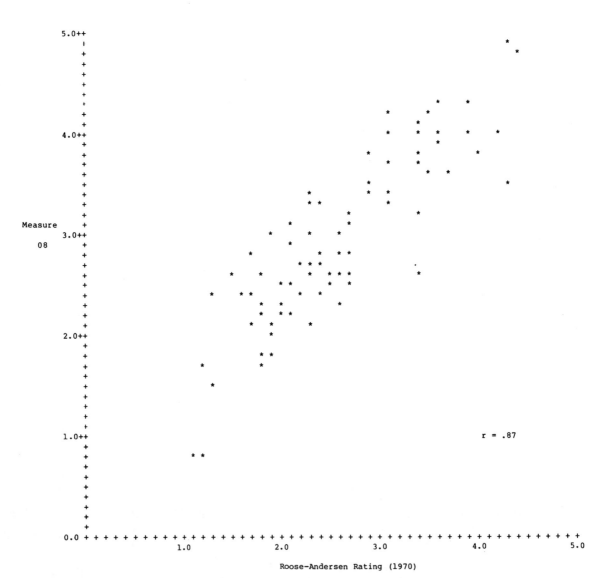

FIGURE 9.4 Mean rating of scholarly quality of faculty (measure 08) versus mean rating of faculty in the Roose-Andersen study--82 programs in microbiology.

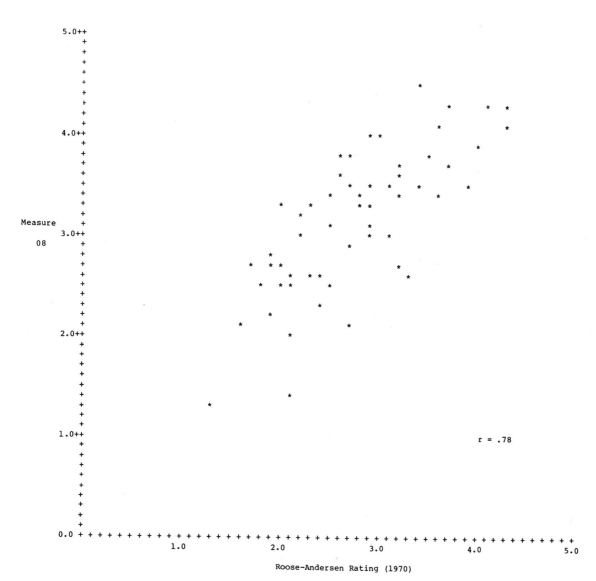

FIGURE 9.5 Mean rating of scholarly quality of faculty (measure 08) versus mean rating of faculty in the Roose-Andersen study--63 programs in physiology.

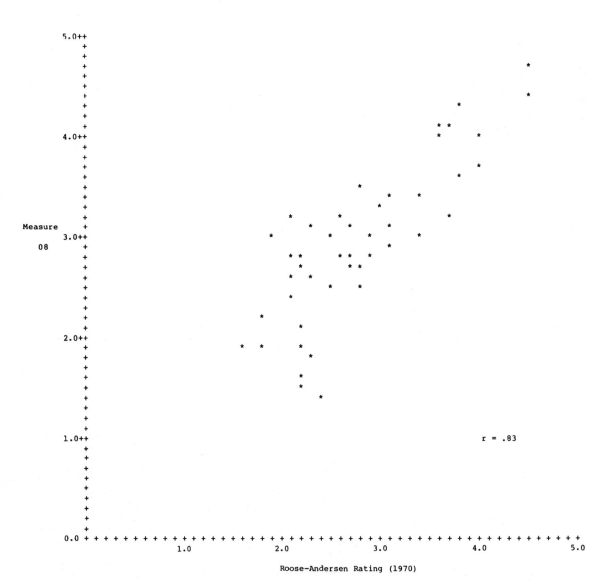

FIGURE 9.6 Mean rating of scholarly quality of faculty (measure 08) versus mean rating of faculty in the Roose-Andersen study--48 programs in zoology.

study programs were identified by institution and discipline (but not by department), the matching of results from this survey with those from the committee's survey is not precise. For universities represented in the latter survey by more than one program in a particular discipline, the mean rating for the program with the largest number of graduates (measure 02) is the only one plotted here. Although the results of both surveys are reported on identical scales, some caution must be taken in interpreting differences in mean ratings a program received in the two evaluations. It is impossible to estimate what effect all of the differences described above may have had on the results of the two surveys. Furthermore, one must remember that the reported scores are based on the opinions of different groups of faculty members and were provided at different time periods. In 1969, when the Roose-Andersen survey was conducted, graduate departments in most universities were still expanding and not facing the enrollment and budget reductions that many departments have had to deal with in recent years. Consequently, a comparison of the overall findings from the two surveys tells us nothing about how much graduate education has improved (or declined) in the past decade. Nor should the reader place much stock in any small differences in the mean ratings that a particular program may have received in the two surveys. On the other hand, it is of particular interest to note the high correlations between the results of the evaluations. For programs in biochemistry, cellular/molecular biology, and microbiology, the correlation coefficients range between .87 and .92; in botany, physiology, and zoology, the coefficients range between .78 and .83. The high correlations found here may suggest to some readers that reputational standings of programs in these disciplines have changed very little in the last decade. However, differences are apparent for some institutions. Also, one must keep in mind that the correlations are based on the reputational ratings of only approximately two-thirds of the programs evaluated in this assessment in these disciplines and do not take into account the emergence of many new programs that did not exist or were too small to be rated in the Roose-Andersen study.

FUTURE STUDIES

One of the most important objectives in undertaking this assessment was to test new measures not used extensively in past evaluations of graduate programs. Although the committee believes that it has been successful in this effort, much more needs to be done. First and foremost, studies of this kind should be extended to cover other types of programs and other disciplines not included in this effort. As a consequence of budgeting limitations, the committee had to restrict its study to 32 disciplines, selected on the basis of the number of doctorates awarded in each. Among those omitted were programs in developmental biology, entomology, pharmacology, and population biology, all of which were included in the Roose-Andersen study; a multidimensional assessment of research-doctorate programs in these and many other important disciplines would be of value. Consideration should also be given to embarking on evaluations of programs offering other types of graduate and professional degrees. As a matter of fact, plans for including master's-degree programs in this assessment were originally contemplated, but because of a lack of available information about the resources and graduates of programs at the master's level, it was decided to focus on programs leading to the research doctorate.

Perhaps the most debated issue the committee has had to address concerned which measures should be reported in this assessment. In fact, there is still disagreement among some of its members about the relative merits of certain measures, and the committee fully recognizes a need for more reliable and valid indices of the quality of graduate programs. First on a list of needs is more precise and meaningful information about the product of research-doctorate programs--the graduates. For example, what fraction of the program graduates have gone on to be productive investigators--either in the academic setting or in government and industrial laboratories? What fraction have gone on to become outstanding investigators--as measured by receipt of major prizes, membership in academies, and other such distinctions? How do program graduates compare with regard to their publication records? Also desired might be measures of the quality of the students applying for admittance to a graduate program (e.g., Graduate Record Examination scores, undergraduate grade point averages). If reliable data of this sort were made available, they might provide a useful index of the reputational standings of programs, from the perspective of graduate students.

A number of alternative measures relevant to the quality of program faculty were considered by the committee but not included in the assessment because of the associated difficulties and costs of compiling the necessary data. For example, what fraction of the program faculty were invited to present papers at national meetings? What fraction had been elected to prestigious organizations/groups in their field? What fraction had received senior fellowships and other awards of distinction? In addition, it would be highly desirable to supplement the data presented on NSF, NIH, and ADAMHA research grant awards (measure 13) with data on awards from other federal agencies (e.g., Department of Agriculture, Department of Defense, Department of Energy, National Aeronautics and Space Administration) as well as from major private foundations.

As described in the preceding pages, the committee was able to make several changes in the survey design and procedures, but further improvements could be made. Of highest priority in this regard is the expansion of the survey sample to include evaluators from outside the academic setting (in particular, those in government and industrial laboratories who regularly employ graduates of the programs to be evaluated). To add evaluators from these sectors would require a major effort in identifying the survey population from which a sample could be selected. Although such an effort is likely to involve considerable costs in both time and financial resources, the committee believes that the addition of evaluators from the government and industrial settings would be of value in providing a different perspective to the reputational assessment and that comparisons between the ratings supplied by academic and nonacademic evaluators would be of particular interest.

Minority Statement

The inclusion of several different and independent possible measures reflecting the quality of graduate education in this report seems to us a substantial addition and a significant improvement to previous such studies. However, we are concerned with the possibility that there are perhaps too many measures, some of which have little or no bearing on the objectives of the present study. In particular, measures 06 and 07 (on the employment plans of graduates) are not informative, have little or nothing to do with the quality of the program, and yield numbers that are not very dependable. Both measures come from data in the NRC's Survey of Earned Doctorates. Measure 06, the fraction of FY1975-79 program graduates with definite employment or study plans at time of doctorate, is vague because the "time of doctorate" may vary considerably from the time of year when, say, academic appointments are offered--and this in turn can vary substantially among institutions. This measure may be associated with the prosperity of the program, but its connection with quality is tenuous. Measure 07, the fraction of FY1975-79 program graduates planning to take positions in Ph.D.-granting universities, is even more nebulous. What is meant by "planning"? How firm are those plans? (We can't know; all there is is a check somewhere on a questionnaire.) What about the variation in quality among different Ph.D.-granting universities. It can be considerable, and such considerable differences are precisely those the whole study is attempting to measure. Such data obscure the differences. Further, measure 07 betrays the inherent bias of the present study and previous ones in that the "program graduates planning to take positions in Ph.D.-granting universities" is tacitly offered as a measure of the "goodness" of the program. In the late 1970's and 1980's nothing can be farther from the truth. The kindest evaluation of measures 06 and 07 is that they are irrelevant.

These two measures do not result from careful plans made by the committee for this study in order to find other useful new measures. Such plans were considered, but for various good reasons could not be carried out. These two particular measures just happen to be available in the vast data collected and recorded (but not critically evaluated) over the years by the Commission on Human Resources of the National Research Council. Their inclusion in this report might be explained by bureaucratic inertia, but this inclusion adds nothing to the report.

SAUNDERS MAC LANE

C. K. N. PATEL

ERNEST S. KUH

Appendixes

LETTER TO INSTITUTIONAL COORDINATORS

COMMITTEE ON AN ASSESSMENT OF QUALITY-RELATED CHARACTERISTICS OF RESEARCH-DOCTORATE PROGRAMS IN THE UNITED STATES

Established by the Conference Board of Associated Research Councils

Office of the Staff Director / National Research Council / 2101 Constitution Avenue, N.W. / Washington, D.C. 20418

(202) 389-6552

December 5, 1980

Dear

We are pleased to learn that you have been designated to coordinate the efforts of your institution in assisting our committee with an assessment of the characteristics and effectiveness of research-doctorate programs in U.S. universities. A prospectus describing the goals and procedures for this study has already been distributed to university presidents and graduate deans. The cooperation of universities and their faculties is essential for the assessment to be carried out in an objective and accurate fashion.

The study is being conducted under the aegis of the Conference Board of Associated Research Councils and is housed administratively within the National Research Council. Financial support has been provided by the Andrew W. Mellon Foundation, the Ford Foundation, the National Science Foundation, and the National Institutes of Health. The study will examine more than 2,600 programs in 31 fields in the physical sciences, engineering, life sciences, social sciences, and humanities. Approximately 10,000 faculty members will be asked to evaluate programs in their own fields. In addition to the reputational evaluations by faculty, information will be compiled from national data banks on the achievements of both the faculty involved in each program and the program graduates.

The product of this study will be a series of reports with descriptive data on institutional programs in each of 31 fields to be covered. These reports will present several different measures of the quality-related characteristics of each program being evaluated. Some of the measures will be adjusted for program size. With the cooperation of your institution and that of other universities, we plan to produce these reports by late spring of 1982. At that time the detailed data that have been compiled on research-doctorate programs within your institution will be made available to you for a nominal cost. These data should prove to be quite valuable for an assessment of the particular strengths and weaknesses of individual programs at your institution.

For the past three months the committee has deliberated over what fields are to be covered in the study and which programs within each field are to be evaluated. The financial resources available limit us to an assessment of approximately 2,600 programs in 31 fields. The fields to be included have been determined on the basis of the total number of doctorates awarded by U.S. universities during the FY1976-78 period and the feasibility of identifying and evaluating comparable programs in a particular field. Within each of the 31 fields, programs which awarded more than a specified number of doctorates during the period have been designated for inclusion in the study.

For each of the programs at your institution that are to be evaluated, we ask that you furnish the names and ranks of all faculty members who participate significantly in education toward the research doctorate, along with some basic information (as indicated) about the program itself. A set of instructions and a computer-printed roster (organized by field) are enclosed. In addition, you are given an opportunity to nominate other programs at your institution that are not on the roster, but that you believe have significant distinction and should be included in our evaluation. Any program you nominate must belong in one of the 31 fields covered by the study.

The information supplied by your institution will be used for two purposes. First, a sample of the faculty members identified with each program will be selected to evaluate research-doctorate programs in their fields at other universities. The selection will be made in such a way as to ensure that all institutional programs and faculty ranks are adequately represented in each field category. Secondly, a list of names of faculty and some of the program information you supply will be provided to evaluators selected from other institutions. Thus, it is important that you provide accurate and up-to-date information. You may wish to ask department chairmen or other appropriate persons at your institution to assist in providing the information requested. If you do so, we ask that your office coordinate the effort by collecting the information on each program and sending a single package to us in the envelope provided.

We hope that you will be able to complete this request by December 15. Should you have any questions regarding our request, please call (collect) Porter Coggeshall, the study director, at (202)389-6552. Thank you for your help in this effort.

Sincerely,

Lyle V. Jones
Co-Chairman

Gardner Lindzey
Co-Chairman

INSTRUCTIONS

General Instructions

- Provided on the first page of the accompanying roster is a list of the 31 program fields to be covered in this study. Those program fields for which you are requested to furnish information have been designated with an asterisk (*).

- For every designated field there is a separate set of roster pages. Please provide all of the information requested on these pages.

- If your institution offers more than one research-doctorate program in a designated field, we ask that you copy the roster pages furnished for that field category and provide a separate set of information for each program. For example, if your university offers one doctoral program in statistics and another in biostatistics, these should be listed separately. For this purpose, programs offered by different departments (or other administative units) that are advertised as distinct programs in your catalogues would be listed separately. Do not consider different specialty areas within a department to be separate programs.

- If your institution currently does not offer a research-doctorate program in an asterisked field or if, in your judgment, a doctoral program offered fails to fit the designated field category, please so indicate on the roster pages provided for that field.

List of Faculty Members (as of December 1, 1980)

- On each program roster please provide the names of faculty members who participate significantly in doctoral education.

- Included should be individuals who (a) are members of the regular academic faculty (typically holding the rank of assistant, associate, or full professor) and (b) regularly teach doctoral students and/or serve on doctoral committees.

- Members of the faculty who are currently on leave of absence but meet the above criteria should be included.

- Visiting faculty members should not be included.

- Emeritus or adjunct faculty members (or faculty with other comparable ranks) should also be excluded unless they currently participate significantly in doctoral education.

- Members of the faculty who participate significantly in doctoral education in more than one program should be listed on the roster for each program in which they participate.

- In many instances the list of faculty for a program may be identical to an institutional list of graduate faculty.

- Faculty names should be provided in the form in which they are most likely to be recognized by colleagues in the field. We prefer that, within each academic rank, you list faculty alphabetically by last name.

Nomination of Faculty to Serve as Program Evaluators
(Column 3 of Faculty Roster)

- Please check the names of at least two faculty members in each academic rank within each program who would be available and, in your opinion, well-qualified to evaluate research-doctorate programs in their field.

- A sample of evaluators will be selected from the list of faculty you provide for each program. In selecting evaluators preference will be given to those whose names you have checked. If no names are checked, a random sample will be selected from the faculty list.

Faculty Who Do Not Hold Ph.D. Degrees From U.S. Universities
(Column 4 of Faculty Roster)

- In order to help us match the faculty names you provide with records in the Doctorate Records File (maintained by the National Research Council), we ask that you identify those faculty members who do not hold a Ph.D. or equivalent research-doctorate from a university in the United States.

- This information will be used only for the purposes of collating records and will not be released to those who are selected to evaluate your institution's programs. Nor will this information affect in any way the selection of program evaluators from your institution's faculty.

Nomination of Additional Programs

- We recognize the possibility that we may have omitted one or more research-doctorate programs at your institution that belong to (non-asterisked) fields listed on the first page of the roster and that you believe should be included in this study.

- The last two pages of the accompanying roster are provided for the nomination of an additional program. You are asked to provide the names of faculty and other information about each program you nominate. Should you decide to nominate more than one program, it will be necessary to make additional copies of these two pages of the roster.

- Please restrict your nominations to programs in your institution that you consider to be of uncommon distinction and that have awarded no fewer than two doctorates during the past two years.

- Only programs which fall under one of the 31 field categories listed on the first page of the accompanying roster will be considered for inclusion in the study.

PLEASE RETURN COMPLETED ROSTER IN
THE ENCLOSED ENVELOPE TO:

COMMITTEE ON AN ASSESSMENT OF
   QUALITY-RELATED CHARACTERISTICS
   OF RESEARCH-DOCTORATE PROGRAMS
NATIONAL RESEARCH COUNCIL, JH-711
2101 CONSTITUTION AVENUE, N.W.
WASHINGTON, D.C. 20418

FIELDS INCLUDED IN THE STUDY

ARTS AND HUMANITIES
* ART HISTORY
* CLASSICS
* ENGLISH LANGUAGE AND LITERATURE
* FRENCH LANGUAGE AND LITERATURE
* GERMAN LANGUAGE AND LITERATURE
  LINGUISTICS
  MUSIC
* PHILOSOPHY
* SPANISH AND PORTUGUESE LANGUAGE AND LITERATURE

BIOLOGICAL SCIENCES
* BIOCHEMISTRY
  BOTANY (INCLUDING PLANT PHYSIOLOGY, PLANT PATHOLOGY, MYCOLOGY).
* CELLULAR BIOLOGY/MOLECULAR BIOLOGY
* MICROBIOLOGY (INCLUDING IMMUNOLOGY, BACTERIOLOGY, PARASITOLOGY, VIROLOGY)
* PHYSIOLOGY (ANIMAL, HUMAN)
  ZOOLOGY

ENGINEERING
* CHEMICAL ENGINEERING
* CIVIL ENGINEERING
* ELECTRICAL ENGINEERING
* MECHANICAL ENGINEERING

PHYSICAL SCIENCES
* CHEMISTRY
* COMPUTER SCIENCES
* GEOSCIENCES (INCLUDING GEOLOGY, GEOCHEMISTRY, GEOPHYSICS, GENL EARTH SCI)
* MATHEMATICS
* PHYSICS (EXCLUDING ASTRONOMY, ASTROPHYSICS)
  STATISTICS (INCLUDING BIOSTATISTICS)

SOCIAL AND BEHAVIORAL SCIENCES
* ANTHROPOLOGY
* ECONOMICS
* HISTORY
* POLITICAL SCIENCE
* PSYCHOLOGY
* SOCIOLOGY

* DESIGNATES FIELDS FOR WHICH YOU ARE REQUESTED TO PROVIDE INFORMATION
  ON RESEARCH-DOCTORATE PROGRAMS IN YOUR INSTITUTION. (SEE INSTRUCTION
  SHEET REGARDING NOMINATION OF ADDITIONAL PROGRAMS TO BE INCLUDED IN
  THE STUDY) .

```
****************************************************
***                                      - PART A  ***
****************************************************
```

PLEASE ANSWER EACH OF THE FOLLOWING QUESTIONS ABOUT THE RESEARCH-DOCTORATE PROGRAM

     IN _____

(1) WHAT IS THE NAME OF THE DEPARTMENT (OR EQUIVALENT ACADEMIC UNIT) IN WHICH
    THIS RESEARCH-DOCTORATE PROGRAM IS OFFERED ?

          •••••••••••••••••••••••••••••••••••••••

(2) HOW MANY PH.D.'S (OR EQUIVALENT RESEARCH-DOCTORATES) HAVE BEEN AWARDED IN THE
    PROGRAM IN EACH OF THE LAST FIVE ACADEMIC YEARS ?

        1975-76 ••••••••

        1976-77 ••••••••

        1977-78 ••••••••

        1978-79 ••••••••

        1979-80 ••••••••

(3) APPROXIMATELY HOW MANY FULL-TIME AND PART-TIME GRADUATE STUDENTS ENROLLED
    IN THE PROGRAM AT THE PRESENT TIME (FALL 1980) INTEND TO EARN DOCTORATES ?

        FULL-TIME STUDENTS ••••••••

        PART-TIME STUDENTS ••••••••

               TOTAL ••••••••

(4) IN APPROXIMATELY WHAT YEAR WAS THIS RESEARCH-DOCTORATE PROGRAM INITIATED ?
    (IF PROGRAM WAS DISCONTINUED AND SUBSEQUENTLY REINSTATED, PLEASE GIVE YEAR
    IT WAS REINSTATED) .

        ••••••••

```
****************************************************
***  _                              - PART B  ***
****************************************************
```

(1)	(2)	(3)	(4)
LIST BELOW ALL FACULTY WHO PARTICIPATE SIGNIFICANTLY IN DOCTORAL EDUCATION IN THIS PROGRAM (SEE INSTRUCTIONS SHEET). PLEASE PRINT OR TYPE NAMES IN FOLLOWING FORMAT:	INDICATE THE ACA- DEMIC RANK OF EACH FACULTY MEMBER (PROF., ASSOC. PROF., ASST. PROF., ETC.).	CHECK BELOW AT LEAST 2 FACULTY IN EACH RANK AVAILABLE AND WELL-QUALIFIED TO EVALUATE OTHER PROGRAMS (SEE INSTRUC- TIONS SHEET).	CHECK BELOW ANY FACULTY WHO DO NOT HOLD A PH.D. OR OTHER RESEARCH- DOCTORATE FROM A UNIVERSITY IN THE U.S. (SEE INSTRUCTIONS SHEET).

```
        EXAMPLE: MARY A. JONES
                 A. B. SMITH, JR.
```

01	..	( )	( )
02	..	( )	( )
03	..	( )	( )
04	..	( )	( )
05	..	( )	( )
06	..	( )	( )
07	..	( )	( )
08	..	( )	( )
09	..	( )	( )
10	..	( )	( )
11	..	( )	( )
12	..	( )	( )
13	..	( )	( )
14	..	( )	( )
15	..	( )	( )
16	..	( )	( )
17	..	( )	( )
18	..	( )	( )
19	..	( )	( )
20	..	( )	( )

(PART B CONTINUED ON NEXT PAGE)

APPENDIX B

SURVEY OF EARNED DOCTORATES

(Conducted by the National Research Council under the sponsorship of the National Science Foundation, the Department of Education, the National Institutes of Health, and the National Endowment for the Humanities.)

This annual survey of new recipients of Ph.D. or equivalent research doctorates in all fields of learning contains information describing their demographic characteristics, educational background, graduate training, and postgraduation plans. The source file includes nearly complete data from all 1958-81 doctorate recipients and partial information for all 1920-57 doctoral graduates.

SURVEY OF EARNED DOCTORATES

NSF Form 558 1977
OMB No. 99-R0290
Approval Expires June 30, 1979

This form is to be returned to the GRADUATE DEAN, for forwarding to .... Board on Human-Resource Data and Analyses
Commission on Human Resources
National Research Council
2101 Constitution Avenue, Washington, D. C. 20418

Please print or type.

A. Name in full: .... (9-30)
        (Last Name)   (First Name)   (Middle Name)

    Cross Reference: Maiden name or former name legally changed .... (31)

B. Permanent address through which you could always be reached: (Care of, if applicable) ....

....
     (Number)   (Street)   (City)

....
    (State)   (Zip Code)   (Or Country if not U.S.)

C. U.S. Social Security Number: __ __ __ – __ __ – __ __ __ __   (32-40)

D. Date of birth: ....   Place of birth: ....
   (41-45)   (Month)   (Day)   (Year)   (46-47)   (State)   (Or Country if not U.S.)

E. Sex: 1 ☐ Male   2 ☐ Female   (48)

F. Marital status: 1 ☐ Married   2 ☐ Not married (including widowed, divorced)   (49)

G. Citizenship: 0 ☐ U.S. native   2 ☐ Non U.S., Immigrant (Permanent Resident)
             1 ☐ U.S. naturalized   3 ☐ Non-U.S., Non-Immigrant (Temporary Resident)   (50)
             If Non-U.S., indicate country of present citizenship .... (51-52)

H. Racial or ethnic group: (Check all that apply.) *A person having origins in —*
    0 ☐ American Indian or Alaskan Native .....any of the original peoples of North America, and who maintain cultural identification through tribal affiliation or community recognition.
    1 ☐ Asian or Pacific Islander ....any of the original peoples of the Far East, Southeast Asia, the Indian Subcontinent, or the Pacific Islands. This area includes, for example, China, Japan, Korea, the Philippine Islands, and Samoa.
    2 ☐ Black, not of Hispanic Origin ....any of the black racial groups of Africa.
    3 ☐ White, not of Hispanic Origin ....any of the original peoples of Europe, North Africa, or the Middle East.
    4 ☐ Hispanic ....Mexican, Puerto Rican, Central or South American, or other Spanish culture or origins, regardless of race.   (53-55)

I. Number of dependents: Do not include yourself. (Dependent = someone receiving at least one half of his or her support from you) ....(56)

J. U.S. veteran status: 0 ☐ Veteran   1 ☐ On active duty   2 ☐ Non-veteran or not applicable   (57)

EDUCATION

K. High school last attended: .... (58-59)
             (School Name)   (City)   (State)
    Year of graduation from high school: ....   (60-61)

L. List in the table below all collegiate and graduate institutions you have attended including 2-year colleges. List chronologically, and include your doctoral institution as the last entry.

Institution Name	Location	Years Attended		Major Field		Minor Field	Degree (if any)		
		From	To	Use Specialties List		Number	Title of Degree	Granted	
				Name	Number			Mo.	Yr.

M. Enter below the title of your doctoral dissertation and the most appropriate classification number and field. If a project report or a musical or literary composition (not a dissertation) is a degree requirement, please check box. ☐   (44)

Title ....   Classify using Specialties List

....   Number   Name of field

....

N. Name the department (or interdisciplinary committee, center, institute, etc.) and school or college of the university

which supervised your doctoral program: ....
                      (Department/Institute/Committee/Program)   (School)

O. Name of your dissertation adviser: ....
                 (Last Name)   (First Name)   (Middle Initial)

continued on next page

SURVEY OF EARNED DOCTORATES, Cont.

P. Please enter a "1" beside your primary source of support during graduate study. Enter a "2" beside your secondary source of support during graduate study. Check all other sources from which support was received.

58 ___ NSF Fellowship	66 ___ GI Bill	72 ___ Research Assistantship	76 ___ Spouse's earnings
59 ___ NSF Traineeship	67 ___ Other Federal support	73 ___ Educational fund of industrial or business firm	77 ___ Family contributions
60 ___ NIH Fellowship	(specify)		
61 ___ NIH Traineeship	68 ___ Woodrow Wilson Fellowship	74 ___ Other institutional funds (specify)	78 ___ Loans (NDSL direct)
62 ___ NDEA Fellowship	69 ___ Other U.S. national fellowship		79 ___ Other loans
63 ___ Other HEW			80 ___ Other (specify)
64 ___ AEC/ERDA Fellowship	(specify)		
	70 ___ University Fellowship	75 ___ Own earnings	....
65 ___ NASA Traineeship	71 ___ Teaching Assistantship		

Q. Please check the space which most fully describes your status during the year immediately preceding the doctorate.

0 ☐ Held fellowship
1 ☐ Held assistantship
2 ☐ Held own research grant
3 ☐ Not employed
4 ☐ Part-time employed

Full-time Employed in: (Other than 0, 1, 2)

5 ☐ College or university, teaching
6 ☐ College or university, non-teaching
7 ☐ Elem. or sec. school, teaching
8 ☐ Elem. or sec. school, non-teaching
9 ☐ Industry or business
(11)☐ Other (specify) ....
(12)☐ Any other (specify) .... (9)

R. How many years (full-time equivalent basis) of professional work experience did you have prior to the doctorate? (include assistantships as professional experience) ....(10-11)

POSTGRADUATION PLANS

S. How well defined are your postgraduation plans?
0 ☐ Have signed contract or made definite commitment
1 ☐ Am negotiating with a specific organization, or more than one
2 ☐ Am seeking appointment but have no specific prospects
3 ☐ Other (specify) .... (12)

T. What are your immediate postgraduation plans?
0 ☐ Postdoctoral fellowship?
1 ☐ Postdoctoral research associateship?
2 ☐ Traineeship?
3 ☐ Other study (specify) ....
4 ☐ Employment (other than 0, 1, 2, 3)
5 ☐ Military service?
6 ☐ Other (specify)..................... (13)

Go to Item "U"
Go to Item "V"

U. If you plan to be on a postdoctoral fellowship, associateship, traineeship or other study

What will be the field of your postdoctoral study? Classify using Specialties List.
Number   Field

....(14-16)

What will be the primary source of support?
0 ☐ U.S. Government
1 ☐ College or university
2 ☐ Private foundation
3 ☐ Nonprofit, other than private foundation
4 ☐ Other (specify)
.... (17)
6 ☐ Unknown
      Go to Item "W"

V. If you plan to be employed, enter military service, or other — What will be the type of employer?
0 ☐ 4-year college or university other than medical school
1 ☐ Medical school
2 ☐ Jr. or community college
3 ☐ Elem. or sec. school
4 ☐ Foreign government
5 ☐ U.S. Federal government
6 ☐ U.S. state government
7 ☐ U.S. local government
8 ☐ Nonprofit organization
9 ☐ Industry or business
(11)☐ Self-employed
(12)☐ Other (specify) .... (18)

Indicate *primary* work activity with "1" in appropriate box; *secondary* work activity (if any) with "2" in appropriate box.
0 ☐ Research and development
1 ☐ Teaching
2 ☐ Administration
3 ☐ Professional services to individuals
5 ☐ Other (specify)......................... (19-20)

In what field will you be working?
Please enter number from Specialties List .... (21-23)

      Go to Item "W"

W. What is the name and address of the organization with which you will be associated?

....
(Name of Organization)

....
(Street)   (City, State)   (Or Country if not U.S.)   (24-29)

BACKGROUND INFORMATION

X. Please indicate, by circling the highest grade attained, the education of

your father:	none	1 2 3 4 5 6 7 8	9 10 11 12	1 2 3 4	MA, MD PhD	Postdoctoral (30)
		Elementary school	High school	College	Graduate	
your mother:	none	1 2 3 4 5 6 7 8	9 10 11 12	1 2 3 4	MA, MD PhD	Postdoctoral (31)
	0	1 2 3	4 5	6 7	8 9	(11)

Signature .... Date completed ....
(32-34)

APPENDIX C

LETTER TO EVALUATORS

COMMITTEE ON AN ASSESSMENT OF QUALITY-RELATED CHARACTERISTICS OF RESEARCH-DOCTORATE PROGRAMS IN THE UNITED STATES

Established by the Conference Board of Associated Research Councils

Office of the Staff Director / National Research Council / 2101 Constitution Avenue, N.W. / Washington, D.C. 20418

April 14, 1981

Dear

As you may already know, our committee has undertaken an assessment of research-doctorate programs in U.S. universities. The study is examining approximately 2,650 programs in 31 fields in the arts and humanities, biological sciences, engineering, physical and mathematical sciences, and social sciences. A study prospectus is provided on the reverse of this page. You have been selected from a faculty list furnished by your institution to evaluate programs offering research-doctorates in the field of Biochemistry.

On the first page of the attached form is a list of the 139 programs that are being evaluated in this field. These programs produce more than 90 percent of the doctorate recipients in the field. In order to keep the task manageable, you are being asked to consider a randomly selected subset of 50 of these programs. These are designated with an asterisk in the list on the next page and are presented in random sequence on the evaluation sheets that follow. Please read the accompanying instructions carefully before attempting your evaluations.

We ask that you complete the attached survey form and return it in the enclosed envelope within the next three weeks. The evaluations you and your colleagues render will constitute an important component of this study. Your prompt attention to this request will be very much appreciated by our committee.

Sincerely,

Gardner Lindzey

Lyle Jones
For the Study Committee

Enclosures

COMMITTEE MEMBERS

Lyle V. Jones, Co-Chairman
Gardner Lindzey, Co-Chairman
Paul A. Albrecht

Marcus Alexis
Robert M. Bock
Philip E. Converse
James H. M. Henderson
Ernest S. Kuh

Winfred P. Lehmann
Saunders Mac Lane
Nancy S. Milburn
Lincoln E. Moses
James C. Olson

Kumar Patel
Michael J. Pelczar, Jr.
Jerome B. Schneewind
Duane C. Spriestersbach
Harriet A. Zuckerman

213

RESEARCH-DOCTORATE PROGRAMS IN THE FIELD OF BIOCHEMISTRY
(* DESIGNATES THE PROGRAMS WHICH YOU ARE ASKED TO EVALUATE ON THE FOLLOWING PAGES.)

INSTITUTION - DEPARTMENT/ACADEMIC UNIT

```
  UNIV OF ALABAMA SCH OF MED, BIRMINGHAM - BIOCHEMISTRY
  UNIVERSITY OF ARIZONA, TUCSON - BIOCHEMISTRY
  UNIV OF ARKANSAS MEDICAL CENTER, LITTLE ROCK - BIOCHEMISTRY
  AUBURN UNIVERSITY - CHEMISTRY/ANIMAL AND DAIRY SCIENCES
  BAYLOR COLLEGE OF MEDICINE, HOUSTON - BIOCHEMISTRY
  BOSTON UNIVERSITY - MEDICAL AND DENTAL SCIENCES
  BOSTON UNIVERSITY - INTERDEPARTMENTAL BIOCHEMISTRY PROGRAM
  BRANDEIS UNIVERSITY - BIOCHEMISTRY
  BROWN UNIVERSITY - BIOLOGY AND MEDICINE
  BRYN MAWR COLLEGE - BIOLOGY/CHEMISTRY
  UNIVERSITY OF CALIFORNIA, BERKELEY - BIOCHEMISTRY
* UNIVERSITY OF CALIFORNIA, DAVIS - BIOCHEMISTRY
  UNIVERSITY OF CALIFORNIA, IRVINE - MOLECULAR BIOLOGY AND BIOCHEMISTRY/ BIOLOGICAL CHEM
  UNIVERSITY OF CALIFORNIA, LOS ANGELES - CHEMISTRY/BIOLOGICAL CHEMISTRY
  UNIVERSITY OF CALIFORNIA, RIVERSIDE - BIOCHEMISTRY
  UNIVERSITY OF CALIFORNIA, SAN DIEGO - BIOLOGY
* UNIVERSITY OF CALIFORNIA, SAN DIEGO - CHEMISTRY
  UNIVERSITY OF CALIFORNIA, SAN FRANCISCO - BIOCHEMISTRY
  UNIVERSITY OF CALIFORNIA, SANTA BARBARA - BIOCHEMISTRY AND MOLECULAR BIOLOGY
  CASE WESTERN RESERVE UNIVERSITY - BIOCHEMISTRY
  UNIVERSITY OF CHICAGO - BIOCHEMISTRY
* UNIVERSITY OF CINCINNATI - BIOLOGICAL CHEMISTRY
* CUNY, THE GRADUATE SCHOOL - BIOCHEMISTRY
  COLORADO STATE UNIVERSITY, FT COLLINS - BIOCHEMISTRY
* UNIVERSITY OF COLORADO, BOULDER - BIOCHEMISTRY/BIOPHYSICS/GENETICS
  COLUMBIA UNIV-GRAD SCHOOL OF ARTS & SCI - BIOCHEMISTRY
* UNIVERSITY OF CONNECTICUT, STORRS - BIOLOGICAL SCIENCES
  CORNELL UNIVERSITY, ITHACA - BIOCHEMISTRY, MOLECULAR AND CELL BIOLOGY
  CORNELL UNIVERSITY MEDICAL CENTER, NYC - BIOCHEMISTRY
* DARTMOUTH COLLEGE - BIOCHEMISTRY
  UNIVERSITY OF DELAWARE, NEWARK - CHEMISTRY
* DUKE UNIVERSITY - BIOCHEMISTRY
  EMORY UNIVERSITY - BIOCHEMISTRY
  GEORGE WASHINGTON UNIVERSITY - BIOCHEMISTRY
  GEORGETOWN UNIVERSITY - BIOCHEMISTRY
  UNIVERSITY OF GEORGIA, ATHENS - BIOCHEMISTRY
* HARVARD UNIVERSITY - BIOCHEMISTRY AND MOLECULAR BIOLOGY (GRADUATE SCHOOL)
* HARVARD UNIVERSITY - BIOLOGICAL CHEMISTRY (MEDICAL SCH)
* UNIVERSITY OF HAWAII - BIOCHEMISTRY AND BIOPHYSICS
* UNIV OF HEALTH SCI/CHICAGO MEDICAL SCHOOL - BIOCHEMISTRY
  UNIVERSITY OF HOUSTON - BIOPHYSICAL SCIENCES
  HOWARD UNIVERSITY - BIOCHEMISTRY
* ILLINOIS INSTITUTE OF TECHNOLOGY - BIOLOGY
  UNIV OF ILLINOIS AT URBANA-CHAMPAIGN - BIOCHEMISTRY
* UNIV OF ILLINOIS AT THE MED CTR, CHICAGO - BIOLOGICAL CHEMISTRY
  INDIANA UNIV-PURDUE UNIV AT INDIANAPOLIS - BIOCHEMISTRY
* IOWA STATE UNIVERSITY, AMES - BIOCHEMISTRY AND BIOPHYSICS
  UNIVERSITY OF IOWA, IOWA CITY - BIOCHEMISTRY
  JOHNS HOPKINS UNIVERSITY - BIOCHEMISTRY
  KANSAS STATE UNIVERSITY, MANHATTAN - BIOCHEMISTRY
  UNIVERSITY OF KANSAS - BIOCHEMISTRY (GRADUATE SCHOOL)
* UNIVERSITY OF KANSAS - BIOCHEMISTRY (SCHOOL OF MEDICINE AT KANSAS CITY)
* UNIVERSITY OF KENTUCKY - BIOCHEMISTRY
  LOMA LINDA UNIVERSITY - BIOCHEMISTRY
* LOUISIANA STATE UNIVERSITY, BATON ROUGE - BIOCHEMISTRY
  UNIVERSITY OF LOUISVILLE - BIOCHEMISTRY
  LOYOLA UNIVERSITY OF CHICAGO - BIOCHEMISTRY AND BIOPHYSICS
* UNIVERSITY OF MARYLAND, COLLEGE PARK - CHEMISTRY
  UNIV OF MARYLAND, BALTIMORE PROF SCHOOLS - BIOLOGICAL CHEMISTRY
* MASSACHUSETTS INSTITUTE OF TECHNOLOGY - BIOLOGY
  UNIVERSITY OF MASSACHUSETTS, AMHERST - BIOCHEMISTRY
  MEDICAL UNIVERSITY OF SOUTH CAROLINA, CHARLESTON - BIOCHEMISTRY
* COL OF MED & DENT OF NEW JERSEY (NEWARK) - BIOCHEMISTRY
* UNIVERSITY OF MIAMI (FLORIDA) - BIOCHEMISTRY
* MICHIGAN STATE UNIVERSITY, EAST LANSING - BIOCHEMISTRY
* UNIVERSITY OF MICHIGAN, ANN ARBOR - BIOLOGICAL CHEMISTRY
  UNIVERSITY OF MINNESOTA - BIOCHEMISTRY (GRADUATE SCHOOL AND MEDICAL SCHOOL)
  UNIVERSITY OF MISSOURI, COLUMBIA - BIOCHEMISTRY
  UNIVERSITY OF NEBRASKA, LINCOLN - CHEMISTRY/SCHOOL OF LIFE SCIENCES
  UNIVERSITY OF NEW HAMPSHIRE - BIOCHEMISTRY
  NEW MEXICO STATE UNIVERSITY, ALAMAGORDO - CHEMISTRY
* NEW YORK UNIVERSITY - BASIC MEDICAL SCIENCES
* UNIVERSITY OF NORTH CAROLINA, CHAPEL HILL - BIOCHEMISTRY AND NUTRITION
```

NORTH CAROLINA STATE UNIVERSITY, RALEIGH - BIOCHEMISTRY
NORTH DAKOTA STATE UNIVERSITY, FARGO - BIOCHEMISTRY
* UNIVERSITY OF NORTH DAKOTA, GRAND FORKS - BIOCHEMISTRY
NORTHERN ILLINOIS UNIVERSITY, DE KALB - CHEMISTRY
NORTHWESTERN UNIVERSITY - BIOCHEMISTRY AND MOLECULAR BIOLOGY/ BIOCHEMISTRY
UNIVERSITY OF NOTRE DAME - CHEMISTRY
OHIO STATE UNIVERSITY - PHYSIOLOGICAL CHEMISTRY
OHIO STATE UNIVERSITY - BIOCHEMISTRY
OKLAHOMA STATE UNIVERSITY, STILLWATER - BIOCHEMISTRY
UNIVERSITY OF OKLAHOMA - BIOCHEMISTRY AND MOLECULAR BIOLOGY
UNIVERSITY OF OREGON, EUGENE - BIOLOGY/CHEMISTRY
OREGON STATE UNIVERSITY, COVALLIS - BIOCHEMISTRY AND BIOPHYSICS
PENNSYLVANIA STATE UNIVERSITY - BIOLOGICAL CHEMISTRY (MEDICAL CTR)
* PENNSYLVANIA STATE UNIVERSITY - BIOCHEMISTRY (GRADUATE SCHOOL)
UNIVERSITY OF PENNSYLVANIA - BIOCHEMISTRY
UNIVERSITY OF PITTSBURGH - BIOCHEMISTRY (SCHOOL OF MEDICINE)
UNIVERSITY OF PITTSBURGH - BIOLOGICAL SCIENCES (ARTS AND SCIENCES)
* PRINCETON UNIVERSITY - BIOCHEMICAL SCIENCES
* PURDUE UNIVERSITY, WEST LAFAYETTE - BIOLOGICAL SCIENCES
UNIVERSITY OF RHODE ISLAND - BIOCHEMISTRY/BIOPHYSICS
* RICE UNIVERSITY - BIOCHEMISTRY
UNIVERSITY OF ROCHESTER - BIOCHEMISTRY
* ROCKEFELLER UNIVERSITY - BIOCHEMISTRY
* RUTGERS UNIVERSITY, NEW BRUNSWICK - BIOCHEMISTRY
* SAINT LOUIS UNIVERSITY - BIOCHEMISTRY
* UNIVERSITY OF SOUTH DAKOTA, VERMILLION - BIOCHEMISTRY, PHYSIOLOGY, AND PHARMACOLOGY
* UNIVERSITY OF SOUTHERN CALIFORNIA - BIOCHEMISTRY
* SOUTHERN ILLINOIS UNIVERSITY, CARBONDALE - CHEMISTRY AND BIOCHEMISTRY
STANFORD UNIVERSITY - BIOCHEMISTRY
UNIVERSITY OF FLORIDA, GAINESVILLE - BIOCHEMISTRY AND MOLECULAR BIOLOGY
* SUNY AT ALBANY - BIOLOGICAL SCIENCES
SUNY AT BUFFALO - BIOCHEMISTRY (SCHOOL OF MEDICINE)
SUNY AT BUFFALO - BIOCHEMISTRY (ROSWELL PARK GRADUATE DIVISION)
* SUNY AT STONY BROOK - BIOCHEMISTRY
SUNY, DOWNSTATE MEDICAL CENTER (BROOKLYN) - BIOCHEMISTRY
SUNY, UPSTATE MEDICAL CENTER (SYRACUSE) - BIOCHEMISTRY
* SYRACUSE UNIVERSITY - BIOLOGY
SUNY, COL OF ENVIR SCI & FORESTRY (SYRACUSE) - SCHOOL OF BIOLOGY, CHEMISTRY, AND ECOLOGY
TEMPLE UNIVERSITY - BIOCHEMISTRY
UNIVERSITY OF TENNESSEE, KNOXVILLE - BIOCHEMISTRY
UNIV OF TENNESSEE-CTR FOR HEALTH SCI, MEMPHIS - BIOCHEMISTRY
TEXAS A&M UNIVERSITY - BIOCHEMISTRY AND BIOPHYSICS
* UNIVERSITY OF TEXAS, AUSTIN - CHEMISTRY
* UNIV OF TEXAS, MED BRANCH AT GALVESTON - HUMAN BIOLOGICAL CHEMISTRY AND GENETICS
UNIV OF TEXAS, HLTH SCI CTR AT HOUSTON - BIOCHEM & MOLECULAR BIO(MED SCH)/ BIOCHEM(ANDERSON HOSP)
* UNIV OF TEXAS, HLTH SCI CTR AT SAN ANTONIO - BIOCHEMISTRY
THOMAS JEFFERSON UNIVERSITY - BIOCHEMISTRY
* TULANE UNIVERSITY - BIOCHEMISTRY
* ALBANY MEDICAL COLLEGE - BIOCHEMISTRY
UNIVERSITY OF UTAH, SALT LAKE CITY - BIOCHEMISTRY
VANDERBILT UNIVERSITY - BIOCHEMISTRY
UNIVERSITY OF VERMONT - BIOCHEMISTRY
VIRGINIA COMMONWEALTH UNIVERSITY - BIOCHEMISTRY
VIRGINIA POLYTECHNIC INSTITUTE AND STATE UNIV - BIOCHEMISTRY AND NUTRITION
UNIVERSITY OF VIRGINIA - BIOCHEMISTRY
WAKE FOREST UNIVERSITY - BIOCHEMISTRY
WASHINGTON STATE UNIVERSITY, PULLMAN - BIOCHEMISTRY AND BIOPHYSICS
* UNIVERSITY OF WASHINGTON, SEATTLE - BIOCHEMISTRY
WAYNE STATE UNIVERSITY - BIOCHEMISTRY
WEST VIRGINIA UNIVERSITY - MEDICAL BIOCHEMISTRY
* WEST VIRGINIA UNIVERSITY - AGRICULTURAL BIOCHEMISTRY
UNIVERSITY OF WISCONSIN, MADISON - PHYSIOLOGICAL CHEMISTRY
UNIVERSITY OF WISCONSIN, MADISON - BIOCHEMISTRY
* UNIVERSITY OF WYOMING - BIOCHEMISTRY
YALE UNIVERSITY - MOLECULAR BIOPHYSICS AND BIOCHEM/ PHARMACOLOGY/ BIOLOGY
ALBERT EINSTEIN COLLEGE OF MEDICINE - BIOCHEMISTRY

INSTRUCTIONS

At the top of the next page please provide the information requested on the highest degree you hold and your current field of specialization. You may be assured that all information you furnish on the survey form is to be used for purposes of statistical description only and that the confidentiality of your responses will be protected.

On the pages that follow you are asked to judge 50 programs (presented in random sequence) that offer the research-doctorate. Each program is to be evaluated in terms of: (1) scholarly quality of program faculty; (2) effectiveness of program in educating research scholars/scientists; and (3) change in program quality in the last five years (see below). Although the assessment is limited to these factors, our committee recognizes that other factors are relevant to the quality of doctoral programs, and that graduate programs serve important purposes in addition to that of educating doctoral candidates.

A list of the faculty members signficantly involved in each program, the name of the academic unit in which the program is offered, and the number of doctorates awarded in that program during the last five years have been printed on the survey form (whenever available). Although this information has been furnished to us by the institution and is believed to be accurate, it has not been verified by our study committee and may have a few omissions, misspellings, or other errors.

Before marking your responses on the survey form, you may find it helpful to look over the full set of programs you are being asked to evaluate. In making your judgments about each program, please keep in mind the following instructions:

(1) Scholarly Quality of Program Faculty. Check the box next to the term that most closely corresponds to your judgment of the quality of faculty in the research-doctorate program described. Consider only the scholarly competence and achievements of the faculty. It is suggested that no more than five programs be designated "distinguished."

(2) Effectiveness of Program in Educating Research Scholars/Scientists. Check the box next to the term that most closely corresponds to your judgment of the doctoral program's effectiveness in educating research scholars/scientists. Consider the access-ibility of the faculty, the curricula, the instructional and research facilities, the quality of graduate students, the performance of the graduates, and other factors that contribute to the effectiveness of the research-doctorate program.

(3) Change in Program Quality in Last Five Years. Check the box next to the term that most closely corresponds to your esti-mate of the change that has taken place in the research-doctorate program in the last five years. Consider both the scholarly quality of the program faculty and the effectiveness of the program in educating research scholars/scientists. Com-pare the quality of the program today with its quality five years ago--not the change in the program's relative standing among other programs in the field.

In assessing each of these factors, mark the category "Don't know well enough to evaluate" if you are unfamiliar with that aspect of the program. It is quite possible that for some programs you may be knowledgeable about the scholarly quality of the faculty, but not about the effectiveness of the program or change in program quality.

For each of the programs identified, you are also asked to indicate the extent to which you are familiar with the work of members of the program faculty. For example, if you recognize only a very small fraction of the faculty, you should mark the category "Little or no familiarity."

Please be certain that you have provided a set of responses for each of the programs identified on the following pages. The fully completed survey form should be returned in the enclosed envelope to:

Committee on an Assessment of Quality-Related
Characteristics of Research-Doctorate Programs
National Research Council, JH-638
2101 Constitution Avenue, N.W.
Washington, D.C. 20418

Our committee will be most appreciative of your thoughtful assessment of these research-doctorate programs. We welcome any comments you may wish to append to the completed survey form.

PLEASE PROVIDE THE FOLLOWING INFORMATION: FORM NO. 2203-51

HIGHEST DEGREE YOU HOLD: ( ) PH.D.   ( ) OTHER (PLEASE SPECIFY): _____

YEAR OF HIGHEST DEGREE: _____

INSTITUTION OF HIGHEST DEGREE: _____

YOUR CURRENT FIELD OF SPECIALIZATION (CHECK ONLY ONE):

A. ( ) ANATOMY   M. ( ) MOLECULAR BIOLOGY

B. ( ) ANIMAL SCIENCES   N. ( ) NUTRITION/FOOD SCIENCE

C. ( ) BIOCHEMISTRY   O. ( ) PATHOLOGY

D. ( ) BIOPHYSICS   P. ( ) PHARMACOLOGY/TOXICOLOGY

E. ( ) BOTANY   Q. ( ) PHYSIOLOGY, ANIMAL/HUMAN

F. ( ) CELL BIOLOGY   R. ( ) PHYSIOLOGY, PLANT

G. ( ) ECOLOGY   S. ( ) PHYTOPATHOLOGY

H. ( ) ENTOMOLOGY   T. ( ) PUBLIC HEALTH/EPIDEMIOLOGY

I. ( ) GENERAL BIOLOGY   U. ( ) ZOOLOGY

J. ( ) GENETICS   V. ( ) OTHER (PLEASE SPECIFY):

K. ( ) IMMUNOLOGY

L. ( ) MICROBIOLOGY/BACTERIOLOGY   _____

INSTITUTION: UNIVERSITY OF CINCINNATI   FORM NO. 2203-01
DEPARTMENT/ACADEMIC UNIT: BIOLOGICAL CHEMISTRY
TOTAL DOCTORATES AWARDED 1976-80: 12

PROFESSORS: James H. FREISHEIM, Richard JACKSON, Jerry B. LINGREL, Harry RUDNEY

ASSOCIATE PROFESSORS: Richard W. ARMENTROUT, W. David BEHNKE, Eric I. GRUENSTEIN, Judith A. K. HARMONY, Robert C. KRUEGER, James D. OGLE, Amadeo J. PESCE

ASSISTANT PROFESSORS: Kenneth M. BLUMENTHAL, Ronald D. BROWN, Donal LUSE, Bruce MOULTON

SCHOLARLY QUALITY OF PROGRAM FACULTY

1. ( ) DISTINGUISHED
2. ( ) STRONG
3. ( ) GOOD
4. ( ) ADEQUATE
5. ( ) MARGINAL
6. ( ) NOT SUFFICIENT FOR DOCTORAL EDUCATION

0. ( ) DON'T KNOW WELL ENOUGH TO EVALUATE

FAMILIARITY WITH WORK OF PROGRAM FACULTY

1. ( ) CONSIDERABLE FAMILIARITY
2. ( ) SOME FAMILIARITY
3. ( ) LITTLE OR NO FAMILIARITY

EFFECTIVENESS OF PROGRAM IN EDUCATING RESEARCH SCHOLARS/SCIENTISTS

1. ( ) EXTREMELY EFFECTIVE
2. ( ) REASONABLY EFFECTIVE
3. ( ) MINIMALLY EFFECTIVE
4. ( ) NOT EFFECTIVE

0. ( ) DON'T KNOW WELL ENOUGH TO EVALUATE

CHANGE IN PROGRAM QUALITY IN LAST FIVE YEARS

1. ( ) BETTER THAN FIVE YEARS AGO
2. ( ) LITTLE OR NO CHANGE IN LAST FIVE YEAR
3. ( ) POORER THAN FIVE YEARS AGO

0. ( ) DON'T KNOW WELL ENOUGH TO EVALUATE

INSTITUTION: **MICHIGAN STATE UNIVERSITY, EAST LANSING**   FORM NO. 2203-02
DEPARTMENT/ACADEMIC UNIT: **BIOCHEMISTRY**
TOTAL DOCTORATES AWARDED 1976-80: 34

PROFESSORS: Richard ANDERSON, Charles ARNTZEN, Steven AUST, Loran BIEBER, William DEAL, James FAIRLEY, Philip FILNER, Paul KINDEL, Hans LILLEVIK, Richard LUECKE, Veronica MAHER, David MCCONNELL, Justin MCCORMICK, Allan MORRIS, Fritz ROTTMAN, John SPECK, Clarence SUELTER, Charles SWEELEY, N. E. TOLBERT, Jack WATSON, William WELLS, John WILSON, Willis WOOD

ASSOCIATE PROFESSORS: Deborah DELMER, Pamela FRAKER, William SMITH

ASSISTANT PROFESSORS: Jerry DODGSON, Edward FRITSCH, Roger KOBES, Hsing Jien KUNG, Shelagh Ferguson MILLER, Arnold REVZIN, Melvin SCHINDLER, Karel SCHUBERT, John WANG

OTHER STAFF: Susan HAWKES, John HOLLAND

SCHOLARLY QUALITY OF PROGRAM FACULTY

1. ( ) DISTINGUISHED
2. ( ) STRONG
3. ( ) GOOD
4. ( ) ADEQUATE
5. ( ) MARGINAL
6. ( ) NOT SUFFICIENT FOR DOCTORAL EDUCATION

0. ( ) DON'T KNOW WELL ENOUGH TO EVALUATE

FAMILIARITY WITH WORK OF PROGRAM FACULTY

1. ( ) CONSIDERABLE FAMILIARITY
2. ( ) SOME FAMILIARITY
3. ( ) LITTLE OR NO FAMILIARITY

EFFECTIVENESS OF PROGRAM IN EDUCATING RESEARCH SCHOLARS/SCIENTISTS

1. ( ) EXTREMELY EFFECTIVE
2. ( ) REASONABLY EFFECTIVE
3. ( ) MINIMALLY EFFECTIVE
4. ( ) NOT EFFECTIVE

0. ( ) DON'T KNOW WELL ENOUGH TO EVALUATE

CHANGE IN PROGRAM QUALITY IN LAST FIVE YEARS

1. ( ) BETTER THAN FIVE YEARS AGO
2. ( ) LITTLE OR NO CHANGE IN LAST FIVE YEAR
3. ( ) POORER THAN FIVE YEARS AGO

0. ( ) DON'T KNOW WELL ENOUGH TO EVALUATE

INSTITUTION: **UNIV OF ILLINOIS AT THE MED CTR, CHICAGO**   FORM NO. 2203-03
DEPARTMENT/ACADEMIC UNIT: **BIOLOGICAL CHEMISTRY**
TOTAL DOCTORATES AWARDED 1976-80: 25

PROFESSORS: Michael BARANY, Clyde C. DOUGHTY, Henry GEWURZ, Mary Sue HANLON, Thomas O. HENDERSON, Henry JEFFAY, Janos MOLNAR, Terrell C. MYERS, Mariano TAO, Edward B. TITCHENER, James VARY, Bernard WEISSMAN

ASSOCIATE PROFESSORS: Charalampos ARSENIS, Bernard FRIEDENSON, Paul MORRIS, Tarakad RAJKUMAR, Newton RESSLER

ASSISTANT PROFESSORS: Robert V. STORTI

SCHOLARLY QUALITY OF PROGRAM FACULTY

1. ( ) DISTINGUISHED
2. ( ) STRONG
3. ( ) GOOD
4. ( ) ADEQUATE
5. ( ) MARGINAL
6. ( ) NOT SUFFICIENT FOR DOCTORAL EDUCATION

0. ( ) DON'T KNOW WELL ENOUGH TO EVALUATE

FAMILIARITY WITH WORK OF PROGRAM FACULTY

1. ( ) CONSIDERABLE FAMILIARITY
2. ( ) SOME FAMILIARITY
3. ( ) LITTLE OR NO FAMILIARITY

EFFECTIVENESS OF PROGRAM IN EDUCATING RESEARCH SCHOLARS/SCIENTISTS

1. ( ) EXTREMELY EFFECTIVE
2. ( ) REASONABLY EFFECTIVE
3. ( ) MINIMALLY EFFECTIVE
4. ( ) NOT EFFECTIVE

0. ( ) DON'T KNOW WELL ENOUGH TO EVALUATE

CHANGE IN PROGRAM QUALITY IN LAST FIVE YEARS

1. ( ) BETTER THAN FIVE YEARS AGO
2. ( ) LITTLE OR NO CHANGE IN LAST FIVE YEAR
3. ( ) POORER THAN FIVE YEARS AGO

0. ( ) DON'T KNOW WELL ENOUGH TO EVALUATE

APPENDIX D

THE ARL LIBRARY INDEX

(SOURCE: Mandel, Carol A., and Mary P. Johnson, ARL Statistics 1979-80, Association of Research Libraries, Washington, D.C., 1980, pp. 23-24.)

The data tables at the beginning of the ARL Statistics display figures reported by ARL member libraries in 22 categories that, with the exception of the measures of interlibrary loan activity, describe the size of ARL libraries in terms of holdings, expenditures, and personnel. The rank order tables provide an overview of the ranges. and medians for 14 of these categories, or variables, among ARL academic libraries as well as quantitatively comparing each library with other ARL member institutions. However, none of the 22 variables provides a summary measure of a library's relative size within ARL or characterizes the ARL libraries as a whole.

The ARL Library Index has been derived as a means of providing this summary characterization, permitting quantitative comparisons of ARL academic libraries, singly and as a group, with other academic libraries. Through the use of statistical techniques known as factor analysis, it can be determined that 15 of the variables reported to ARL are more closely correlated with each other than with other categories. Within this group of 15 variables, some are subsets or combinations of materials. When the subsets and combinations are eliminated, 10 variables emerge as characteristic of ARL libary size. These are: volumes held, volumes added (gross), microform units held, current serials received, expenditures for library materials, expenditures for binding, total salary and wage expenditures, other operating expenditures, number of professional staff, and number of nonprofessional staff.

These 10 categories delineate an underlying dimension, or factor, of library size. By means of principal component analysis, a technique that is a variant of factor analysis, it is possible to calculate the correlations of each of the variables with this hypothetical factor of library size. From this analysis a weight for each variable can be determined based on how closely that variable is correlated with the overall dimension of library size defined by all 10 categories. A high correlation indicates that much of the variation in ARL library size is accounted for by the variable in question, implying a characteristic in which ARL libraries are relatively alike. The component score coefficients, or weights, for

219

the 1979-80 ARL academic library data are as follows:

Volumes held	.12108
Volumes added (gross)	.11940
Microforms held	.07509
Current serials received	.12253
Expenditures for library materials	.12553
Expenditures for binding	.11266
Expenditures for salaries and wages	.12581
Other operating expenditures	.10592
Number of professional staff	.12347
Number of nonprofessional staff	.11297

From these weights an individual library can compute an index score that will indicate its relative position among ARL libraries with respect to the overall factor of library size. The data for each of the 10 variables are converted to standard normal form and multiplied by the appropriate weight. The resulting scores are expressed in terms of the number of standard deviations above or below the mean index score for ARL academic libraries. Thus, the formula* for calculating a library's 1979-80 index score is as follows:

$$.12108 \text{ (log of volumes held} - 6.2916)/.2172$$
$$+.11940 \text{ (log of volumes added gross} - 4.8412)/.2025$$
$$+.07509 \text{ (log of microforms} - 6.0950)/.1763$$
$$+.12253 \text{ (log of current serials} - 4.3432)/.2341$$
$$+.12553 \text{ (log of expenditures for materials} - 6.2333)/.1636$$
$$+.11266 \text{ (log of expenditures for binding} - 5.0480)/.2475$$
$$+.12581 \text{ (log of total salaries} - 6.4675)/.2103$$
$$+.10592 \text{ (log of operating expenditures} - 5.6773)/.2635$$
$$+.12347 \text{ (log of professional staff} - 1.8281)/.1968$$
$$+.11297 \text{ (log of nonprofessional staff} - 2.1512)/.2046$$

The index scores for the 99 academic libraries that were members of ARL during 1979-80 are shown on the following page. It is important to emphasize that these scores are only a summary description of library size, distributing ARL libraries along a normal curve, based on 10 quantitative measures that are positively correlated with one another in ARL libraries. The scores are in no way a qualitative assessment of the collections, services, or operations of these libraries.

---

*For calculation on a hand calculator, the formula can be mathematically simplified to: (.55746 x log of volumes held) + (.58963 x log of volumes added gross) + (.42592 x log of microforms) + (.52341 x log of current serials) + (.76730 x log of expenditures for materials) + (.45519 x log of expenditures for binding) + (.59824 x log of total salaries) + (.40197 x log of operating expenditures) + (.62739 x log of professional staff) + (.55215 x log of nonprofessional staff) - 26.79765.

APPENDIX E

FACULTY RESEARCH SUPPORT

The names of National Science Foundation (NSF) research grant awardees were obtained from a file maintained by the NSF Division of Information Systems. The file provided to the committee covered all research grant awards made in FY1978, FY1979, and FY1980 and included the names of the principal investigator and co-principal investigators for each award. Also available from this file was information concerning the field of science/engineering of the research grant and the institution with which the investigator was affiliated. This information was used in identifying which research grant recipients were on the program faculty lists provided by institutional coordinators.

The names of National Institutes of Health (NIH) and Alcohol, Drug Abuse, and Mental Health Administration (ADAMHA) research grant recipients (principal investigators only) were obtained from the NIH Information for Management Planning, Analysis, and Coordination System. This system contains a detailed record of all applications and awards in the various training and research support programs of these agencies. For the purposes of this study, information analogous to that available from the NSF file was extended for FY1978-80 research grant awardees and their records were matched with the program faculty lists. Measure 13 constitutes the fraction of program faculty members who had received one or more research grant awards from NSF (including both principal investigators and co-principal investigators), NIH, or ADAMHA during the FY1978-80 period.

R&D EXPENDITURES

Total university expenditures for R&D activities are available from the NSF Survey of Scientific and Engineering Expenditures at Universities and Colleges. A copy of the survey form appears on the following pages.

221

NSF FORM 411 (Dec. 1979)

FORM APPROVED
OMB No. 99-R0279

NATIONAL SCIENCE FOUNDATION
Washington, D.C. 20550

SURVEY OF SCIENTIFIC AND ENGINEERING
EXPENDITURES AT UNIVERSITIES AND COLLEGES, FY 1979

(Current and Capital Expenditures for Research,
Development, and Instruction in the Sciences and Engineering)

Organizations are requested to complete and return this form to:

NATIONAL SCIENCE FOUNDATION
1800 G Street, N.W.
Washington, D.C. 20550
Attn: UNISG

This form should be returned by February 1, 1980.
Your cooperation in returning the survey questionnaire
promptly is very important.

Financial data are requested for your institution's
1979 fiscal year.

This information is solicited under the authority of the
National Science Foundation Act of 1950, as amended.
All information you provide will be used for statistical
purposes only. Your response is entirely voluntary and
your failure to provide some or all of the information
will in no way adversely affect your institution.

All financial data requested on this form should be reported in thousands of dollars; for example, an expenditure of $25,342 should be rounded to the nearest
thousand dollars and reported as $25.

Where exact data are not available, estimates are acceptable. Your estimates will be better than ours.

Please correct if name or address has changed

(Includes aggregate data from 567
universities and colleges but excludes 19 university-administered
FFRDC's)

Include data for branches and all organizational units of your institution, such as
medical schools and agricultural experiment stations. Also include hospitals or clinics
owned, operated, or controlled by universities, and integrated operationally with the
clinical programs of your medical schools. Exclude data for federally funded research
and development centers (FFRDC's). A separate questionnaire is included in this package if your institution administers an FFRDC. **If you have any questions please contact
Jim Hoehn (202-634-4674).**

Please enter the beginning and ending dates of your institution's fiscal year for which
you are reporting on this form:

_____ through _____

Please note in space below:
(1) Any suggestions to improve the design of the survey questionnaire, (2) any suggestions to improve
the instructions, or (3) any comments on significant change in R&D in your institution.

(Attach additional sheets, if necessary.)

PLEASE TYPE OR PRINT NAME OF PERSON SUBMITTING THIS FORM	TITLE	AREA CODE	EXCH	NO.	EXT

NAME OF PERSON WHO PREPARED THIS SUBMISSION (If different from above)	TITLE	AREA CODE	EXCH	NO.	EXT

Please check and correct if necessary the name and address of your institution shown on the mailing label.   DATE

ITEM 1. CURRENT EXPENDITURES FOR SEPARATELY BUDGETED RESEARCH AND DEVELOPMENT (R&D) IN THE SCIENCES AND ENGINEERING, BY SOURCE OF FUNDS AND BASIC RESEARCH, FY 1979 (Include indirect costs)

ITEMS 1. & 2. INSTRUCTIONS

Separately budgeted research and development (R&D) includes all funds expended for activities specifically organized to produce research outcomes and commissioned by an agency either external to the institution or separately budgeted by an organizational unit within the institution. **Include** equipment purchased under research project awards as part of "current funds." Research funds subcontracted to outside organizations should also be included. **Exclude** training grants, public service grants, demonstration projects, etc.

Under a. **Federal Government.** Report grants and contracts for R&D by all agencies of the Federal Government including indirect costs from these sources.

Under b. **State and local governments.** Include funds for R&D from State, county, municipal, or other local governments and their agencies. Include here State funds which support R&D at agricultural experiment stations.

Under c. **Industry.** Include all grants and contracts for R&D from profitmaking organizations, whether engaged in production, distribution, research, service, or other activities. Do not include grants and contracts from nonprofit foundations financed by industry, which should be reported under **All other sources.**

Under d. **Institutional funds.** Report funds which your institution spent for R&D activities including indirect costs from the following sources: (1) General-purpose State or local government appropriations; (2) general-purpose grants from industry, foundations, or other outside sources; (3) tuition and fees; (4) endowment income. In addition, estimate your institution's contribution to unreimbursed indirect costs incurred in association with R&D projects financed by outside organizations, and mandatory cost sharing on Federal and other grants. To estimate unreimbursed indirect costs, many institutions use a university-wide negotiated indirect cost rate multiplied by the base (e.g., direct salaries and wages, etc.) minus actual indirect cost recoveries. If your institution now separately budgets what was previously classified as departmental research, these data should be included in line d.

Under e. **All other sources.** Include foundations and voluntary health agencies grants for R&D, as well as all other sources not elsewhere classified. Funds from foundations which are affiliated with or grant solely to your institution should be included under d. Institutional funds. Funds for R&D received from a health agency that is a unit of a State or local government should be reported under State and local governments. Also include gifts from individuals that are restricted by the donor to research.

Please exclude from your response any R&D expenditures in the fields of education, law, humanities, music, the arts, physical education, library science, and all other nonscience fields.

Source of funds		(1) Total R&D expenditures (Dollars in thousands)	(2) Basic research (Percent of column 1)
a. Federal Government	1110	$ 3,431,538	73.4 %
*b. State and local governments	1125	467,311	Basic research is directed toward an increase of knowledge; it is research where the primary aim of the investigator is a fuller knowledge or understanding of the subject under study rather than a practical application thereof.
c. Industry	1150	193,794	
d. Institutional funds	1160	716,241	
(1) Separately budgeted	1161	357,926	
(2) Underrecovery of indirect costs and cost sharing	1162	358,315	
*e. All other sources	1175	373,845	
f. TOTAL (sum of a through e)	1100	$ 5,182,729	68.5 %

*Combined data cell (See instructions for b and e).

Total R&D expenditures reported in line 1100 column (1) and line 1400 column (1) should be the same.
Federally financed R&D expenditures reported in line 1100 column (1) and line 1400 column (2) should be the same.

CONFIDENTIALITY

Information received from individual institutions in lines 1161 and 1162, or estimates for basic research expenditures, will **not** be published or released; only aggregate totals will appear in publications.

ITEM 2. TOTAL AND FEDERALLY FINANCED EXPENDITURES FOR SEPARATELY BUDGETED RESEARCH AND DEVELOPMENT, BY FIELD OF SCIENCE, FY 1979 (Include indirect costs and equipment).

Field of science	Illustrative disciplines		(Dollars in thousands)	
			(1) Total	(2) Federal
a. ENGINEERING (TOTAL)	Aeronautical, agricultural, chemical, civil, electrical, industrial, mechanical, metallurgical, mining, nuclear, petroleum, bio- and biomedical, energy, textile, architecture	1410	$ 715,454	$ 474,866
b. PHYSICAL SCIENCES (TOTAL)		1420	559,566	448,992
(1) Astronomy	Astrophysics, optical and radio, x-ray, gamma-ray, neutrino	1421	39,026	26,862
(2) Chemistry	Inorganic, organo-metallic, organic, physical, analytical, pharmaceutical, polymer science (exclude biochemistry)	1422	204,062	154,031
(3) Physics	Acoustics, atomic and molecular, condensed matter, elementary particles, nuclear structure, optics, plasma	1423	275,680	236,872
(4) Other	Used for multidisciplinary projects within physical sciences and for disciplines not requested separately	1424	40,798	31,227
c. ENVIRONMENTAL SCIENCES (TOTAL)	ATMOSPHERIC SCIENCES: Aeronomy, solar weather modification, meteorology, extra-terrestrial atmospheres GEOLOGICAL SCIENCES: Engineering geophysics, geology, geodesy, geomagnetism, hydrology, geochemistry, paleomagnetism, paleontology, physical geography, cartography, seismology, soil sciences OCEANOGRAPHY: Chemical, geological, physical, marine geophysics, marine biology, biological oceanography	1430	429,129	307,493
d. MATHEMATICAL AND COMPUTER SCIENCES (TOTAL)		1440	145,087	94,534
(1) Mathematics	Algebra, analysis, applied mathematics, foundations and logic, geometry, numerical analysis, statistics, topology	1441	65,637	49,043
(2) Computer sciences	Design, development, and application of computer capabilities to data storage and manipulation, information science	1442	79,450	45,491
e. LIFE SCIENCES (TOTAL)		1450	2,814,824	1,810,729
(1) Biological sciences	Anatomy, biochemistry, biophysics, biogeography, ecology, embryology, entomology, genetics, immunology, microbiology, nutrition, parasitology, pathology, pharmacology, physical anthropology, physiology, botany, zoology	1451	949,993	690,805
(2) Agricultural	Agricultural chemistry, agronomy, animal science, conservation, dairy science, plant science, range science, wildlife	1452	565,697	168,849
(3) Medical	Anesthesiology, cardiology, endocrinology, gastroenterology, hematology, neurology, obstetrics, opthalmology, preventive medicine and community health, psychiatry, radiology, surgery, veterinary medicine, dentistry, pharmacy	1453	1,214,442	890,612
(4) Other	Used for multidisciplinary projects within life sciences	1454	84,692	60,463
f. PSYCHOLOGY (TOTAL)	Animal behavior, clinical, educational, experimental, human development and personality, social	1460	99,732	72,256
g. SOCIAL SCIENCES (TOTAL)		1470	290,057	153,674
(1) Economics	Econometrics, international, industrial, labor, agricultural, public finance and fiscal policy	1471	85,415	40,641
(2) Political science	Regional studies, comparative government, international relations, legal systems, political theory, public administration	1472	39,029	18,452
(3) Sociology	Comparative and historical, complex organizations, culture and social structure, demography, group interactions, social problems and welfare, theory	1473	72,669	46,739
(4) Other	History of science, cultural anthropology, linguistics, socio-economic geography	1474	92,944	47,842
h. OTHER SCIENCES, n.e.c. (TOTAL)*	To be used when the multidisciplinary and interdisciplinary aspects make the classification under one primary field impossible	1480	128,880	68,994
i. TOTAL (SUM of a through h) Check to insure that column totals are identical with data reported in item 1.		1400	5,182,729	3,431,538

*PLEASE EXCLUDE FROM YOUR RESPONSE ANY R&D EXPENDITURES IN THE FIELDS OF EDUCATION, LAW, HUMANITIES, MUSIC, THE ARTS, PHYSICAL EDUCATION, LIBRARY SCIENCE, AND ALL OTHER NONSCIENCE FIELDS.

ITEM 3. CAPITAL EXPENDITURES FOR SCIENTIFIC AND ENGINEERING FACILITIES AND
EQUIPMENT FOR RESEARCH, DEVELOPMENT, AND INSTRUCTION,
BY FIELD OF SCIENCE AND SOURCE OF FUNDS, FY 1979

ITEM 3. INSTRUCTIONS

Report funds for facilities which were in process or completed during FY 1979. Expenditures for administration buildings, steam plants, residence halls, and other such facilities should be excluded unless utilized principally for research, development, or instruction in engineering or in the sciences. Land costs should be **excluded**. Exclude small equipment items in your current fund account costing approximately $300 or less per unit or as recommended by the Joint Accounting Group (JAG) or as determined by your institutional policy; these are to be reported under items 1 and 2.

Facilities and equipment expenditures **include** the following: (a) Fixed equipment such as built-in equipment and furnishings; (b) movable scientific equipment such as oscilloscopes and pulse-height analyzers; (c) movable furnishings such as desk; (d) architect's fees, site work, extension of utilities, and the building costs of service functions such as integral cafeterias and bookstores of a facility; (e) facilities constructed to house separate components such as medical schools and teaching hospitals; and (f) special separate facilities used to house scientific apparatus such as accelerators, oceanographic vessels, and computers.

Field of science		Total (1)	Federal (2)	All other sources (3)
		(Dollars in thousands)		
a. Engineering	1710	$ 95,399	$ 22,060	$ 73,339
b. Physical sciences	1720	64,551	32,439	32,112
c. Environmental sciences	1730	25,293	8,970	16,323
d. Mathematical and computer sciences	1740	27,465	3,049	24,416
e. Life sciences	1750	456,477	92,567	363,910
f. Psychology	1760	7,803	1,767	6,036
g. Social sciences	1770	20,932	2,069	18,863
h. Other sciences, n.e.c.	1780	31,984	5,054	26,930
i. **Total (sum of a through h)**	1700	$ 729,904	$ 167,975	$ 561,929

APPENDIX F

DATA ON PUBLICATION RECORDS

Data for these measures were provided by a subcontractor, Computer Horizons, Inc. A detailed description of the derivation of these measures and examples of their use is given in:

Francis Narin, Evaluative Bibliometrics: The Use of Publications and Citations Analysis in the Evaluation of Scientific Activity, Report to the National Science Foundation, March 1976.

The following pages have been excerpted from Chapters VI and VII of this report and describe operational considerations in compiling the publication records included here (measure 15) and the methodology used in determining the "influence" of published articles (measure 16).

VI.   OPERATIONAL CONSIDERATIONS

A.   Basics of Publication and Citation Analysis

The first section of this chapter discusses the major stages of publication and citation analysis techniques in evaluative bibliometrics. Later sections of the chapter consider publication and citation count parameters in further detail, including discussions of data bases, of field-dependent characteristics of the literature, and of some cautions and hazards in performing citation analyses for individual scientists.

The basic stages which must be kept in mind when doing a publication or citation analysis are briefly summarized in Figure 6-1.

1.   Type of Publication

For a publication analysis the fundamental decision is which type of publication to count. A basic count will include all regular scientific articles. However, notes are often counted since some engineering and other journals often contain notes with significant technical content. Reviews may be included. Letters-to-the-editor must also be considered as a possible category for inclusion, since some important journals are sometimes classified as letter journals. For example, publications in Physical Review Letters were classified as letters by the Science Citation Index prior to 1970, although they are now classified as articles.

For most counts in the central core of the scientific literature, articles, notes and reviews are used as a measure of scientific output. When dealing with engineering fields, where many papers are presented at meetings accompanied by reprints and published proceedings, meeting presentations must also be considered. In some applied fields, i.e., agriculture, aerospace and nuclear engineering, where government support has been particularly comprehensive, the report literature may also be important. Unfortunately, reports generally contain few references, and citations to them are limited so they are not amenable to the normal citation analyses.

Books, of course, are a major type of publication, especially in the social sciences where they are often used instead of a series of journal articles. In bibliometrics a weighting of n articles equal to one book is frequently used; no uniformly acceptable value of n is available. A few of the papers discussed in Chapter V contain such measures.

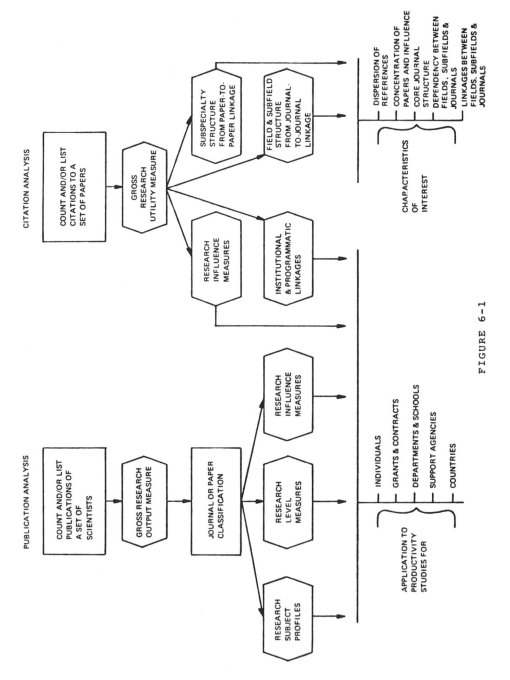

FIGURE 6-1

STAGES OF PUBLICATION AND CITATION ANALYSIS

2. Time Spans

A second important decision in making a publication count is to select the time span of interest. In the analysis of the publications of an institution a fixed time span, usually one year or more, is most appropriate. In comparing publication histories of groups of scientists, their professional ages (normally defined as years since attaining the PhD degree) must be comparable so that the build-up of publications at the beginning of a career or the decline at the end will not complicate the results. A typical scientist's first publication appears soon after his dissertation; if he continued working as a scientist, his publications may continue for thirty or more years.

The accurate control of the time span of a count is not as trivial as it might seem. Normally, the publication count is made from secondary sources (abstracting or indexing services) rather than from scanning the publications individually. Since most abstracting and indexing sources have been expanding their coverage over time, any publication count covering more than a few years must give careful consideration to changes in coverage. Furthermore, the timeliness of the secondary sources varies widely, with sources dependent on outside abstractors lagging months or even years behind. Since these abstracting lags may depend upon language, field and country of origin, they are a particular problem in international publication counts.

The Science Citation Index is one of the most current secondary sources, with some 80% to 90% of a given year's publications in the SCI for that year.

Of course, no abstracting or indexing service can be perfect, since some journals are actually published months after their listed publication dates. Nevertheless, variations in timeliness are large from one service to another.

3. Comprehensiveness of Source Coverage

An important consideration in making a publication count is the comprehensiveness of the source coverage. Most abstracting and indexing sources cover some journals completely, cover other journals selectively, and omit some journals in their field of interest. The Science Citation Index is an exception in that it indexes each and every important entry from any journal it covers. This is one of the major advantages in using the SCI as a data base. Chemical Abstracts and Biological Abstracts have a group of journals which they abstract completely, coupled with a much larger set of journals from which they abstract selectively, based upon the appropriateness of the article to the subject coverage. In some cases the abstractor or indexer may make a quality judgment, based on his estimate of the importance or the quality of the article or upon his knowledge of whether similar information has appeared elsewhere; Excerpta Medica is a comprehensive abstracting service for which articles are included only if they meet the indexers' quality criteria.

Some data on the extent of coverage of the major secondary sources is presented in Section D of this chapter.

4.   Multiple Authorships and Affiliations

Attributing credits for multiple authorships and affili- ations is a significant problem in publication and citation anal- ysis. In some scientific papers the authors are listed alpha- betically; in others the first author is the primary author; still others use different conventions. These conventions have been been discussed by Crane[1] and by other social scientists.[2] There does not seem to be any reasonable way to deal with the attribution problem, except to attribute a fraction of a publi- cation to each of the authors. For example, an article which has three authors would have one-third of an article attributed to each author. The amount of multiple authorship unfortunately differs from country to country and from field to field. Several studies have investigated the problem, but no comprehensive data exists.[3]

Multiple authorship takes on particular importance when counting an individual's publications since membership on a large research team may lead to a single scientist being a co- author of ten or more publications per year. This number of publications is far in excess of the normal publication rate of one to two articles per year per scientist.

Multiple authorship problems arise less often in institu- tional publication counts since there are seldom more than one or two institutions involved in one publication.

A particularly vexing aspect of multiple authorship is the first author citation problem: almost all citations are to the first author in a multi-authored publication. As a result, a researcher who is second author of five papers may receive no

---

[1]Diana Crane, "Social Structure in a Group of Scientists: A Test of the 'Invisible College' Hypothesis," American Socio- logical Review 34 (June 1969):335-352.

[2]James E. McCauly, "Multiple Authorship," Science 141 (August 1963):579.

Beverly L. Clark, "Multiple Authorship Trends in Scientific Papers," Science 143 (February 1964):822-824.

[3]Harriet Zuckerman, "Nobel Laureates in Science: Patterns of Productivity, Collaboration, and Authorship," American Sociolgoical Review 32 (June 1967):391-403.

citations under his own name, even though the papers he co-author-
ed may be highly cited. Because of this, a citation count for a
person must account for the citations which appear under the
names of the first authors of publications for which the author
of interest was a secondary author. This can lead to a substantial amount of tedious additional work, since a list of first
authors must be generated for all of the subjects' multi-authored papers. Citations to each of these first authors must then
be found, the citations of interest noted, and these citations
fractionally attributed to the original author. Since multiple
years of the Citation Index are often involved, the amount of
clerical work searching from volume to volume and from author
to author, and citation to citation can be quite large.

A note of caution about the handling of multiple authorship in the Corporate Index of the Science Citation Index: SCI
lists a publication giving all the corporate affiliations, but
always with the first author's name. Thus a publication by
Jones and Smith where Jones is at Harvard and Smith is at Yale
would be listed in the Corporate Index under Harvard with the
name Jones and also under Yale with the name Jones. To find
the organization with which the various authors are affiliated,
the original article must be obtained.

Although the publisher of the Science Citation Index, the
Institute for Scientific Information, tries to maintain a consistent policy in attributing institutional affiliations, when
authors have multiple affiliations the number of possible var-
iants is large. In the SCI data base on magnetic tape, sufficient information is included to assign a publication with authors from a number of different institutions in a reasonably
fair way to those institutions; however, in the printed Corporate Index, one has to refer to the Source Index to find the
actual number of authors, or to the paper itself to find the
affiliations of each of the authors.

5.   Completeness of Available Data

Another consideration in a publication analysis is the
completeness of data available in the secondary source, since
looking up hundreds or thousands of publications individually
is tedious and expensive. One difficulty here is that most of
the abstracting and indexing sources are designed for retrieval
and not for analysis. As a result, some of the parameters which
are of greatest analytical importance, such as the affiliation
of the author and his source of financial support, are often
omitted. Furthermore, some of the abstracting sources are
cross-indexed in complex ways, so that a publication may only
be partially described at any one point, and reference must be
made to a companion volume to find even such essential data
as the author's name. While intellectually trivial, these

searches can be exceedingly time consuming when analyzing large numbers of publications.

The specific data which are consistently available in the secondary sources are the basic bibliographic information: i.e., authors' name, journal or report title, volume, page, etc. This information is the basic data used for retrieval, and since the abstracting and indexing services are retrieval oriented, this bibliographic information is always included.

Data which are less consistently available in the secondary source are the authors' affiliation and the authors' rank or title. Both of these are of interest in analysis. For example, the ranking of universities based on publication in a given subject area is often of interest. This ranking can be tabulated only from a secondary source which gives the authors' university affiliation.

6. Support Acknowledgements

The source of the authors' financial support is seldom given in any secondary source, although it is now being added to the MEDLARS data base. Since this financial data can be used to define the fraction of a subject literature which is being supported by a particular corporate body such as a governmental agency, the data are of substantial evaluative interest.

The amount of acknowledgement of agency support in the scientific literature has changed over time. In a Computer Horizons study completed in 1973 the amount of agency support acknowledgement was tabulated in twenty major journals from five different fields.[4] Table 6-1 summarizes those support acknowledgements for 1969 and 1972.

In 1969, only 67% of the articles in 20 major journals acknowledged financial support. By 1972, the percentage of articles acknowledging financial support had risen to approximately 85%. The table shows that the sources of support differ from one field to another and also shows that the fields of interest to these sources differ as well. For example, the National Science Foundation is the major source of acknowledged support in mathematics, while the National Institutes of Health clearly dominate the support of biology. Chemistry is the field with the largest amount of non-government (private sector) support in the U.S.

Note also that the 20 journals used were major journals in their fields; as less prestigious journals are examined, the amount of support acknowledgement generally decreases.

_____

[4] Computer Horizons, Inc., Evaluation of Research in the Physical Sciences Based on Publications and Citations, Washington, D.C., National Science Foundation, Contract No. NSF-C627, November, 1973.

TABLE 6-1

AGENCY SUPPORT ACKNOWLEDGEMENTS IN 20 LEADING JOURNALS
FROM 5 MAJOR FIELDS - 1969 and 1972

Agency Acknowledged	Mathematics 1969	1972	Physics 1969	1972	Chemistry 1969	1972	Biochemistry 1969	1972	Biology 1969	1972	All Fields 1969	1972
NSF	18%	37%	14%	19%	18%	21%	8%	8%	8%	8%	13%	16%
NIH	2	1	1	1	11	10	37	39	23	32	13	16
AEC	1	1	21	15	10	8	3	2	3	2	11	8
DOD	15	7	19	15	10	10	1	1	2	3	10	9
NASA	1	1	7	9	2	2	1	1	1	2	3	4
Other U.S. Government	1	2	1	2	2	2	1	1	1	3	1	2
Other U.S.	3	10	3	14	8	21	10	10	9	13	7	14
Foreign	5	4	5	15	7	8	16	25	10	24	8	16
Unacknowledged	55	37	31	11	32	18	25	13	42	14	33	15

In an attempt to account for the 15% of unacknowledged papers, a questionnaire was sent to all U.S. authors in the 1972 sample who did not acknowledge agency support. Almost 70% of the authors who had not listed sources of support responded to the questionnaire. Of the authors who responded, over two-thirds were supported by their institutions as part of their regular duties; approximately 20% of the respondents cited specific governmental agencies as sources of support, even though they had not acknowledged these in the article itself. Twelve percent of the respondents listed no agency or institutional support; research done as fulfillment of graduate studies was included in this category.

Overall, the 1972 tabulation and survey showed that 88% of the research reported in these prestigious journals was externally supported, and that 97% of the externally supported work was acknowledged as such.

7.   Subject Classification

Having constructed a basic list of publications, the next step in analysis is normally to subject classify the publications. Either the journals or the papers themselves may be classified. When a large number of papers is to be analyzed, classification of the papers by the field of the journal can be very convenient. Such a classification implies, of course, a degree of homogeneity of publication which is normally adequate when analyzing hundreds of papers. Such a classification may not be sufficient for the analysis of the scientific publications of one or a few individuals.

Subject classification schemes differ from one abstracting and indexing service to another. Therefore, a comparison of a collection of papers based on the classification schemes of more than one abstracting and indexing service is almost hopeless. A classification of papers at the journal level has been used in the influence methodology discussed in Chapters VII through X.

8.   Citation Counts

Citation counts are a tool in evaluative bibliometrics second in importance only to the counting and classification of publications. Citation counts may be used directly as a measure of the utilization or influence of a single publication or of all the publications of an individual, a grant, contract, department, university, funding agency or country. Citation counts may be used to link individuals, institutions, and programs, since they show how one publication relates to another publication.

In addition to these evaluative uses, citations also have important bibliometric uses, since the references from one paper to another define the structure of the scientific literature. Chapter III discusses how this type of analysis may be carried out at a detailed, micro-level to define closely related papers through bibliographic coupling and co-citation. That chapter also describes how citation analysis may be used at a macro-level to link fields and subfields through journal-to-journal mapping. The bibliometric characteristics of the literature also provide a numeric base against which evaluative parameters may be normalized.

Some of the characteristics of the literature which are revealed by citation analysis are noted on Figure 6-1. These characteristics include:

> The dispersion of references: a measure of scientific "hardness", since in fields that are structured and have a central core of accepted knowledge, literature references tend to be quite concentrated.

> The concentration of papers and influence: another measure of centrality in a field, dependent upon whether or not a field has a core journal structure.

> The hierarchic dependency relationships between field, subfield and journals, including the comparison of numbers of references from field A to field B, compared with number of references from field B to field A: this comparison provides a major justification for the pursuit of basic research as a foundation of knowledge utilized by more applied areas.

> The linkages between fields, subfields and journals: a measure of the flow of information, and of the importance of one sector of the scientific mosaic to another.

VII.   THE INFLUENCE METHODOLOGY

A.   Introduction

In this chapter an influence methodology will be described which allows advanced publication and citation techniques to be applied to institutional aggregates of publications, such as those of departments, schools, programs, support agencies and countries, without performing an individual citation count.   In essence, the influence procedure ascribes a weighted average set of properties to a collection of papers, such as the papers in a journal, rather than determining the citation rate for the papers on an individual basis.

The influence methodology is completely general, and can be applied to journals, subfields, fields, institutions or countries.

There are three separate aspects of the influence methodology which are particularly pertinent to journals.   These are

1.   A subject classification for each journal

2.   A research type (level) classification for the biomedical journals, and

3.   Citation influence measures for each journal.

It is the third of these, the citation influence measures, which add a quality or utilization aspect to the analysis.   The influence methodology assumes that, although citations to papers vary within a given journal, aggregates of publications can be characterized by the influence measures of the journals in which they appear.   Chapter IX discusses this assumption in some detail.

Older measures of influence all suffer from some defect which limits their use as evaluative measures.

The total number of publications of an individual, school or country is a measure of total activity only; no inferences concerning importance may be drawn.

The total number of citations to a set of publications, while incorporating a measure of peer group recognition, depends on the size of the set involved and has no meaning on an absolute scale.

The journal "impact factor" introduced by Garfield is a size-independent measure, since it is defined as the ratio of the number of citations the journal receives to the number of publications in a specified earlier time period.[1]   This

---

[1]Eugene Garfield, "Citation Analysis As a Tool in Journal Evaluation," Science 178 (November 3, 1972):471.

measure, like the total number of citations, has no meaning on an absolute scale. In addition the impact factor suffers from three more significant limitations. Although the size of the journal, as reflected in the number of publications, is corrected for, the average length of individual papers appearing in the journal is not. Thus, journals which publish longer papers, namely review journals, tend to have higher impact factors. In fact the nine highest impact factors obtained by Garfield were for review journals. This measure can therefore not be used to establish a "pecking order" for journal prestige.

The second limitation is that the citations are unweighted, all citations being counted with equal weight, regardless of the citing journal. It seems more reasonable to give higher weight to a citation from a prestigious journal than to a citation from a peripheral one. The idea of counting a reference from a more prestigious journal more heavily has also been suggested by Kochen.[2]

A third limitation is that there is no normalization for the different referencing characteristics of different segments of the literature: a citation received by a biochemistry journal, in a field noted for its large numbers of references and short citation times, may be quite different in value from a citation in astronomy, where the overall citation density is much lower and the citation time lag much longer.

In this section three related influence measures are developed, each of which measures one aspect of a journal's influence, with explicit recognition of the size factor. These measures are:

(1) The influence weight of the journal: a size-independent measure of the weighted number of citations a journal receives from other journals, normalized by the number of references the journal gives to other journals.

(2) The influence per publication for the journals: the weighted number of citations each article, note or review in a journal receives from other journals.

(3) The total influence of the journal: the influence per publication times the total number of publications.

---

[2] M.Kochen, *Principles of Information Retrieval*, (New York: John Wiley & Sons, Inc. 1974), 83.

B.   Development of the Weighting Scheme

1.   The Citation Matrix

A citation matrix may be used to describe the interactions among members of a set of publishing entities. These entities may, for example, be journals, institutions, individuals, fields of research, geographical subdivisions or levels of research methodology. The formalism to be developed is completely general in that it may be applied to any such set. To emphasize this generality, a member of a set will be referred to as a _unit_ rather than as a specific type of unit such as a journal.

The citation matrix is the fundamental entity which contains the information describing the flow of influence among units.

The matrix has the form

$$C = \begin{pmatrix} c_{11} & c_{12} & \ldots & c_{1n} \\ c_{21} & c_{22} & \ldots & c_{2n} \\ \cdot & \cdot & & \cdot \\ \cdot & \cdot & & \cdot \\ \cdot & \cdot & & \cdot \\ c_{n1} & c_{n2} & \ldots & c_{nn} \end{pmatrix}$$

A distinction is made between the use of the terms "reference" and "citation" depending on whether the issuing or receiving unit is being discussed. Thus, a term c_{ij} in the citation matrix indicates both the number of references unit i gives to unit j and the number of citations unit j receives from unit i.

The time frame of a citation matrix must be clearly understood in order that a measure derived from it be given its proper interpretation. Suppose that the citation data are based on references issued in 1973. The citations received may be to papers in any year up through 1973. In general, the papers issuing the references will not be the same as those receiving the citations. Thus, any conclusions drawn from such a matrix assume an on-going, relatively constant nature for each of the units. For instance, if the units of study are journals, it is assumed that they have not changed in size relative to each other and represent a constant subject area. Journals in rapidly changing fields and new journals would therefore have to be treated with caution.

A citation matrix for a specific time lag may also be formulated. This would link publications in one time period with publications in some specified earlier time period.

2. Influence Weights

For each unit in the set a measure of the influence of that unit will be extracted from the citation matrix. Because total influence is clearly a size-dependent quantity, it is essential to distinguish between a size-independent measure of influence, to be called the influence weight, and the size-dependent total influence.

To make the idea of a size-independent measure more precise, the following property of such a measure may be specified: if a journal were randomly subdivided into smaller entities, each entity would have the same measure as the parent journal.

The citation matrix may be thought of as an "input-output" matrix with the medium of exchange being the citation. Each unit gives out references and receives citations; it is above average if it has a "positive citation balance", i.e., receives more than it gives out. This reasoning provides a first order approximation to the weight of each unit, which is

$$W_i^{(1)} = \frac{\text{total number of citations to the ith unit from other units}}{\text{total number of references from the ith unit to other units}}.$$

This is the starting point for the iterative procedure for the calculation of the influence weights to be described below.

The denominator of this expression is the row sum

$$S_i = \sum_{j=1}^{n} c_{ij}$$

corresponding to the ith unit of the citation matrix; it may be thought of as the "target size" which this unit presents to the referencing world.

The influence weight, W_i, of the ith unit is defined as

$$W_i = \sum_{k=1}^{n} \frac{W_k \, c_{ki}}{S_i}$$

In the sum, the number of cites to the ith unit from the kth unit is weighted by the weight of kth (referencing) unit. The number of cites is also divided by the target size S_i of

the unit i being cited. The n equations, one for each unit, provide a self consistent "bootstrap" set of relations in which each
unit plays a role in determining the weight of every other unit.
The following summarizes the derivation of those weights.

The equations defining the weights,

$$W_i = \sum_{k=1}^{n} \frac{W_k C_{ki}}{S_i}, \qquad i = 1,..,n \qquad (1)$$

are a special case of a more general system of equations which
may be written in the form

$$\left\{ \sum_{k=1}^{n} W_k \gamma_{ki} \right\} - \lambda W_i = 0, \qquad i = 1,..,n \quad . \qquad (2)$$

Here $\gamma_{ki} = \dfrac{C_{ki}}{S_i}$ and Equation 1 is shown to be

a special case of Equation 2 corresponding to $\lambda = 1$. As will be
explained shortly the system of equations given in (1) will not,
in general, possess a non-zero solution; only for certain values
of λ called the eigenvalues of the system, will there be non-
zero solutions.

With the choice of target size S_i, the value $\lambda = 1$ is
in fact an eigenvalue so that Equation 1 itself does possess a
solution.

Using the notation γ^T for the transpose of γ,

$$\gamma^T_{ik} = \gamma_{ki} \; ; \; \text{introducing the Kronecker delta symbol}$$

defined by
$$\delta_{ik} = \begin{cases} 1 & i = k \\ 0 & i \neq k \end{cases}$$

the equation can then be written

$$\sum_{k=1}^{n} \left(\gamma_{ik}^{T} - \lambda \delta_{ik} \right) w_k = 0 \; . \qquad (3)$$

This is a system of n homogeneous equations for the weights. In order that a solution for such a system exists, the determinant of the coefficients must vanish. This gives an nth order equation for the eigenvalues

$$\begin{vmatrix} \gamma_{11}-\lambda & \gamma_{21} \dots \dots & \gamma_{n1} \\ \gamma_{12} & \gamma_{22}-\lambda \dots \dots & \gamma_{n2} \\ \vdots & \vdots & \vdots \\ \vdots & \vdots & \vdots \\ \gamma_{1n} & \gamma_{2n} \dots \dots & \gamma_{nn}-\lambda \end{vmatrix} = 0 \qquad (4)$$

called the characteristic equation.

Only for values of λ which satisfy this equation, does a non-zero solution for the W's exist. Moreover, Equation 3 does not determine the values of the w_k themselves, but at best determines their ratios. Equivalently the eigenvalue equation may be thought of as a vector equation for the vector unknown $\underline{W} = \{w_1, \dots, w_n\}$

$$\underline{\underline{\gamma}}^{T} \cdot \underline{W} = \lambda \underline{W} \qquad (5)$$

from which it is clear that only the direction of $\underline{W}$ is determined.

The normalization or scale factor is then fixed by the condition that the size-weighted average of the weights is 1, or

$$\frac{\displaystyle\sum_{1}^{n} s_k \ w_k}{\displaystyle\sum_{1}^{n} s_k} \ = \ 1 \qquad\qquad (6)$$

This normalization assures that the weight values have an absolute as well as a relative meaning, with the value 1 representing an average value.

Each root of the characteristic equation determines a solution vector or eigenvector of the equation, but the weight vector being sought is the eigenvector corresponding to the largest eigenvalue. This can be seen from the consideration of an alternative procedure for solving the system of equations, a procedure which also leads to the algorithm of choice.

Consider an iterative process starting with equal weights for all units. The values $W_i^{(0)} = 1$ can be thought of as zeroth order approximations to the weights. The first order weights are then

$$W_i^{(1)} \ = \ \frac{\displaystyle\sum_{k=1}^{n} c_{ki}}{s_i}$$

This ratio (total cites to a unit divided by the target size of the unit) is the simplest size-corrected citation measure and, in fact, corresponds to the impact measure used by Garfield. These values are then substituted into the right hand side of Equation 1 to obtain the next order of approximation. In general, the mth order approximation is

$$W_i^{(m)} = \sum_{k=1}^{n} \frac{W_k^{(m-1)}}{S_i} c_{ki} = \sum_{k=1}^{n} W_k^{(m-1)} \times \gamma_{ki} = \sum_{j=1}^{n} \left(\gamma\right)^m_{ji}$$

The exact weights are therefore

$$W_i = W_i^{(\infty)} = \sum_{j=1}^{n} \left(\lim_{m \to \infty} \gamma^m\right)_{ji}$$

This provides the most convenient numerical procedure for finding the weights, the whole iteration procedure being reduced to successive squarings of the γ matrix.

This procedure is closely related to the standard method for finding the dominant eigenvalue of a matrix. Since $\lambda = 1$ is the largest eigenvalue, repeated squarings are all that is needed. If the largest eigenvalue had a value other than 1, the normalization condition, Equation 6, would have to be reimposed with each squaring. Convergence to three decimal places usually occurs with six squarings, corresponding to raising γ to the 64th power.

APPENDIX G

CONFERENCE ON THE ASSESSMENT OF
QUALITY OF GRADUATE EDUCATION PROGRAMS

September 27-29, 1976
Woods Hole, Massachusetts

Participants

Robert A. ALBERTY   Dean of Science, Massachusetts Institute of
                           Technology
Charles ANDERSEN   Coordinator, Education Statistics, American
                           Council on Education
Richard C. ATKINSON   Acting Director, National Science Foundation
R. H. BING   Chairman, Department of Mathematics, University
                           of Texas at Austin
David W. BRENEMAN   Senior Fellow, The Brookings Institution
John E. CANTLON   Vice-President for Research and Graduate
                           Studies, Michigan State University
Henry E. COBB   Professor, Department of History, Southern
                           University
Monroe D. DONSKER   Professor, Courant Institute of Mathematical
                           Sciences, New York University
David E. DREW   Senior Scientist, Rand Corporation
E. Alden DUNHAM   Program Officer, Carnegie Corporation of
                           New York
David A. GOSLIN   Executive Director, Assembly of Behavioral and
                           Social Sciences, National Research Council
Hanna H. GRAY   Provost, Yale University
Norman HACKERMAN   President, Rice University
Philip HANDLER   President, National Academy of Sciences
David D. HENRY   President Emeritus, University of Illinois
Roger W. HEYNS   President, American Council on Education
Lyle V. JONES   Vice Chancellor and Dean, Graduate School,
                           University of North Carolina at Chapel Hill
Charles V. KIDD   Executive Secretary, Association of American
                           Universities
Winfred P. LEHMANN   Professor, Department of Linguistics,
                           University of Texas at Austin
Charles T. LESTER   Vice-President of Arts and Sciences,
                           Emory University

Gardner LINDZEY	Director, Center for Advanced Study in the Behavioral Sciences (Chairman)
Raymond P. MARIELLA	Dean of the Graduate School, Loyola University
Cora B. MARRETT	Center for Advanced Study in the Behavioral Sciences
Peter S. McKINNEY	Acting Dean, Graduate School of Arts and Sciences, Harvard University
Doris H. MERRITT	Dean, Research and Sponsored Programs, Indiana University/Purdue University
John Perry MILLER	Corporation Officer for Institutional Development, The Campaign for Yale
Lincoln E. MOSES	Professor, Department of Family, Community and Preventive Medicine, Stanford University Medical Center
Frederick W. MOTE	Professor, Department of East Asian Studies, Princeton University
Thomas A. NOBLE	Executive Associate, American Council of Learned Societies
J. Boyd PAGE	President, The Council of Graduate Schools in the United States
C. K. N. PATEL	Director, Physical Research Laboratory, Bell Laboratories
Michael J. PELCZAR, Jr.	Vice-President for Graduate Studies and Research, University of Maryland, College Park
Frank PRESS	Chairman, Department of Earth and Planetary Sciences, Massachusetts Institute of Technology
John J. PRUIS	President, Ball State University
Lorene L. ROGERS	President, University of Texas at Austin
John SAWYER	President, The Andrew W. Mellon Foundation
Robert L. SPROULL	President, University of Rochester
Eliot STELLAR	Provost, University of Pennsylvania
Alfred S. SUSSMAN	Dean, Horace H. Rackham School of Graduate Studies, University of Michigan
Donald C. SWAIN	Academic Vice-President, University of California System
Mack E. THOMPSON	Executive Director, American Historical Association
Charles V. WILLIE	Professor of Education and Urban Studies, The Graduate School of Education, Harvard University
H. Edwin YOUNG	Chancellor, University of Wisconsin, Madison
Harriet A. ZUCKERMAN	Associate Professor, Department of Sociology, Columbia University

SUMMARY

September 27-29, 1976, Woods Hole, Massachusetts

Report of the Conference

A substantial majority of the Conference believes that the earlier assessments of graduate education have received wide and important use: by students and their advisors, by the institutions of higher education as aids to planning and the allocation of educational functions, as a check of unwarranted claims of excellence, and in social science research.

The recommendations which follow attempt to distill the main points of consensus within the conference. This report does not in any sense adequately represent the rich diversity of points of view revealed during the Conference nor the deep and real differences in belief among the participants.

Recommendations

1.   A new assessment of graduate programs is needed, and we believe that the Conference Board is an appropriate sponsor. While we do not propose to specify the details of this assessment, we are prepared to suggest the following guidelines.

2.   The assessment should include a modified replication of the Roose-Andersen study, with the addition of some fields and the subdivision of others.

3.   It is important to provide additional indices relevant to program assessment such as some of those cited by Breneman, Drew, and Page. The Conference directs specific attention to the CGS/ETS Study currently nearing completion and urges that the results of that study be carefully examined and used to the fullest possible extent.

4.   The initial assessment study should be one of surveying the quality of scholarship and research and the effectiveness of Ph.D. programs in the fields selected for inclusion.

     a.   It is intended that the study be carried forward on a continuing basis to provide valuable longitudinal data. This should be implemented along the lines suggested by Moses, involving annual assessment of subsets of programs.

     b.   Every eligible institution should be given the choice of whether to be included in the study.

     c.   Each program is to be characterized by a set of scores, one for each selected index. The presentation of scores for all reported indices should be accompanied by a discussion of their substantive meaning. In addition, appropriate measures of uncertainty should accompany all tables of results.

5. We propose a simultaneous study exploring ways of reviewing goals of graduate education other than research and scholarship. This would involve review of other doctoral programs and selected master's programs.

APPENDIX H

PLANNING COMMITTEE FOR THE
STUDY OF THE QUALITY OF RESEARCH-DOCTORATE PROGRAMS

September 1978

Robert M. Bock
Dean of the Graduate School
University of Wisconsin
  at Madison

Philip E. Converse
Institute for Social Research
University of Michigan

Richard A. Goldsby
Department of Genetics
Stanford University

Hugh Holman
Department of English
University of North Carolina
  at Chapel Hill

Lyle V. Jones
Vice Chancellor and Dean,
  Graduate School
University of North Carolina
  at Chapel Hill

Gardner Lindzey, Co-Chairman
Director
Center for Advanced Study in the
  Behavioral Sciences
Stanford, California

Sterling McMurrin
Dean of the Graduate School
University of Utah

Lincoln E. Moses
Administrator
Energy Information
  Administration
Washington, D.C.

George Pake
Xerox Corporation
Palo Alto, California

C. K. N. Patel
Director, Physical Research
Bell Laboratories

Cornelius Pings
Dean of the Graduate School
California Institute of
  Technology

Gordon Ray
President
The John Simon Guggenheim
  Memorial Foundation

Harriet A. Zuckerman,
  Co-Chairman
Department of Sociology
Columbia University

248

APPENDIX I

REGION AND STATE CODES
FOR THE UNITED STATES AND POSSESSIONS
(and U.S. Government)

REGION 1 - NEW ENGLAND

11 Maine
12 New Hampshire
13 Vermont
14 Massachusetts
15 Rhode Island
16 Connecticut

REGION 2 - MIDDLE ATLANTIC

21 New York
22 New Jersey
23 Pennsylvania

REGION 3 - EAST NORTH CENTRAL

31 Ohio
32 Indiana
33 Illinois
34 Michigan
35 Wisconsin

REGION 4 - WEST NORTH CENTRAL

41 Minnesota
42 Iowa
43 Missouri
44 North Dakota
45 South Dakota
46 Nebraska
47 Kansas

REGION 5 - SOUTH ATLANTIC

51 Delaware
52 Maryland
53 District of Columbia
54 Virginia
55 West Virginia
56 North Carolina
57 South Carolina
58 Georgia
59 Florida

REGION 6 - EAST SOUTH CENTRAL

61 Kentucky
62 Tennessee
63 Alabama
64 Mississippi

REGION 7 - WEST SOUTH CENTRAL

71 Arkansas
72 Louisiana
73 Oklahoma
74 Texas

REGION 8 - MOUNTAIN

81 Montana
82 Idaho
83 Wyoming
84 Colorado
85 New Mexico
86 Arizona
87 Utah
88 Nevada

REGION 9 - PACIFIC

90 Guam
91 Washington
92 Oregon
93 California
94 Alaska
95 Hawaii
96 Virgin Islands
97 Panama Canal Zone
98 Puerto Rico